Longman

Higher Science 2

for GCSE

Mark Levesley

Penny Johnson

Richard O'Regan

Sarah Pitt

Nicky Thomas

Bob Wakefield

with additional material by
Iain Brand, Miles Hudson,
Silvia Newton, Gary Philpott

Contents for Higher Science

G1	Somewhere to live	6
G2	Adaptation	8
G3	Chains and webs	10
G4	Pyramids	12
G5	Energy losses	14
G6	Competition	16
G7	Populations	18
G8	Estimating population sizes	20
G9	Decomposition	22
G10	Nutrient recycling	24
G11	The carbon cycle	26
G12	The nitrogen cycle	28
G13	Population explosion	30
G14	Land pollution	32
G15	Water pollution	34
G16	Air pollution	36
G17	Acid rain	38
G18	The greenhouse effect	40
G19	Global warming	42
G20	Further questions	44

H1	Differences	46
H2	Genes	48
H3	Reproduction in animals	50
H4	Sexual reproduction in animals	52
H5	Fertility	54
H6	Reproduction in plants	56
H7	The discovery of genes	58
H8	Alleles	60
H9	Inherited diseases	62
H10	Sickle-cell anaemia	64
H11	More cloning	66
H12	Genetic engineering	68
H13	Selective breeding	70
H14	Agricultural problems	72
H15	Natural selection	74
H16	Mutations	76
H17	Evolution: Theory	78
H18	Evolution: Evidence	80
H19	Fossils	82
H20	Further questions	84

I1	Rates of reaction	86
I2	Measuring rate of reaction – 1	88
I3	Measuring rate of reaction – 2	90
I4	Effect of concentration	92
I5	Collision theory	94
I6	Effect of temperature	96
I7	Effect of surface area	98
I8	Catalysts	100
I9	Enzymes	102
I10	Uses of enzymes	104
I11	Enzymes and food	106
I12	Energy transfer	108
I13	Reversible reactions	110
I14	Nitrogen – a very useful gas!	112
I15	Making fertilisers – part 1	114
I16	Making fertilisers – part 2	116
I17	Masses and moles	118
I18	More moles	120
I19	Formulae and percentage mass	122
I20	Further questions	124

J1	Elements and compounds	126
J2	Formulae	128
J3	Balancing equations	130
J4	Ideas about atoms	132
J5	Atomic structure	134
J6	Electronic structure	136
J7	The Periodic Table	138
J8	Looking for patterns	140
J9	Metals and non-metals	142
J10	Metallic bonding	144
J11	Ionic bonding	146
J12	Ionic compounds	148
J13	The Group 1 metals	150
J14	Covalent bonding	152
J15	Covalent giant structures	154
J16	The halogens	156
J17	Using sodium chloride	158
J18	Halogen compounds	160
J19	Structures and bonding	162
J20	Further questions	164

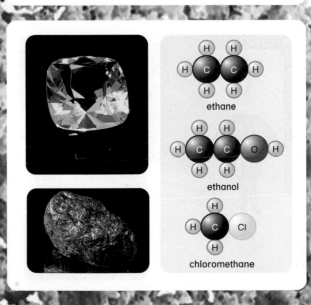

K1	Speed	166
K2	Distance–time graphs	168
K3	Acceleration	170
K4	Velocity–time graphs	172
K5	Balanced forces	174
K6	Unbalanced forces	176
K7	Friction	178
K8	Braking and stopping	180
K9	Moving through fluids	182
K10	Unbalanced forces and acceleration	184
K11	Gravity, mass and weight	186
K12	Terminal velocity	188
K13	Work and energy transfer	190
K14	Kinetic energy	192
K15	The Solar System	194
K16	Satellites and orbits	196
K17	Stars	198
K18	The Universe	200
K19	Life in the Universe	202
K20	Further questions	204

L1	Introducing waves	206
L2	Speed of waves	208
L3	Comparing waves	210
L4	Reflection and refraction	212
L5	Waves and the Earth	214
L6	Sound and ultrasound	216
L7	Total internal reflection	218
L8	Dispersion	220
L9	Diffraction	222
L10	Long wavelength electromagnetic waves	224
L11	Analogue and digital signals	226
L12	Short wavelength electromagnetic waves	228
L13	Radiation and living cells	230
L14	Ionisation	232
L15	Ionising radiation	234
L16	Isotopes	236
L17	Half-lives	238
L18	Using radioactive isotopes	240
L19	Atomic models	242
L20	Further questions	244

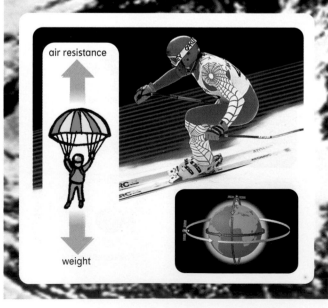

Matching chart for AQA Dual Award Specification

Name of module	AQA specification number	Higher Science module
Humans as Organisms	01	A (Book 1)
Maintenance of Life	02	B (Book 1)
Environment	03	G (Book 2)
Inheritance and Evolution	04	H (Book 2)
Metals	05	C (Book 1)
Earth Materials	06	D (Book 1)
Patterns of Chemical Change	07	I (Book 2)
Structures and Bonding	08	J (Book 2)
Energy	09	E (Book 1)
Electricity	10	F (Book 1)
Forces	11	K (Book 2)
Waves and Radiation	12	L (Book 2)

Full topic by topic matching charts are available on the companion web site
www.higherscience.co.uk

Somewhere to live

What are habitats, communities and populations?

Animals and plants live in many different places. The place where an animal or plant lives is called its **habitat** (e.g. a woodland, desert or lake). An organism's surroundings are called its **environment**. There are two parts to an environment: living organisms (**living environmental factors**) and non-living things (**physical factors**).

A woodland habitat. **A**

1 What is a habitat?

2 Describe your environment at the moment.

Organisms can only live, grow and reproduce in habitats where conditions are suitable. The physical factors which may affect organisms include:

● temperature
● amount of light
● availability of water
● availability of oxygen and carbon dioxide.

A woodland in winter. **B**

These factors may vary according to the time of day and also to the season of the year.

3 Describe three environmental factors in a wood that will be different in summer and winter.

All the living organisms in a habitat are called a **community**. Together, a habitat and a community make up an **ecosystem**. For example, in a desert ecosystem there is a community of plants and animals and the desert is the habitat.

A desert ecosystem.

4 **a)** What is a community?
  b) Write down the names of some members of the community in a desert ecosystem.
  c) Describe the physical factors in a desert habitat.

An animal's habitat must give it:

● food
● somewhere to shelter and be safe from other animals
● a place to breed and bring up its young (**offspring**).

 Rabbits eat grass and other plants. They live in burrows underground.

5 a) Why do rabbits live underground in burrows?
  b) Why do they dig their burrows in fields or woodland?

6 Why do herons live near lakes, rivers or the sea?

Herons live near lakes, rivers or the sea. **E**

A plant's environment must give it:

- sunlight
- carbon dioxide
- water and nutrients.

7 Why are many more plants found in woodland than in the desert?

F *A hedgerow is an ecosystem.*

P How could you investigate a hedgerow community?

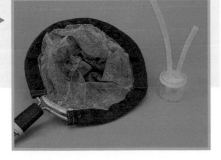

G

A Year 11 class looked at what animals and plants they could find living in a hawthorn hedge around a field. They found grass, dandelions, ferns and nettles. There was also an oak tree with moss and lichen growing on its bark. One group spotted a sparrow's nest in the branches. Another group found woodlice, beetles, ladybirds, ants, slugs and worms in the undergrowth. Wasps and butterflies were feeding from the wild flowers. Although no one saw any rabbits, they did find lots of rabbit droppings.

All the animals or plants of one kind make up a **population**. The community in the hedge had many different populations. All the woodlice living there made a population of woodlice. All the nettles growing there made a population of nettles.

8 Name five animals and five plants which are part of the community living in the hedge.

9 Explain the difference between a community and a population.

10 How do you think the changes in the seasons affect the animals and plants that live in the hedgerow? Explain in as much detail as you can.

Summary

Draw a concept map using all the words in bold on this spread. Include on your concept map the things that plants and animals need to survive and reproduce.

Adaptation

How can some animals and plants survive in difficult conditions?

Millions of different animals and plants live on the Earth. Most of them can only live in certain places. They are suited to the habitat that they live in. Scientists say that they are **adapted** to where they live. **Adaptation** means that animals and plants have things about them which help them to survive in their habitat.

A

 1 What is adaptation?

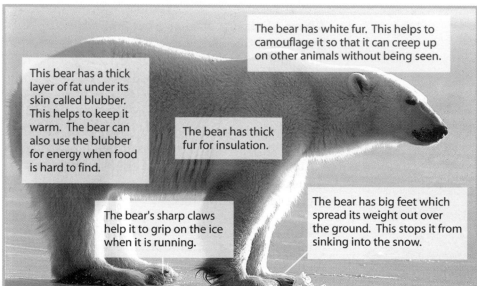

The bear has white fur. This helps to camouflage it so that it can creep up on other animals without being seen.

This bear has a thick layer of fat under its skin called blubber. This helps to keep it warm. The bear can also use the blubber for energy when food is hard to find.

The bear has thick fur for insulation.

The bear's sharp claws help it to grip on the ice when it is running.

The bear has big feet which spread its weight out over the ground. This stops it from sinking into the snow.

2 Look at photograph A. Why does a polar bear have:
   a) a thick layer of blubber
   b) big feet
   c) white fur?

! Cod living in the Antarctic have a kind of antifreeze to stop their blood freezing.

3 Copy and complete the sentences here by choosing the right ending from the box.

   a) The camel has a sandy colour . . .
   b) The camel makes very little urine . . .
   c) The camel can drink . . .
   d) The camel does not have a layer of body fat . . .
   e) The camel's big feet spread its weight out . . .
   f) The camel stores fat . . .
   g) The camel has long eyelashes to stop sand . . .

. . . so that it does not sink into the sand.
. . . up to 100 litres of water at once and store it in its stomach.
. . . in its hump which it can use for energy when there is not much food.
. . . or sweat so that it does not lose too much water.
. . . to camouflage it in the desert.
. . . blowing into its eyes.
. . . as this would keep heat in and stop it cooling down.

B

Animals that live in hot countries tend to have large surface areas compared with their volumes. This means they have as much skin as possible in contact with the air. As blood flows through the skin it loses heat to the air. This helps to cool the animal down. An African elephant makes its surface area bigger by having very big ears and lots of folds in its skin. Although a polar bear is a big animal, it is very compact and has a small surface area compared to its volume. This cuts down heat loss.

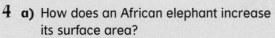

4 a) How does an African elephant increase its surface area?

b) Why do polar bears have very small ears?

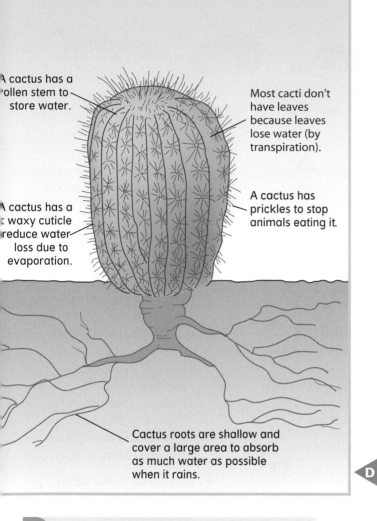

A cactus has a swollen stem to store water.

A cactus has a waxy cuticle reduce water loss due to evaporation.

Most cacti don't have leaves because leaves lose water (by transpiration).

A cactus has prickles to stop animals eating it.

Cactus roots are shallow and cover a large area to absorb as much water as possible when it rains.

A cactus plant's swollen stem reduces the plant's surface area compared to its volume, so it has a relatively small surface area through which water can be lost.

5 Look at diagram D. Why has the cactus got:
  a) no leaves
  b) roots which cover a large area
  c) a swollen stem
  d) sharp prickles?

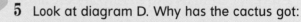

6 How might the adaptations listed below help the animals or plants to survive?
  a) Rabbits have very good hearing and eyesight.
  b) A chameleon can change the colour of its skin.
  c) Seaweed has air sacs which help it float (*Hint*: think how a plant gets its energy).

P How could you investigate why penguins from polar regions are larger than their relatives from warmer climates.

Summary

Make brief notes to explain how animals and plants are adapted to survive in arctic and desert habitats. Include the following terms in your notes: adaptation, camouflage, insulation, surface area and volume.

Chains and webs

What are food chains and food webs?

A **food chain** tells you what different animals eat. The food chain in picture A tells you that a fox eats hedgehogs, that hedgehogs eat snails and that snails eat cabbages. The arrows in a food chain show the direction of transfer of **energy** from one organism to another.

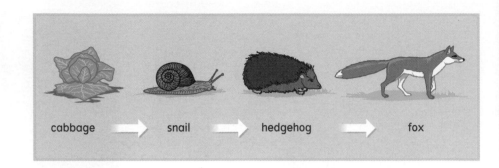

cabbage ⟹ snail ⟹ hedgehog ⟹ fox

A

1 What do food chains tell you?

2 What do the arrows in a food chain show?

Producers are organisms that produce food for the rest of a food chain. **Consumers** are organisms that eat other organisms. Consumers can be **carnivores** or **herbivores**. Carnivores are animals that eat other animals and herbivores are animals that eat plants.

Diagram B shows you how plants make food by photosynthesis. All living organisms depend on energy from the Sun. Plants could not make food to start food chains without sunlight. Plants convert light energy into chemical energy, which is then locked up in substances like starch and protein in their cells and tissues. This energy is passed along the food chain to herbivores and then to carnivores.

B

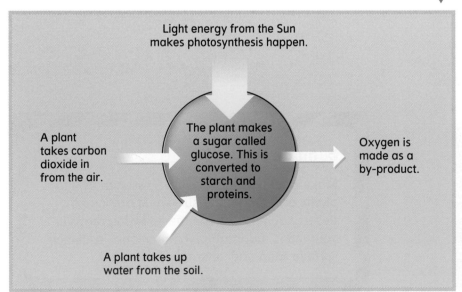

Light energy from the Sun makes photosynthesis happen.

A plant takes carbon dioxide in from the air.

The plant makes a sugar called glucose. This is converted to starch and proteins.

Oxygen is made as a by-product.

A plant takes up water from the soil.

3 **a)** Why are plants called producers?

b) Why are animals called consumers?

4 **a)** What gas do plants use up from the air?

b) What do plants take up from the soil?

c) What do plants make as their food?

d) What gas do plants make?

e) Plants need energy to photosynthesise. Where do they get this energy from?

5 Why do all living things depend on light energy for their food?

Food chain A tells you that a snail eats cabbages and a hedgehog eats snails and a fox eats hedgehogs. However, in the wild hedgehogs eat other things as well as snails, and foxes eat other animals as well as hedgehogs.

If you want to see everything that an animal eats in a habitat, you have to look at a **food web**.

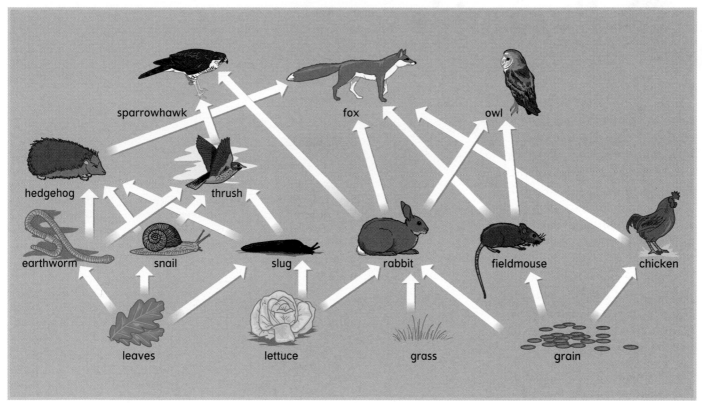

 A food web.

6 Look at food web C.
   a) Name the four producers.
   b) How many consumers are there?
   c) Name six herbivores from the web.
   d) Name five carnivores from the web.

7 Food webs are made from different food chains linked together. Write out five food chains from food web C.

8 Make your own food web using the information in the box below.

> The two producers in a pond are water weeds and green algae. Snails feed on water weeds and water fleas feed on the green algae. The tadpoles eat either producer. Minnows are small fish which eat tadpoles and water fleas. Perch are bigger fish which eat minnows and tadpoles. The frogs in the pond eat snails. Herons which live nearby eat frogs and perch. Pike are very big fish which also eat perch.

9 a) Look at food web C. What would happen to the number of thrushes if all the rabbits died of disease? Explain your answer.
   b) How might this affect the number of worms and slugs? Explain your answer.

10 The amount of energy available to each organism decreases as you go along a food chain. Suggest why.

Summary

Produce a leaflet with diagrams to explain how all animals and plants depend on energy from the Sun for survival. Include the following words in your leaflet: carnivore, consumer, herbivore, producer.

Pyramids

What do pyramids of numbers and biomass tell you?

Look at the food chain in picture A and think about how many animals or plants are eaten at each step of the food chain in a week. Each big fish may eat four small fish. Each small fish may eat 10 tadpoles. This means that there must be at least 40 tadpoles to feed the small fish. Each tadpole may eat 100 cells of algae. This means there must be at least 4000 cells of algae to feed the tadpoles.

You can draw a food chain as a **pyramid of numbers**. The size of each box in the pyramid gives you an idea of how many plants or animals there are at that step of the food chain. They are called *pyramids* of numbers because they are usually shaped liked a pyramid.

!
A robin can eat up to 50 worms in one day.

A

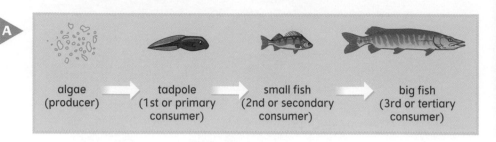

algae (producer) → tadpole (1st or primary consumer) → small fish (2nd or secondary consumer) → big fish (3rd or tertiary consumer)

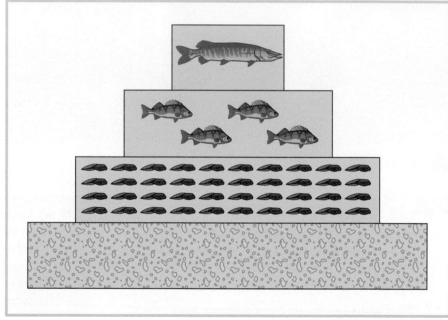

B

1 Look at the pyramid of numbers in diagram B. Complete the following sentences.
   a) As you go up a pyramid of numbers there are usually fewer…
   b) As you go up a pyramid of numbers the sizes of animals or plants…

2 Draw pyramids of numbers for these food chains.
   a) grass —→ grasshopper —→ frog
   b) dandelion —→ woodmouse —→ barn owl

3 Use the information below to write out a food chain and then draw a pyramid of numbers to go with it.
   ● Lots of aphids feed on one rosebush.
   ● Sparrows feed on lots of aphids.

Diagram C shows the pyramid of numbers for this food chain.

oak tree → caterpillar → blackbird

In a pyramid of numbers, an oak tree counts as one plant although an oak tree is very large and could feed hundreds of caterpillars.

Pyramids of numbers do not take into account the size of the animals or plants at each step of the food chain. This is why some of them have strange shapes.

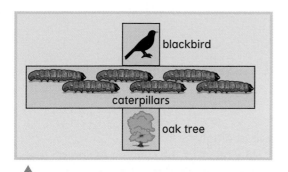

The word **biomass** means the mass of living material. A **pyramid of biomass** shows you the mass of living material at each step of the food chain. In other words it shows you how much mass all the animals or plants at each step would have if you put them all together.

 4 a) What does biomass mean?
  b) Which has a bigger biomass, an oak tree or a grass plant?

5 What does a pyramid of biomass tell you?

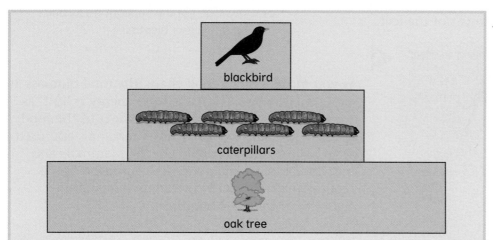

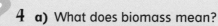

blackbird

caterpillars

oak tree

A pyramid of biomass shows the mass of living material at each step of the food chain.

The pyramid of biomass in diagram D looks very different from its pyramid of numbers in diagram C. This is because it takes into account the mass of the oak tree. There is still only one oak tree but it has a big biomass. There may be 1000 caterpillars, but 1000 caterpillars do not have much mass when compared to an oak tree! Pyramids of biomass are nearly always shaped like a pyramid.

6 The table gives information about two food chains.

Producer	Primary consumer	Secondary consumer	Tertiary consumer
600 dandelions	10 rabbits	1 fox	500 fleas
1 apple tree	100 aphids	2 ladybirds	

a) Draw a pyramid of numbers for each food chain.
b) The mean masses of each organism are: dandelion (250 g), rabbit (1 kg), fox (5 kg), flea (0.03 g), apple tree (40 kg), aphid (0.06 g), ladybird (1 g). Use this information to draw a pyramid of biomass for each food chain.

7 When biomass is measured, the measurements are taken at a certain time. Phytoplankton are small plants that live in the sea. Zooplankton are small animals that eat phytoplankton. Explain why this pyramid of biomass is upside down.

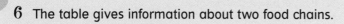

zooplankton

phytoplankton

Summary

A Explain the difference between pyramids of numbers and pyramids of biomass.

B Which one gives a more accurate picture of food chains?

Energy losses

What happens to the Sun's energy as it passes along a food chain?

Look at this food chain:

leaf ⟶ slug ⟶ hedgehog ⟶ fox

When the slug eats the leaf, it is taking in energy that was originally light energy captured by the leaf during **photosynthesis**. Some of this energy is stored as chemical energy in the substances of the leaf.

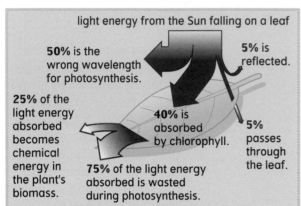

light energy from the Sun falling on a leaf A

50% is the wrong wavelength for photosynthesis.

5% is reflected.

25% of the light energy absorbed becomes chemical energy in the plant's biomass.

40% is absorbed by chlorophyll.

5% passes through the leaf.

75% of the light energy absorbed is wasted during photosynthesis.

 1 Look at diagram A.
  a) How much of the sunlight falling on the leaf is absorbed for photosynthesis?
  b) How much of the sunlight absorbed is used up by the leaf for energy?
  c) How much of the sunlight absorbed becomes new biomass?

As you move along a food chain, the total biomass at each step gets less. This is because energy is 'lost' as it passes from one organism to the next in the food chain. The energy is lost as waste materials and used up in **respiration** to supply energy. Mammals and birds lose a lot of energy to their surroundings as heat because they keep their body temperature higher than their surroundings.

B

10% of the leaf is used to make new cells as the slug grows. This part of the leaf becomes new biomass.

40% of the leaf passes straight through the slug and is lost as waste.

50% of the leaf is used up by the slug for energy.

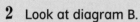 2 Look at diagram B.
  a) How much of the leaf is lost from the food chain as waste?
  b) How much of the leaf is used up by the slug for energy?
  c) How much of the leaf becomes new biomass in the slug?

3 Look at diagram C.
  a) How much of the slug is lost from the food chain as waste?
  b) How much of the slug is used up by the hedgehog for energy?
  c) How much of the slug becomes new biomass in the hedgehog?

4 Look at diagrams B and C.
  a) If the slug ate 100 grams of leaves, how many grams of leaf would be turned into part of the slug's body?
  b) If the hedgehog ate 500 grams of slugs, how many grams of slug would be turned into part of the hedgehog's body?

The slug only stores a small amount of the energy it gets from the leaf. This energy is stored in the slug's cells and is the only energy passed on to the hedgehog in the food chain.

 C

10% of the slug is used to make new cells as the hedgehog grows. This part of the slug becomes new biomass.

40% of the slug passes straight through the hedgehog and is lost as waste.

50% of the slug is used up by the hedgehog for energy.

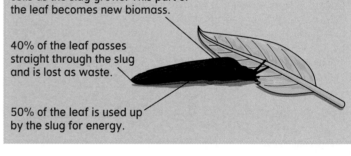

5 Why is there less energy stored in biomass at each step in a food chain?

Intensive farming of pigs by restricting space.

Reducing the energy loss

Modern farming has become more intensive as farmers try to produce as much food as possible. Most farm animals are mammals or birds. As the animals feed they grow, but they also use a lot of energy in moving and keeping warm. The animals use less energy if they are kept in warm conditions and are prevented from moving about too much.

6 How does keeping animals like pigs crowded together in barns benefit farmers?

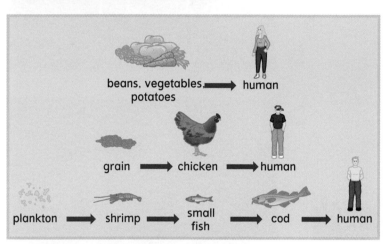

beans, vegetables, potatoes ➞ human

grain ➞ chicken ➞ human

plankton ➞ shrimp ➞ small fish ➞ cod ➞ human

Food chains.

If we eat more plants and less meat and fish, less energy is lost because there are fewer stages in the food chains.

7 Which one of the following food chains is more efficient in providing food for humans? Explain your choice.
 A grass ➞ cow ➞ human
 B soya bean ➞ cow ➞ human
 C soya bean ➞ human

Food producers can use **hormones** to control the ripening of fruit like apples and bananas, both on the plant and while it is being transported to consumers.

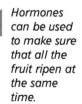
Hormones can be used to make sure that all the fruit ripen at the same time.

8 How does using hormones make food production more efficient?

9 Explain why there are rarely more than five steps in a food chain.

10 Fish do not keep their body temperature constant. It varies with the temperature of the surroundings. Explain why fish need less food than birds and mammals of the same mass.

11 Find out about 'free range' and 'intensive' farming for food production.

Summary

A Write a letter to your local newspaper explaining why farmers should not rear cattle in barns (intensive farming) and how eating more plants and less meat would provide more food for more people.

B Write a reply to your letter from a farmer explaining why he or she uses intensive farming.

Competition

What is competition and what do living things compete for?

Many different animals may live in a habitat. Sometimes they may want to eat the same things. Sometimes they may want to breed or shelter in similar places. **Competition** is when different animals want the same things. Different animals may compete for the same food or for the same space to build their homes.

1 What is competition?

2 What do animals compete for?

3 Look at food web C on page 11.
   a) Which three animals compete for leaves?
   b) Which three animals compete for rabbits?
   c) Which two animals compete for slugs?

4 Look at photographs A and B. What do the squirrel and the bird compete for?

 Gulls nesting.

5 Look at photograph C.
   a) What do you think the birds are competing for?
   b) What will happen to birds that cannot find a nesting site?

Competition does not matter when there is plenty of food and space for everyone. Competition *does* matter when there is not much food to go round or when space is scarce. When food is scarce, the animals which are best adapted to find or catch it will survive and the other animals may starve. If space is limited, then some animals may not find anywhere to breed or shelter.

An anteater is adapted for catching ants. It can stick its tongue into the middle of an ant hill.

6 Look at photograph D. Many animals eat ants. What advantage would the anteater have over other competitors if ants were in short supply?

Plants compete for sunlight, water and nutrients. Some plants have big leaves to catch as much light as they can. Their leaves can put other plants in the shade. Other plants have long roots which go deep into the soil. Plants with shorter roots cannot compete when water and nutrients are in short supply.

A Year 11 class were looking at competition between two different plants, A and B. They planted 20 seedlings of plant A in one tray and 20 seedlings of plant B in another. Every 10 days they measured the mean (average) mass of each plant to see how quickly they were growing. Graph E shows how well the two plants grew.

The class then planted 20 seedlings of each plant altogether in one tray. Again, they measured the mean mass of each plant every 10 days to see how quickly they were growing. Graph F shows how well the two plants grew when they were grown together.

7 **a)** What do plants compete for?
b) Why do some plants have large leaves?
c) Why do some plants have long roots?

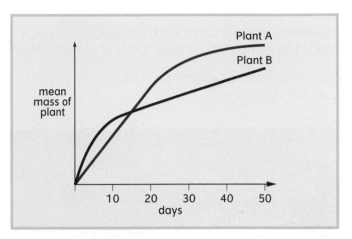

E This graph shows how the plants grew when they were in separate trays.

8 **a)** Which plant grew quicker to start with when they were grown separately?
b) What happened when the two plants were grown together?

Look at diagram G. It shows what the two plants looked like. **G**

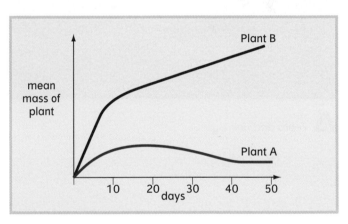

F This graph shows how the plants grew when they were together in the same tray.

Summary

Make lists of all the things that plants and animals compete for.

c) What do you think the two plants were competing for when they were grown together?
d) Why do you think plant B survived and not plant A?

9 Why do some woodland plants grow in the spring before all the trees get their leaves?

Populations

What controls the size of a population?

Predators are animals that hunt and kill other animals for food. The animals that they kill and eat are called **prey**.

Predators have adaptations which help them to hunt and kill their prey.

A *Zebra and lion.*

B *Artic fox and lemming.*

The number of predators in a community will depend on the numbers of prey. If there are lots of prey, the predators will have a lot to eat. If there is plenty of food, their young will survive and the population of predators will increase. If there are only a few prey, the predators will not have much food and some will die.

C

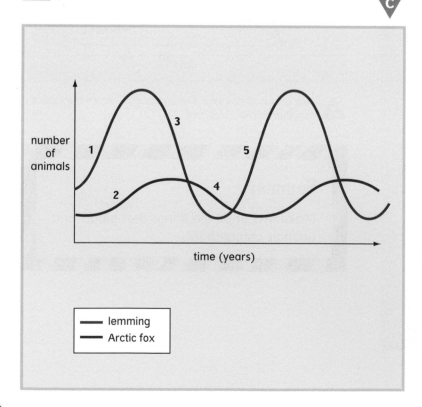

number of animals

time (years)

— lemming
— Arctic fox

?

1 **a)** What is a predator?
   b) What are prey?

2 Complete the sentences below to explain why the lion is a good predator.

   a) The lion is a fast runner . . .
   b) It has sharp claws and teeth . . .
   c) It has a sandy yellow colour to camouflage it . . .
   d) It has good eyesight . . .

The lemming and the Arctic fox live in Alaska. The Arctic fox is a predator which feeds on the lemming. Graph C shows what happened to the number of lemmings and Arctic foxes in one habitat over a number of years.

3 Which of the five labels below match up to each of the points 1 to 5 on graph C?

a) The number of Arctic foxes increases as there are lots of prey for them to eat.

b) The number of lemmings starts to fall as there are now lots of Arctic foxes hunting and killing them.

c) There are now only a few Arctic foxes left. The number of lemmings increases as there are fewer predators. The whole cycle starts again.

d) There are not many lemmings left. As food is scarce, the number of Arctic foxes gets less.

e) In the beginning, the lemmings have plenty of food. They start to breed and have young. The number of lemmings increases.

D *Diseases can spread rapidly through farmed crops.*

5
a) Why is competition between plants for water more of a problem in the summer?

b) How can overcrowding affect smaller plants?

c) Why does disease spread quicker through an overcrowded population?

6 Predators such as frogs do not eat plants, but they depend on plants for their food. Explain why.

7 Predators are adapted to hunting and killing their prey. What adaptations could the prey have that would help them escape?

8 Some plants make sure that their seeds are spread a long way from the parent. Why does this give the seeds a better chance of surviving?

A **population** of animals in a habitat does not keep on getting bigger. The size of a population is usually controlled by a number of different things.

4 Look at the list below. Copy out the factors which will limit the size of a population and stop it from getting too big.

- There is a shortage of food and water.
- The number of predators falls.
- Disease spreads through the population.
- There is less competition from other animals.
- The population runs out of space.
- There is plenty of food available.
- There is more competition from other animals.
- The number of predators increases.
- The climate changes and gets much hotter or colder.

A population of plants will not keep on growing forever either.

- If the population gets too big, there may not be enough water or nutrients.
- Overcrowding means bigger plants may put smaller ones in the shade. Plants that don't get enough light will die.
- Diseases spread quickly through an overcrowded population as the plants are a lot closer together.
- An increase in the number of herbivores feeding on the plants will keep the population down.

Summary

Give four factors that may limit the size of an animal population and four factors that may limit the size of a plant population. For each factor explain the effect it has on the population's growth.

Estimating population sizes

How can you work out the size of a population?

Sometimes scientists want to work out how big a population of animals is. This is not very easy as animals move about and may be spread over a big habitat. Sometimes animals hide so they can't be seen. Some animals only come out at night.

You can estimate the size of animal populations by **mark**, **release** and **recapture**.

- Trap a sample of the population.
- **Mark** them in some way to show that they have already been caught once. Small animals such as insects can be marked by a small spot of paint. Birds often have a small ring put round one leg.
- **Release** the animals back into the habitat to mix with the rest of the population.
- Trap a sample of the population again.
- See how many of the sample have been **recaptured** by counting how many of them are already marked.

 1 Why is it difficult to estimate the size of a population of animals?

A

E Estimate the size of the population using this calculation.

$$\text{population} = \frac{\substack{\text{number of animals} \\ \text{in first catch}} \times \substack{\text{number of animals} \\ \text{in second catch}}}{\substack{\text{number of animals that} \\ \text{were marked in second catch}}}$$

A group of pupils were investigating the size of different populations in a woodland habitat. Table C shows their results.
C

B *Yoghurt pots or small plastic cups are often used as simple traps. Food is left in the bottom of the trap to attract small animals.*

Animals	Number in first catch	Number in second catch	Number of marked animals in second catch
Woodlice	10	15	5
Snails	6	4	2
Beetles	12	10	6
Centipedes	8	6	2

Worked example

$$\substack{\text{population} \\ \text{of woodlice}} = \frac{10 \times 15}{5} = \frac{150}{5} = 30$$

 2 What do scientists use mark, release and recapture for?

3 a) How are birds marked?
   b) How are small insects marked?

4 Why is food often left in the trap?

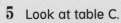

5 Look at table C.
  a) Work out the population of each animal. The size of the woodlice population has already been worked out to start you off.
  b) Draw a bar chart to show the population size of each animal.

 D

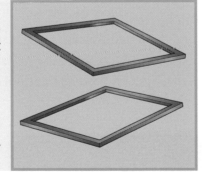

P How could you investigate a plant population?

F

Scientists estimate the size of a plant population using a **quadrat**. A quadrat is a metal or wooden frame. The quadrat is placed on the ground at random a number of times. You then simply count the plants found inside the frame at each place.

A group of pupils were using a quadrat to estimate the number of buttercups in a garden. The garden was 100 m². The quadrat size was 1 m². They threw the quadrat 10 times. Each time the quadrat landed they counted the number of buttercups inside the frame. Their results are shown in table E.

E

Sample	1	2	3	4	5	6	7	8	9	10
No. Buttercups	0	0	10	5	0	3	3	0	4	0

6 What is a quadrat used for?

7 Look at table E.
  a) How many m² of garden had the pupils sampled altogether?
  b) How many buttercups did they find?
  c) How big was the garden?
  d) The pupils estimated that there would be 250 buttercups in the garden. How did they work out this answer?

8 Why is it important that quadrat samples are taken all over a habitat and not just in one small area?

9 A group of pupils were estimating the size of a bluebell population in a wood which was 500 m² big. They used a 1 m² quadrat and threw it 25 times. Altogether they counted 22 bluebells. Estimate how many bluebells were in the wood.

10 If you were sampling two habitats to compare them, which factors would you want to keep the same?

Summary

Imagine you have just returned from a field trip to a forest. Prepare a report to explain how you were able to estimate the numbers of beetles and blackberry plants.

G9 Decomposition

What happens to animals and plants when they die?

A

Have you ever wondered where the dead leaves go when they fall off the trees in Autumn? Are they all swept up or do they just disappear? The answer is that they rot away or **decompose**. All living things decompose when they die. If they didn't, the Earth would be piled high with the bodies of dead animals and plants. Materials that can decompose or decay are called **biodegradable**.

1 What happens to living organisms when they die?

Decomposition happens in two stages. Dead animals and plants and waste materials such as urine or faeces are called **detritus**. In the first stage, **detritus feeders** (**detritivores**) such as shrimps, earthworms and woodlice feed on the dead tissue or waste material. They break up the dead organisms and waste materials into smaller pieces with a large surface area.

In the second stage, **decomposers** such as **bacteria** and **fungi** digest the dead tissue and waste materials into soluble substances which are absorbed by the decomposers for food.

The maggots which hatch from the eggs laid by these flies will feed on this cow pat. B

2 a) What is a detritivore?
b) Name three detritivores.

3 a) What is a decomposer?
b) Which types of microorganisms are decomposers?

 C

Small animals such as maggots, woodlice and earthworms start decomposition. They break down dead tissue and waste material into smaller pieces.

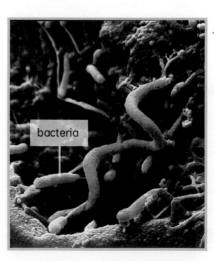 D

Microorganisms such as bacteria and fungi feed on these smaller pieces of tissue and waste.

bacteria

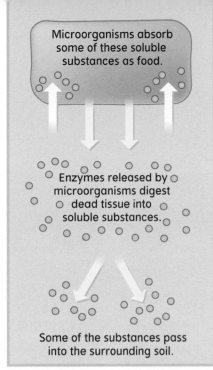

Microorganisms absorb some of these soluble substances as food.

Enzymes released by microorganisms digest dead tissue into soluble substances.

Some of the substances pass into the surrounding soil.

E *Microorganisms* release *enzymes* to digest the dead tissue and waste material.

P How could you investigate the effect of temperature on decomposition?

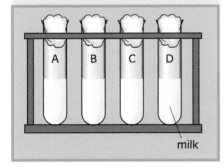

A B C D

milk

4 Look at diagram E.
   a) What do microorganisms release to digest their food?
   b) What is the dead tissue or waste material digested into?
   c) What happens to these products of digestion?

Detritivores and decomposers get energy from their food using **aerobic respiration** just like we do. They use the energy to stay alive and grow. This is the word equation for aerobic respiration:

$$\text{oxygen} + \text{glucose} \longrightarrow \text{carbon dioxide} + \text{water} \ (+ \text{energy})$$

Microorganisms grow best in warm, moist conditions. Many microorganisms also require a plentiful supply of oxygen. Dead tissue will decompose faster under these conditions as the microorganisms will be feeding and growing quickly.

5 **a)** Why do living organisms respire?
   b) What gas do organisms need for aerobic respiration?
   c) What waste gas do organisms make in aerobic respiration?

F This man's body was found frozen in ice.

G No air could get to this leaf as it was covered by sediment. The leaf has become a fossil.

6 Why does dead tissue decompose quickly when it is warm and damp?

7 Look at photograph F. Why did the dead body not decompose?

8 Look at photograph G. Why did the leaf not decompose properly?

9 Explain why freezing, drying or canning food helps to preserve it.

10 The three types of enzymes involved in digestion are proteases, amylases (carbohydrases) and lipases. Find out what each enzyme does.

Summary

Look back at the food web on page 11.
A Write out a food chain to include a named detritivore.

B Write out another food chain to include a named decomposer. (*Hint*: Slugs and snails eat fungi.)

C Explain how energy from the Sun is used by detritivores and decomposers for growth.

Nutrient recycling

Why is decomposition important?

Nearly all of the living tissue which makes up an animal or plant is made from just six elements. These are carbon, hydrogen, oxygen, nitrogen, phosphorus and sulphur. When living things grow, they lock these elements up in their cells. The elements become part of their bodies. When they die, their bodies decompose and these important elements are put back into the environment for other living things to use again. If animals and plants did not decompose, we would soon run out of the elements to make new living things!

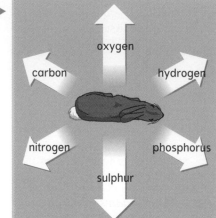

A

1 Name the six main elements which make up living tissue.

2 a) Why is decomposition important?
b) What would happen if dead bodies did not decompose?

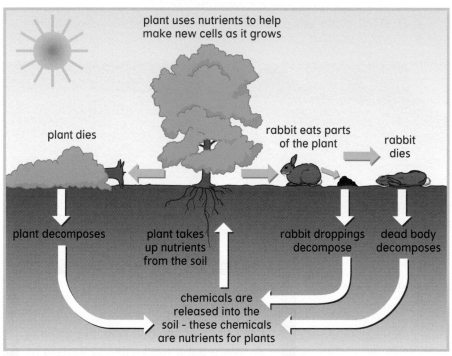

B   *Nutrient recycling in an ecosystem.*

Use the information in diagram B to answer these questions.

3 a) Where does the plant get its nutrients from?
b) What does the plant use the nutrients for?

4 a) How are the nutrients passed on from the plant to the rabbit?
b) How would nutrients be passed on from a rabbit to a fox?

5 How are the nutrients from dead organisms released back into the soil?

Have you ever wondered why gardeners put horse manure on their roses or why farmers spread cow manure or slurry on their fields? Horse manure and cow muck are natural fertilisers! When the waste decomposes it releases nutrients into the soil which are needed by plants for healthy growth.

6 Why do farmers spray cow manure on their fields?

C

Compost

Gardeners often dump dead plant material like grass cuttings in a big heap in the corner of the garden. Sometimes other plant material, like potato peelings or banana skins, is thrown on the heap too. As this plant material decomposes, important nutrients such as **nitrates** are released. This rotted plant material is called **compost**. Compost acts like a natural fertiliser. Gardeners dig the compost into the soil so that the nutrients will help plants to grow.

A compost heap.

Sewage

Sewage is human waste. Sewage works use microorganisms to decompose human waste and make it harmless. At the sewage works the sewage is left in sludge tanks where solid matter settles out. The sludge is first digested by **anaerobic bacteria**, which do not need oxygen for respiration. As they digest the sewage these bacteria produce methane gas which can be used as a fuel for cooking and heating. The remaining liquid and semi-solid sewage is then sprinkled onto a coke bed (coke is made from coal). Each piece of coke is covered by a layer of **aerobic bacteria** which need oxygen for respiration. Sprinkling the sewage over the coke bed increases the amount of oxygen in the sewage. As the sewage trickles through the coke bed it is digested by the microorganisms.

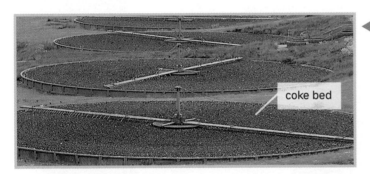

coke bed

7 **a)** What things are thrown on a compost heap?
   b) Why do gardeners add compost to their soil?
   c) Gardeners often 'turn' their compost heaps with a fork to allow air into the middle. Why do you think they do this?

8 Compost heaps are usually warm. Where does the heat energy in the compost heap come from?

microorganisms digest the sewage

piece of coke

9 **a)** What is sewage?
   b) What happens in sludge tanks?
   c) What happens to the waste as it trickles through the coke beds?
   d) Why does increasing the amount of oxygen in the sewage help to break it down?

10 **a)** What gas is produced by the anaerobic decomposition of sewage?
   b) What can this gas be used for?

11 What is the difference between aerobic and anaerobic decomposition?

12 Find out about fermentation (anaerobic respiration in yeast). How is it different from anaerobic respiration in humans?

Summary

A Produce an advertisement leaflet for a 'compost accelerator' which helps compost to rot faster. In your leaflet, explain how gardeners can save money on fertilisers by using compost.

B Draw a labelled flowchart to explain how sewage is broken down.

The carbon cycle

What is the carbon cycle?

All living organisms need **carbon**. They need it to make carbohydrates, fats and proteins. They use some of these chemicals to make new cells as they grow. They use some of the chemicals for respiration to give them energy.

Carbon is passed from one living thing to another in the **carbon cycle**.

An average person contains enough carbon to make nearly 13 kg of coal.

1 What do living organisms use carbohydrates, fats and proteins for?

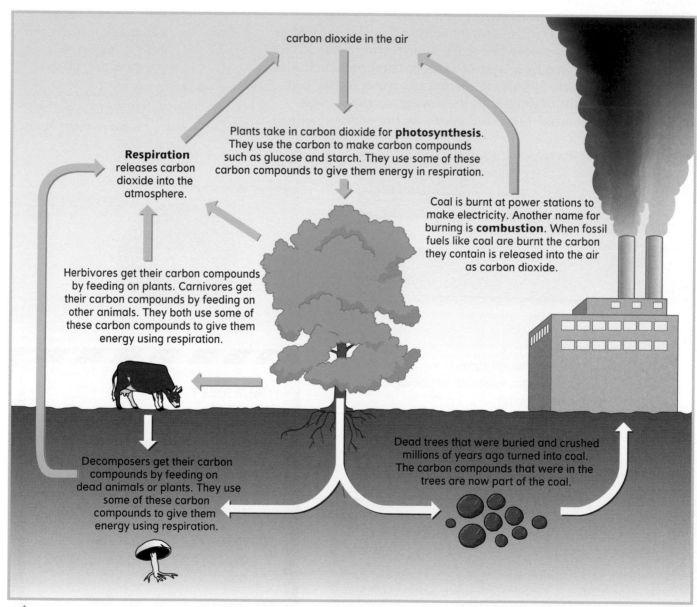

carbon dioxide in the air

Plants take in carbon dioxide for **photosynthesis**. They use the carbon to make carbon compounds such as glucose and starch. They use some of these carbon compounds to give them energy in respiration.

Respiration releases carbon dioxide into the atmosphere.

Coal is burnt at power stations to make electricity. Another name for burning is **combustion**. When fossil fuels like coal are burnt the carbon they contain is released into the air as carbon dioxide.

Herbivores get their carbon compounds by feeding on plants. Carnivores get their carbon compounds by feeding on other animals. They both use some of these carbon compounds to give them energy using respiration.

Decomposers get their carbon compounds by feeding on dead animals or plants. They use some of these carbon compounds to give them energy using respiration.

Dead trees that were buried and crushed millions of years ago turned into coal. The carbon compounds that were in the trees are now part of the coal.

A The carbon cycle.

Living organisms respire to get energy from their food. **Respiration** is a series of chemical reactions and can be summarised as a word equation. Most organisms need oxygen to respire. They use **aerobic respiration**.

Plants photosynthesise to make their food. **Photosynthesis** is also a series of chemical reactions and can be summarised as a word equation.

oxygen + glucose ⟶ carbon dioxide + water (+ energy)

oxygen is taken in for respiration

carbon dioxide is given out as a waste product

carbon dioxide + water (+ light energy) ⟶ glucose + oxygen

carbon dioxide is taken in for photosynthesis

oxygen is given out as a waste product

2 **a)** Why do plants photosynthesise?
  b) What gas do plants use as a raw material for photosynthesis?
  c) What gas is made in photosysnthesis?

3 How was coal formed?

4 **a)** What is combustion?
  b) What gas is given out when fossil fuels are burnt?

5 **a)** How do herbivores get their carbon?
  b) How do carnivores get their carbon?
  c) How do decomposers get their carbon?

6 **a)** Why do all living things respire?
  b) What gas do they use up in aerobic respiration?
  c) What waste gas is given out?

7 Do each of these processes add carbon dioxide to the air or use it up?
  a) respiration
  b) photosynthesis
  c) combustion

8 Explain how the following affect the amount of carbon dioxide in the atmosphere.
  a) cutting down the rain forests
  b) burning more fossil fuels

P How can you show that you are respiring?

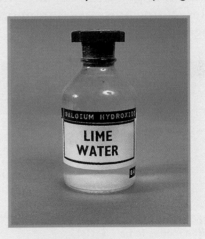

9 Many living organisms use up oxygen all the time. How is the oxygen replaced so that it doesn't run out?

10 How would the composition of the air above a wheat field change during a hot sunny day in early summer? Explain your answer.

Summary

Draw a diagram or flow chart to show how carbon is recycled. Include the following terms in your diagram: combustion, consumer, decomposer, photosynthesis, producer, respiration.

The nitrogen cycle

What is the nitrogen cycle?

All living organisms need a source of **nitrogen**. Plants need it to make compounds called **amino acids** which are used to make **proteins**. Animals get their nitrogen from the proteins in plants or other animals. Proteins are used to make new cells. They are also used to make **enzymes** which catalyse (speed up) all the chemical reactions that go on inside living organisms.

The air contains nearly 80% nitrogen, but nitrogen gas is no use to living organisms. It has to be changed into **nitrates** before it can be used by plants. **Nitrogen-fixing bacteria** in the soil are able to combine nitrogen from the air with other elements to make nitrates. Nitrogen is passed from one organism to another in the **nitrogen cycle**.

 1 Why do living organisms need nitrogen?

 A The nitrogen cycle.

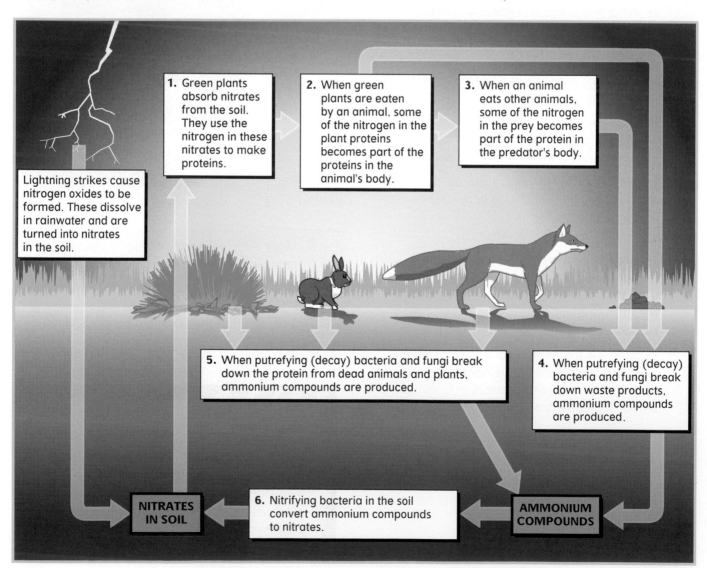

1. Green plants absorb nitrates from the soil. They use the nitrogen in these nitrates to make proteins.

2. When green plants are eaten by an animal, some of the nitrogen in the plant proteins becomes part of the proteins in the animal's body.

3. When an animal eats other animals, some of the nitrogen in the prey becomes part of the protein in the predator's body.

Lightning strikes cause nitrogen oxides to be formed. These dissolve in rainwater and are turned into nitrates in the soil.

5. When putrefying (decay) bacteria and fungi break down the protein from dead animals and plants, ammonium compounds are produced.

4. When putrefying (decay) bacteria and fungi break down waste products, ammonium compounds are produced.

NITRATES IN SOIL

6. Nitrifying bacteria in the soil convert ammonium compounds to nitrates.

AMMONIUM COMPOUNDS

2 How do the following get their nitrogen?
   a) plants
   b) herbivores
   c) carnivores
   d) decomposers

3 What do decomposers change proteins into?

4 What do nitrifying bacteria do?

B

5 How are bacteria important in the nitrogen cycle?

6 Explain how the following benefit the next year's crop.
   a) After beans and peas have been harvested, farmers dig the plants into the ground.
   b) Farmers often add artificial fertilisers to the soil when they plant crops.

7 Why do you think the nitrogen cycle works better in well aerated soil (soil that has lots of oxygen in it)?

8 During a flood or heavy rain, nitrates in the soil get washed into rivers and streams. What effect do you think this will have on plants in the rivers?

9 If a farmer adds no fertiliser to the land, the crop yield will fall within a few years. In natural ecosystems, like a forest, there is no fertiliser added, yet its production does not decline. Explain why.

In a natural ecosystem, such as a forest or meadow, plants eventually die and rot away. The nitrogen in the plants is recycled by decomposers. When farmers harvest crops they prevent nitrogen being returned to the soil. Farmers need to add **fertilisers** to the soil to help their crops grow.

C

Summary

Draw a diagram or flow chart to show how nitrogen is recycled. Include the following terms in your diagram: ammonium compounds, consumer, decomposer, nitrates, producer.

Population explosion

Will the Earth's resources last for ever?

The world's population is growing extremely rapidly. Over the last 100 years it has gone up from 2 billion to nearly 6 billion people. As the population increases we use up more and more of the Earth's **raw materials**.

! Every year the World's population grows by more than the whole population of the UK.

A *Limestone is dug out of the Earth's crust at quarries.*

B *Iron ore is used to make steel.*

C *In the rainforests, trees like mahogany are cut down to make furniture and window frames.*

D *Oil and gas need to be extracted from deep underground.*

Raw materials are natural materials which we get from the Earth. We use raw materials to make things. Limestone is a raw material which we use to make cement and glass. Limestone is dug out of the Earth's crust at quarries. Metal ores such as iron ore are also dug out of the Earth's crust. Iron ore is used to make steel. Wood is the raw material we use to make paper and furniture. The fossil fuels oil, coal and natural gas are all raw materials. Scientists think that we will run out of oil in about 30 years time if no new deposits are found.

?

1 What are raw materials?

2 a) Name six raw materials.
   b) What is made from limestone?
   c) What is made from iron ore?

3 Why are we cutting down trees from the rainforests?

4 Why do scientists think we may run out of oil?

Many things we throw away can be **recycled** and used again. People now recycle glass bottles, plastics, cans and paper. Bottles are crushed and melted into new glass. Recycled paper is used to make newspapers. Aluminium cans are melted down so that we can use the aluminium again. Recycling saves scarce raw materials.

E

5 a) What happens to glass bottles that are recycled?

   b) What is recycled paper used for?

   c) Why are aluminium cans melted down?

   d) Why is recycling a good idea?

F

As the population grows we are using up more and more land. We need more houses, roads, shops, factories, schools and hospitals. We also need to grow more food so large areas of land are being used for farming. As land is used up we are destroying many natural habitats. The animals and plants that lived there now face **extinction**. This means there will be none of them left.

G

6 a) Give two reasons why we are using up so much land.

   b) What new building work is taking place near your home or school?

7 a) What does it mean if an animal or plant becomes extinct?

   b) Why are many animals and plants facing extinction?

8 Think of as many reasons as you can why the Earth's population has increased so much over the last hundred years.

9 Explain the statement: 'When the Earth's human population was much smaller, the effects of human activity were usually small and local.'

10 Find out what is meant by the term 'sustainable development'.

Summary

Write a letter to your local paper explaining why the Earth's resources are running out. In your letter suggest how we can help to conserve scarce raw materials.

Land pollution

How are we polluting our land?

As our population grows we make more and more waste. A lot of this waste is just dumped into big holes in the ground. These rubbish tips are called **landfill sites**. Some of this rubbish is **biodegradable** and rots down. This can take a long time. Sometimes **toxic** chemicals are dumped on rubbish tips. If they leak out into the soil they can poison the wildlife.

As towns keep on growing, local councils have to find more landfill sites to get rid of our rubbish. This can be quite difficult as most people do not want a rubbish tip near their house. Most of the rubbish is **non-biodegradable** and will be unchanged after hundreds of years. Tips can be very smelly and they are not very nice to look at!

 **A** *A landfill site.*

 In the UK we produce over 100 million tonnes of rubbish every year.

 1 What is a landfill site?

2 Why should poisonous chemicals not be dumped on rubbish tips?

3 Why don't people want rubbish tips near their homes?

Many farmers spray toxic chemicals such as **herbicides** and **pesticides** on their land. Herbicides are chemicals which kill weeds. Weeds compete with the farmer's crop for water, nutrients and light. Pesticides are chemicals which kill pests such as insects that feed on the crop.

Many herbicides and pesticides are described as **persistent**. This means they do not break down naturally. They may be taken in by animals and accumulate (build up) in the cells of the animal. Eventually the concentration of chemicals may become so high that the animal is poisoned. Diagram C shows what happened when a pesticide called dieldrin was used in the 1950s.

B

4 **a)** What are herbicides?
b) Why do farmers want to kill weeds?

5 Why do farmers use pesticides?

C *As the poison passes along the food chain, it becomes more concentrated at each stage.*

Seeds were soaked in dieldrin to poison small animals that might eat them.

Each time a shrew ate some of the seeds, poison accumulated in its body fat.

The poison was passed along the food chain.

Each time a bird such as a falcon or a sparrowhawk ate poisoned prey, some of the poison accumulated in its body fat. The dieldrin also made the shells of their eggs very thin. Many eggs broke and the young did not survive.

6 Look at diagram C.
Why were seeds soaked in dieldrin?

7 a) What is a persistent pesticide?
b) How were the sparrowhawks and falcons poisoned?
c) Why were fewer young born?

D *A spoil tip.*

Mining produces lots of waste. Mining waste is called **spoil**. The spoil is just dumped on the Earth's surface. Eventually some spoil tips become so big that they look like hills. Spoil contains large amounts of poisonous metals like lead, copper and zinc. Compounds of these metals dissolve and leak into the soil.

Spoil tips look very ugly. People tried to grow grass and other plants on the tips to make them look nicer. Unfortunately the plants were poisoned by the metals and died. Scientists have now found some types of grass which are **tolerant** to the waste. This means that the plants are not affected by the poisonous metals. These grasses grow well on spoil tips, even though their cells and tissues contain a lot of the metal waste.

8 a) What is spoil?
b) What does spoil contain?

9 Why wouldn't most plants grow on the spoil tips?

10 What does it mean if a plant is tolerant to metals?

11 Look at food chain E. Why can't farmers graze their sheep or cows on the metal-tolerant grass?

E

The cells and tissues of the tolerant grasses contain a lot of the metal waste.

Traces of metal will be found in the meat and the milk of any cattle that feed on the grass.

P How can you investigate the effect of metals on plants?
F

12 Metals such as copper are poisonous because they cause enzymes to change shape (denature). Explain why this could affect an organism.

13 Many governments are now using biological control to limit the populations of pests which damage crops. In Holland, lice were damaging trees so the Government imported specially bred ladybirds which fed on lice.
a) Why did the Government introduce ladybirds into the community?
b) What is biological control?
c) Name one advantage of using biological control.

14 Explain why 'organic food' is more expensive than 'non-organic' food.

Summary

Write brief notes to answer the topic question at the top of page 32.

G15 Water pollution

How do we pollute our lakes and rivers?

A

Sewage is human waste. Sometimes untreated sewage is poured into rivers. Bacteria feed on the sewage and reproduce very quickly. Soon there are billions of them. The bacteria use up the oxygen in the water for **respiration**. Eventually there is no oxygen left and the fish and other aquatic animals die.

 1 a) What is sewage?
   b) What happens to the sewage that is poured into rivers?
   c) What happens to the number of bacteria in the river?
   d) How does this kill the fish?

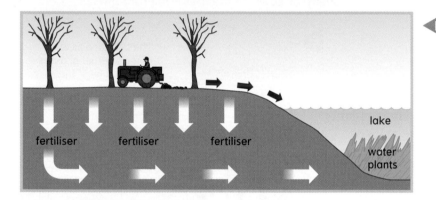

B

 2 a) Why do farmers add fertilisers to their crops?
   b) What do we call rapid plant growth in nutrient-rich water?
   c) Draw a flow chart to explain how this process happens.

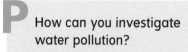
P How can you investigate water pollution?

Farmers add **fertilisers** to the soil to help their crops grow. Sometimes the fertilisers are washed out of the soil into lakes and rivers. Once in the water, fertilisers help water plants and algae to grow. Many plants and algae die because competition for light is so great. Bacteria feed on the dead plants and algae and their numbers increase rapidly, once again using up the oxygen in the water for respiration. This process is called **eutrophication**.

Farmers also spray herbicides and pesticides onto their crops. Sometimes these chemicals are washed into the rivers too. Diagram C shows what happened when a pesticide called DDT drained into a lake.

 3 How did the DDT kill the grebes?

C

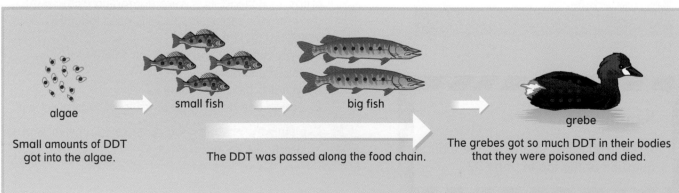

algae
Small amounts of DDT got into the algae.

small fish

big fish

The DDT was passed along the food chain.

grebe
The grebes got so much DDT in their bodies that they were poisoned and died.

Many factories tip poisonous chemicals into the water. There was a fishing town in Japan where a plastics factory was tipping waste mercury into the sea. The factory opened in 1952. People started dying from a mystery illness in 1953. Table D shows how many people died between 1952 and 1962.

4
a) What happened when fishing was banned in 1957?
b) What happened when fishing was allowed again in 1959?
c) What happened when fishing was banned in 1960?
d) How was the waste mercury poisoning people?

Year	Number of deaths
1952	0
1953	1
1954	12
1955	18
1956	53
1957 (fishing banned)	7
1958	5
1959 (fishing allowed again)	20
1960 (fishing banned)	4
1961	2
1962	1

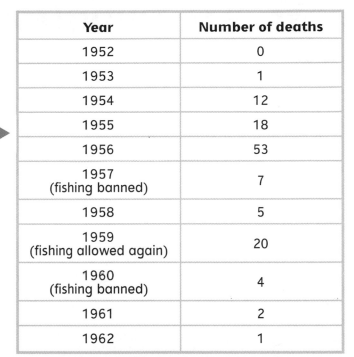

Oil is carried around the world in huge tankers. Sometimes tankers run aground on rocks and crude oil pours into the sea and is washed onto beaches. Oil kills the wildlife that lives there. It sticks to the feathers of birds such as gulls. It sticks to the fur of animals such as seals. The animals try to clean themselves and swallow the **toxic** oil.

! In 1989, the Exxon Valdez spilt 11 million gallons of crude oil into the sea around Alaska.

The Exxon Valdez oil disaster.

5
a) Name two animals which are harmed by oil pollution.
b) How are the animals harmed by the oil?

6 Look back at table D. Draw a bar chart to show the number of people who died from mercury poisoning between 1952 and 1962. Label your chart to show the dates when fishing was banned and allowed again.

7 Suggest ways that farmers could try to reduce the amount of fertilisers being washed out of soils.

Summary

You have been asked to write an introduction for a radio programme on the causes and effects of water pollution. Make notes to help you write the introduction.

Air pollution

How are we polluting our air?

When fossil fuels burn they make **smoke** and harmful gases such as **sulphur dioxide** and **carbon dioxide**. Smoke is made of solid fuel particles which don't burn and float off into the air instead. You can see the effects of smoke if you look at the blackened buildings in many towns and cities.

 1 a) What is smoke?
   b) Name two gases that are made when fossil fuels are burnt.

A *The Houses of Parliament before they were cleaned . . .*

B *. . . and after.*

Sometimes smoke mixes with fog to make **smog**. In 1952 there was very bad smog in London. It was so thick that street lamps had to be kept on in the day. The tiny particles in smoke can damage your lungs and cause bronchitis. The London smog killed nearly 4000 people.

C

 2 How can breathing in smoke harm you?

3 a) What is smog?
   b) How many people died in the London smog of 1952?

The main causes of air pollution are cars and lorries. Their exhaust fumes contain many poisonous gases. Before unleaded petrol was available, exhaust fumes also contained lead. If too much lead is breathed in, it can damage the brain and nervous system.

Photochemical smog is common in cities such as Los Angeles, Tokyo and Mexico City. It is caused by the effect of sunlight on exhaust fumes. In Tokyo, many drivers now wear masks and there are special 'clean air' booths where people can get fresh air to breathe when the smog is really bad.

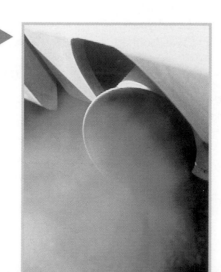

E

D *The table shows the increase in the number of vehicles on Britain's roads.*

Year	Number of vehicles (millions)
1930	2
1940	3
1950	4
1960	9
1970	15
1980	25
1990	38
2000	53

4 Why has unleaded petrol been introduced?

5 **a)** What causes photochemical smog?
 b) Name three cities which suffer from this kind of smog.

 How can you investigate air pollution?

G ! 75% of all air pollution is caused by motor exhaust fumes.

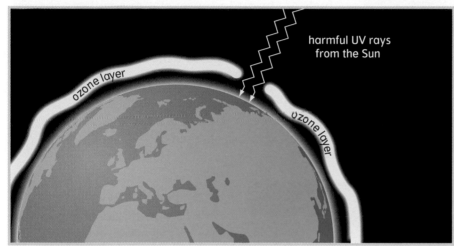

harmful UV rays
from the Sun

ozone layer

ozone layer

The Sun gives out harmful **ultraviolet rays** (UV rays) which can cause skin cancer. We are protected from them by a layer of **ozone** high up in the Earth's atmosphere. The ozone absorbs the UV rays and stops them reaching the Earth's surface.

6 **a)** How can UV rays harm animals?
 b) How does the ozone layer protect us?

CFCs (chlorofluorocarbons) are gases which used to be in spray cans and refrigerators. When these gases are released into the atmosphere they react with the ozone and break it up. This makes a hole in the ozone layer which allows UV rays through. As a result it is dangerous to go out in the Sun without sunscreen in some parts of the world as there is an increased chance of skin cancers. We no longer use CFCs.

H

CFC FREE

7 **a)** What are chlorofluorocarbons better known as?
 b) Why do aerosol cans no longer use these chemicals?

8 Use table D to draw a graph showing how the numbers of cars and lorries have increased over the last 70 years.

9 CF_3Cl is a chlorofluorocarbon. It breaks down to form compounds called free radicals ($Cl^{\bullet}$). These free radicals destroy ozone (O_3) in the following way:

strong sunlight

$$CF_3Cl \longrightarrow CF_3^{\bullet} + Cl^{\bullet}$$
$$Cl^{\bullet} + O_3 \longrightarrow O_2 + ClO^{\bullet}$$
$$ClO^{\bullet} + O^{\bullet} \longrightarrow Cl^{\bullet} + O_2$$

 a) Explain in words what happens.
 b) Why does this not happen at sea level?
 c) Why does this reaction then carry on?

Summary

A Draw a concept map to explain air pollution. Make sure that you include all the words in bold on these two pages.

B Add more information to your map to include land and water pollution.

Acid rain

What is acid rain and what problems does it cause?

A

Coal and oil contain sulphur. When they burn, the sulphur reacts with oxygen to form **sulphur dioxide**. The high temperatures produced when fuels are burnt in power stations and car engines also make nitrogen react with oxygen to form **nitrogen oxides**. Sulphur dioxide and nitrogen oxides are acidic gases which cause **acid rain**.

1
 a) Name two acidic gases.
 b) How is sulphur dioxide made?
 c) How are nitrogen oxides made?

B

Sulphur dioxide dissolves in rain to make sulphuric acid.
Nitrogen oxides dissolve in rain to make nitric acid.

2
 a) What acid is made when sulphur dioxide dissolves in rain?
 b) What acid is made when nitrogen oxides dissolve in rain?

3
 a) What does acid rain do to soil?
 b) How does this affect plant life?

Acid rain makes soil more acidic. Many plants cannot live or grow in acidic soil. Sometimes trees can be killed and forests destroyed. Tree roots hold the soil together on hills and mountain sides. If the trees are killed then the soil is washed away and new plants cannot grow there. Acid rain can make water too acidic for animals to live in. Many lakes and rivers no longer have fish.

C

4
 a) How is the soil held together on hills and mountain sides?
 b) What happens to the soil if the trees are killed by acid rain?

5 Why do many lakes and rivers no longer have fish?

Many power stations now have **acid gas scrubbers** fitted to their chimneys. These remove the harmful gases before the fumes are released into the atmosphere. Modern cars have **catalytic converters** fitted which clean up their exhaust fumes. The only real way to stop acid rain though is by burning fewer fossil fuels.

6 Why are acid gas scrubbers fitted at power stations?

7 Why do modern cars have catalytic converters?

Lichens are very useful organisms because they can tell us how polluted the atmosphere is. They are sensitive to the amount of sulphur dioxide in the air. Scientists can work out how polluted the air is by looking at how many kinds of lichen they can find. If there are not many types of lichen, then there must be a lot of sulphur dioxide in the air. If there are lots of different lichens then the air must be quite clean.

 8 Why are lichens useful to scientists?

 Lichens from an unpolluted area.

Graph G shows how many different lichens were found in and around a city. It also shows how much sulphur dioxide there was in the air.

 9 How many different kinds of lichen were found:
  a) in the city centre **b)** 3 km out
  c) 7 km out **d)** 12 km out?

10 What was the concentration of sulphur dioxide:
  a) in the city centre **b)** 3 km out
  c) 7 km out **d)** 12 km out?

11 How will the following reduce acid rain?
  a) More use of wind and solar power.
  b) Cheap and efficient public transport.

12 Why do you think alkaline lime (calcium hydroxide) is used in the acid gas scrubbers in factory chimneys?

13 Catalytic converters have a thin coating of a catalyst (platinum) spread over a large surface area.
  a) What is a catalyst?
  b) Why is the catalyst spread over a large surface area?

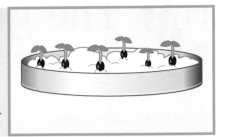
P How can you investigate the effect of acid rain on plants? **D**

 Lichens from a polluted area.

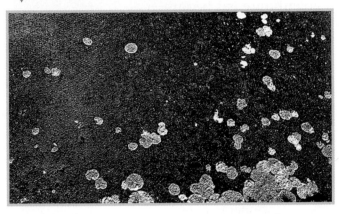

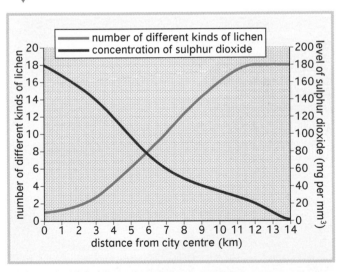

number of different kinds of lichen
concentration of sulphur dioxide

distance from city centre (km)

number of different kinds of lichen

level of sulphur dioxide (mg per mm³)

Summary

A TV company is making a programme about acid rain. You are asked to explain what acid rain is and what problems it causes. Make brief notes to help you remember what to say.

The greenhouse effect

What is the greenhouse effect?

When fossil fuels are burnt, carbon dioxide is released into the atmosphere. Scientists say that carbon dioxide is a **greenhouse gas** because it traps the Sun's heat energy in our atmosphere and makes the Earth warmer. This increase in the Earth's temperature is called **global warming**.

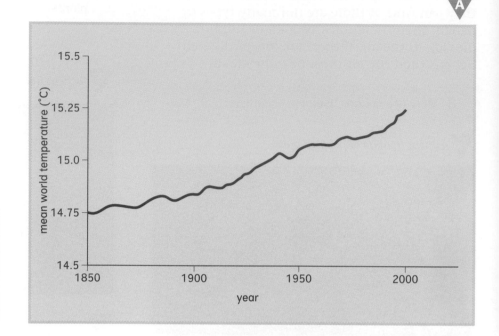

A

1 a) Why is carbon dioxide called a greenhouse gas?
b) What is global warming?

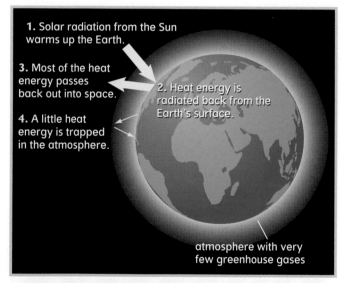

1. Solar radiation from the Sun warms up the Earth.

3. Most of the heat energy passes back out into space.

2. Heat energy is radiated back from the Earth's surface.

4. A little heat energy is trapped in the atmosphere.

atmosphere with very few greenhouse gases

B *Before global warming.*

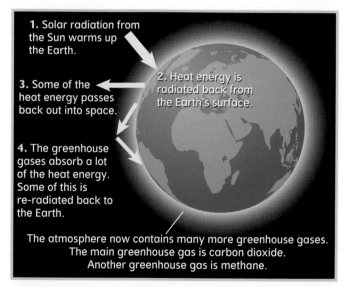

1. Solar radiation from the Sun warms up the Earth.

3. Some of the heat energy passes back out into space.

2. Heat energy is radiated back from the Earth's surface.

4. The greenhouse gases absorb a lot of the heat energy. Some of this is re-radiated back to the Earth.

The atmosphere now contains many more greenhouse gases. The main greenhouse gas is carbon dioxide. Another greenhouse gas is methane.

C *Since global warming.*

2 Look at diagram B (before global warming).
a) Where does the Earth get its heat from?
b) What happens to most of the heat that is radiated from the Earth's surface?

3 Look at diagram C (since global warming).
a) Name two greenhouse gases.
b) Do greenhouse gases allow the Sun's heat into the Earth's atmosphere?
c) How are greenhouse gases making the atmosphere warmer?

Carbon dioxide and methane are called greenhouse gases because they act a bit like the glass in a greenhouse. The glass lets the Sun's radiation (visible light) pass through. The warm Earth radiates heat energy as longer wavelength infrared radiation (IR radiation). The IR radiation is absorbed by the glass, and some of the heat energy is re-radiated back into the greenhouse. This is why it is usually warmer inside a greenhouse than it is outside.

 4 Why is it usually warm inside a greenhouse?

Scientists predict that the Earth's temperature will continue to rise as we make more and more greenhouse gases. They are worried that the polar ice caps will melt and the sea levels around the world will start to rise. This will cause serious flooding in many countries. Changes to the Earth's climate may make other parts of the world too dry to grow crops. This could lead to food shortages and famine.

D

E

F

 5 Why could global warming cause flooding?

6 How could global warming lead to famine?

7 Look at graph A.
  a) Scientists have recorded the mean temperature every year since 1850. How can they use this information to work out the mean temperature for the last 150 years?
  b) By how many degrees has the temperature gone up since 1850?

8 A lot of carbon dioxide is made when fossil fuels are burnt at power stations to make electricity. Think of all the things you could do at home which would help to reduce global warming.

9 The atmosphere on Venus is 96% carbon dioxide and 3% nitrogen. Explain, giving your reasons, what you think conditions on Venus might be like.

Summary

Draw a diagram of the Earth and label it to explain the causes of 'the greenhouse effect'.

Global warming

Why is global warming getting worse?

For many millions of years the amount of carbon dioxide in the air stayed about the same. Animals and plants added carbon dioxide to the air through **respiration**. Plants then used the carbon dioxide up for **photosynthesis**. The amount of carbon dioxide used up in photosynthesis balanced with the amount of carbon dioxide given out in respiration.

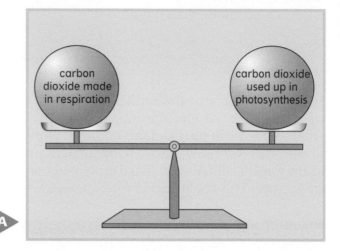

carbon dioxide made in respiration

carbon dioxide used up in photosynthesis

A

 1 **a)** How do living things add carbon dioxide to the air?

b) How do plants remove carbon dioxide from the air?

The amount of carbon dioxide in the atmosphere started to increase around about 1850. This was when we first started to burn fossil fuels to drive engines and machinery.

B

C

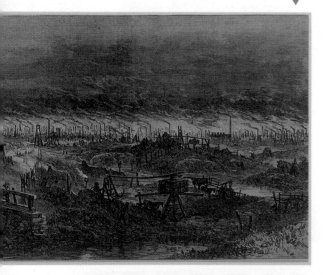

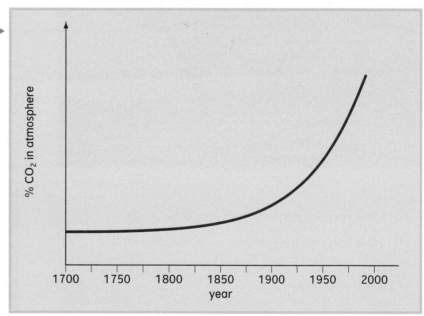

% CO$_2$ in atmosphere

1700   1750   1800   1850   1900   1950   2000
year

 2 Why did carbon dioxide levels start to go up in about 1850?

Since 1850, we have continued to burn more and more fossil fuels. Coal, oil and natural gas are burnt at power stations to make electricity. Petrol, diesel oil and kerosene all come from oil and are used to fuel our cars, lorries, ships and aircraft. We burn so much fossil fuel that we add 20 000 million tonnes of carbon dioxide to the atmosphere every year.

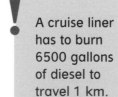

! A cruise liner has to burn 6500 gallons of diesel to travel 1 km.

3 **a)** What are the main reasons for burning fossil fuels?

b) How much carbon dioxide do we add to the air every year?

Not only are we producing more carbon dioxide, but we are also cutting down more and more trees. Every day, hundreds of hectares of tropical rainforest are cut down. This is called **deforestation**. All of these trees would be using up carbon dioxide for us if they were still living.

 4 a) What is deforestation?
b) How is this affecting global warming?

To make matters worse, a lot of the land that is cleared of rainforest is now used to graze cattle. We need more cows to make more burgers! Cows produce huge amounts of methane when they fart. Methane is another greenhouse gas. It traps heat in the atmosphere like carbon dioxide does.

Rice fields in China.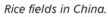

As the population grows we need more food. Rice is the main crop grown in many parts of the world. Rice also produces methane. As more rice is grown, more methane is added to the air.

Every year we produce millions of tonnes of rubbish. A lot of this is dumped in landfill sites. Microbes feed on the rubbish and cause it to decompose. As the rubbish decays in the absence of oxygen it gives off methane gas.

 5 a) What gas do cattle produce when they fart?
b) What gas do rice plants produce?
c) What gas is given out by rotting rubbish?
d) Which organisms cause decay?
e) What type of respiration takes place during decomposition without oxygen?
f) Give two reasons why the proportion of methane in the atmosphere is rising.
g) How does methane make the problem of global warming worse?

6 Find out what you can about the world climate conference and what it is trying to do.

7 Look at this data:

Year	Carbon emitted as CO_2 (billions of tonnes)	Average sea level rise (metres)
1860	0.2	0.05
1910	0.3	0.06
1960	1.6	0.08

a) What does the data tell you?
b) What conclusions could you come to with this data?
c) Why would you not want to use this data alone to decide that carbon dioxide levels are linked to sea-level rise?

Summary

You have been asked to write a simple introduction for a lesson on global warming. You need to explain what global warming is, and what causes it.

1 Copy and complete these sentences:

a) The place where an animal or plant lives is called its ____. (1)

b) All the animals and plants which live together in one place make up a ____. (1)

c) Any group of animals or plants of the same species make up a ____. (1)

d) All the living and non-living things in a habitat make up the ____. (1)

e) Temperature, rainfall and amount of light and water are called ____ ____. (1)

2 Read this information about some of the animals and plants in a woodland community.

A vole may eat 100 caterpillars in a day. The caterpillars feed on the leaves of oak trees. One oak tree has enough leaves to feed many thousands of caterpillars. Owls eat voles. An owl may eat three voles each day.

a) Use this information to draw out:

i) a food chain (1)

ii) a pyramid of numbers (1)

iii) a pyramid of biomass. (1)

b) Why can a pyramid of biomass be more useful than a pyramid of numbers? (1)

3 Look at the food chain.

> plant ⟶ moth ⟶ toad ⟶ owl

a) Why do all the animals and plants in the food chain depend on light energy for their food? (1)

b) For every 10 grams of moths that a toad eats, only 1 gram will be used to make new biomass. What happens to the other 9 grams that the toad has eaten? (2)

4 Look at the food web.

owls

weasel

small bird

shrew

rabbit

insect

worm

leaf

a) What might happen to the number of weasels if all the rabbits died of disease? Explain your answer. (2)

b) What might happen to the number of shrews if all the rabbits died of disease? Explain your answer. (2)

c) Which animals compete for insects? (1)

d) Name *one* other thing that animals compete for apart from food. (1)

e) Name *two* things that plants compete for. (2)

5 How might the following adaptations help a camel to survive in the desert?

a) A camel can store up to 100 litres of water in its stomach. (1)

b) It stores its fat in its hump rather than as a layer under its skin. (1)

c) It produces very little urine or sweat. (1)

d) It has big feet. (1)

6 Some farmers keep their chickens in barns where they have warmth, food and water but cannot move about a lot. Other farmers produce 'free-range' chickens which are allowed to wander about in the fields. What are the advantages and disadvantages of each method of farming? (2)

7 Lynx look a little like cats. They live in cold climates near the Arctic Circle. They hunt and kill hares for their food.

a) What name is given to animals like lynx which hunt and kill other animals for food? (1)

b) What name is given to the animals that are killed and eaten? (1)

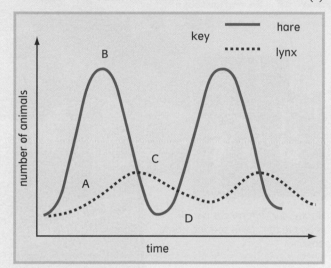

c) The graph shows what happened to the numbers of lynx and hares over a period of time.

   i) Why did the number of lynx start to increase at point A? (1)

   ii) Why did the number of hares start to decrease at point B? (1)

   iii) Why did the number of lynx start to decrease at point C? (1)

   iv) Why did the number of hares start to increase at point D? (1)

d) Name *two* other factors which could cause a population of animals to decrease. (2)

8 a) Which *two* gases are the main causes of the greenhouse effect? (1)

b) Which gas is the main cause of acid rain? (1)

c) How is deforestation affecting global warming? Explain your answer. (2)

d) Name *one* thing we could do to reduce the amount of acid rain. (1)

e) Insects once found only in southern Europe are now appearing in England. Explain why this is evidence of global warming. (1)

9 The graph shows how adding sewage to a river affected the amount of oxygen in the water.

a) What happened to the oxygen concentration when the sewage was added? (1)

b) Explain why this happened. (1)

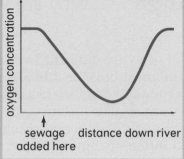

c) Why did the oxygen concentration go back to normal further down the river? (2)

d) Pollution of water by fertilisers can lead to the death of fish. Explain how this happens. (3)

10 The diagram shows part of the carbon cycle.

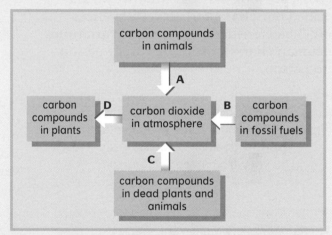

a) Match up each of the words below with the correct letter A to D on the diagram.

   i) decomposition   iii) combustion

   ii) respiration   iv) photosynthesis (4)

b) Why is it very important that plants and animals decompose once they have died? (1)

c) Why do dead animals and plants decompose more quickly in the summer than the winter? (1)

11 Farmers sometimes plant and harvest crops in the same fields year after year. If they do not add manure fertilisers the crop yields gradually decrease.

a) Why do crop yields gradually decrease? (1)

b) Why do some farmers dig the remains of plants into the ground after harvesting? (1)

c) Why is producing food from plants more efficient than from animals? (1)

Differences

Why are we all different?

All of us are different from each other. The most obvious differences are in what we look like but there are many other examples. For instance, different people enjoy doing different things and believe in different things. Despite these differences, we are all human beings.

1 List three ways in which each of us is different.

What we look like and what we do are called our **characteristics**. Differences in characteristics are known as **variations**. Human characteristics vary from person to person.

2 a) Write down a characteristic that is the same in all humans.
   b) How does this characteristic vary from person to person?

A *Despite our differences we all belong to the same species* Homo sapiens.

We all belong to the same **species**. A species is a group of organisms that can reproduce with one another to produce **offspring** that will also be able to reproduce. Between members of different species the characteristics vary a lot. Between members of the same species the characteristics vary a little.

! Sometimes two different species can reproduce with each other. However, their offspring are not able to reproduce. A liger is a cross between a lion and a tiger. **B**

3 Look at photographs C and D.
   a) Name two characteristics that are different between aardvarks and hyenas.
   b) Hyenas do not all have identical characteristics. Choose one characteristic of hyenas and describe how it varies from hyena to hyena.

An aardvark. **C**   **D** *Hyenas.*

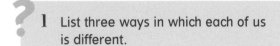

4 What is a species?

Inherited variation

Offspring have similar characteristics to their **parents**. We all have charcteristics like hair on our heads because we are all human. However, any variation in these characteristics (e.g. hair colour) comes from our parents. We all get some characteristics from our mothers and some from our fathers. We say that we **inherit** these characteristics. Since we inherit a mixture of characteristics we look slightly different to our parents. This is called **inherited variation**.

Environmental variation

Variation can also be caused by the surroundings (environment). For example, a plant may not grow as tall as another plant of the same species if it gets less light. The environment causes many differences between humans. These include things like having a broken leg, having a cold, and even the clothes we decide to wear. Differences caused by the surroundings are known as **environmental variation**.

6 List two of your characteristics affected by:
   a) what you inherited
   b) your environment.

7 How tall you grow is affected by characteristics that you inherited and the food that you eat (your environment). Name one other characteristic affected by a mixture of what you inherited and your surroundings.

8 Look at the picture of the liger.
   a) Name one characteristic it has inherited from the lion.
   b) Name one characteristic it has inherited from the tiger.
   c) How can we be sure that lions and tigers are different species?

5 **a)** Young plants and animals have similar characteristics to their parents. What will the organisms in photographs E and F grow into?
   b) Why do young plants and animals look similar to their parents?
   c) What variation is there between the animals in picture E?

E

F

Summary

Explain the meaning of the words in bold on these two pages.

Genes

Where is the information for inherited variation found?

Forensic scientists are people who examine crime scenes. If they find some blood or skin they can get a substance called DNA out of it. Most of the cells in our bodies contain DNA and everybody's DNA is slightly different. DNA from a crime scene can be compared with DNA from the suspects and the scientists can work out if any of the suspects had been there.

 A

Forensic scientists at work trying to solve a mystery.

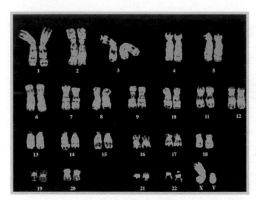

B

Human chromosomes magnified × 1500.

 1 Skin cells fall off our bodies the whole time. Forensic scientists wear white body suits and gloves. Explain why.

DNA is a molecule found in the nucleus of cells. Molecules of DNA are very long and form structures called **chromosomes**. The nucleus of most human cells contains 23 different sorts of chromosomes. There are usually two copies of each chromosome.

Chromosomes are made up of many smaller sections called **genes**. Each chromosome carries a large number of genes and each gene controls the production of a protein used in the body. The proteins that are made by our genes control all our inherited characteristics and these include everything from how tall we grow, to the colour of our eyes and the shapes of our faces. Genes contain the information that causes inherited variation.

 2 a) Draw an animal cell. Label the cell membrane, cytoplasm and nucleus.
b) In which part of the cell are chromosomes found?
c) What are chromosomes made from?

3 How many chromosomes *in total* are usually found in the nucleus of a human cell?

We can't really see genes but, using special dyes, we can stain them to make them show up.

You can think of chromosomes as a set of books. Each book (chromosome) contains chapters of instructions (genes). All the books together contain all the instructions needed to produce a human being. Each of us inherits a slightly different set of instructions (different genes) and so we all look slightly different.

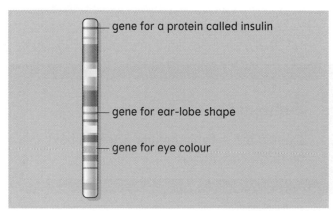

gene for a protein called insulin

gene for ear-lobe shape

gene for eye colour

C *Chromosome 11 showing some of the genes.*

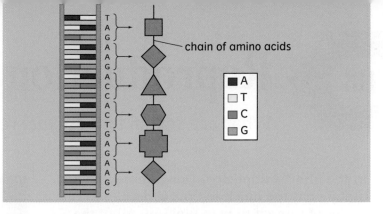

chain of amino acids

■ A
□ T
■ C
■ G

E *Sets of three DNA bases carry the instructions to add one amino acid to a protein chain. The DNA strand has been unravelled to make the drawing clearer.*

! There are about 31 000 different genes in humans.

4 a) Where are genes found?
   b) What do genes do?

5 How do genes allow us to inherit characteristics which vary?

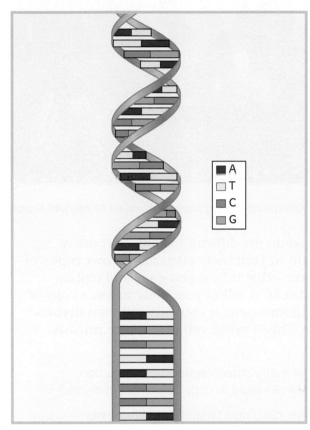

■ A
□ T
■ C
■ G

D *Part of a DNA molecule.*

The DNA code

A DNA molecule is made of two strands joined together by compounds called **bases**. The two strands are twisted around each other to form a double helix. There are four different bases (A, T, C and G) in a molecule of DNA. A gene is a sequence of bases along a strand of DNA.

Proteins are made up of amino acids linked together in a chain. Different proteins contain different sequences of amino acids. For example, the protein amylase which digests starch, found in saliva, is very different from the protein insulin which controls blood glucose levels.

A set of three bases (a **triplet**) in a DNA strand carries the code for one amino acid. So, this means the order or sequence of bases in DNA determines the order in which amino acids are arranged to make a protein.

6 a) What molecule is a chromosome made of?
   b) How many different kinds of bases are found in this molecule?
   c) What is the function of these bases?
   d) What do you notice about how the bases are paired up?

7 a) Name two proteins.
   b) Describe one similarity between these two proteins.

8 a) How many bases code for one amino acid?
   b) A protein consists of 120 amino acids. How many bases would there be in the gene that codes for this protein?
   c) Calculate how many different codes there are for amino acids.
   d) How many amino acids do you think there are? Find out if you are right.
   e) What do you think would happen if just one base in a gene was changed for another?

Summary

Write a short paragraph to explain the relationship between DNA, chromosomes, bases, amino acids and proteins.

H3 Reproduction in animals

What are sexual and asexual reproduction?

In the film 'Multiplicity', Doug Kinney finds that he has too much to do. He decides to get copies of himself to help him out. All of the copies have exactly the same chromosomes carrying the same genes and so have the same inherited characteristics. Exact copies like this are called **clones**.

 A *The four clones of Doug Kinney (all played by Michael Keaton).*

1 What is a clone?

2 If you could make a clone of yourself, what colour eyes would the clone have?

3 Look at photograph A. Write down one example of *environmental* variation you can see between the four clones.

Human adults are difficult to clone, but many of the cells in your body often make exact copies of themselves – that is how you grow and replace damaged cells. A cell in your body makes a copy of all the chromosomes it contains and then **divides** into two. This is called **cell division** or **mitosis**.

4 How many chromosomes does a human body cell need to copy before it can divide?

5 Draw diagrams to show what happens when a cell with four chromosomes reproduces by mitosis.

Single-celled organisms, like bacteria and amoebae, reproduce by mitosis. When a whole organism reproduces like this, it is called **asexual reproduction**. This means 'producing offspring from only one parent'. The offspring produced by asexual reproduction contain identical genes to their parent.

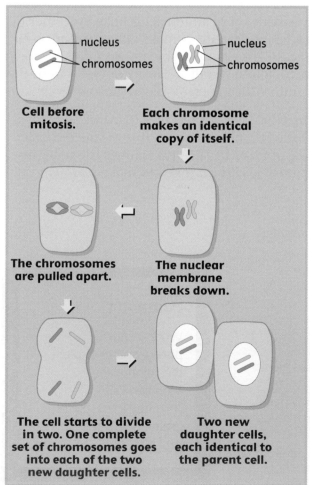

Cell before mitosis.

Each chromosome makes an identical copy of itself.

The chromosomes are pulled apart.

The nuclear membrane breaks down.

The cell starts to divide in two. One complete set of chromosomes goes into each of the two new daughter cells.

Two new daughter cells, each identical to the parent cell.

B *Mitosis – making copies of cells.*

*An amoeba (pronounced 'am-**mee**-ba') dividing.* C

50

Some insects can also reproduce asexually. In the spring, aphids reproduce asexually. The eggs of a female aphid simply grow into new aphids – there is no need for a male aphid!

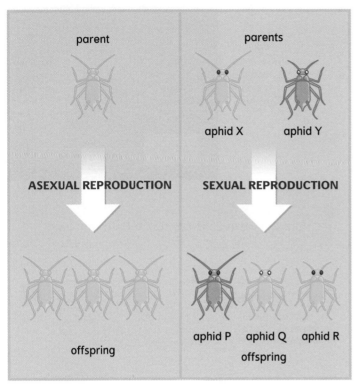

parent

parents

aphid X   aphid Y

ASEXUAL REPRODUCTION   **SEXUAL REPRODUCTION**

offspring

aphid P   aphid Q   aphid R

offspring

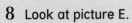 **D** *Aphids can reproduce asexually.*

Aphids can also reproduce sexually. **E**

 6 When aphids reproduce asexually, what do the offspring look like compared to the parent?

 A type of fly, called the cecidomyian gall midge, can also reproduce asexually. However, the offspring grow inside the mother and eat her alive!

In the autumn, aphids reproduce using **sexual reproduction**. A male and a female mate. The fertilised eggs produced have a mixture of chromosomes, half of them from each parent. The offspring will therefore get a mixture of genes and so have a set of characteristics that is different from each parent. Each offspring will have some characteristics from the male parent and some from the female parent.

7 When aphids reproduce *sexually*, what do the offspring look like compared to the parents?

Asexual reproduction is faster than sexual reproduction because the organisms do not need to find a mate. However, asexual reproduction does not produce variation, whereas sexual reproduction does.

8 Look at picture E.
   a) Name one characteristic that each aphid (P, Q and R) has inherited from aphid X.
   b) Name one characteristic that each aphid (P, Q and R) has inherited from aphid Y.

9 Bacteria can reproduce very quickly. They make new cells by splitting in two, a process called binary fission. If a bacterium divides every 20 minutes, how many bacteria would a single cell produce after 4 hours?

10 Explain why variation can be an advantage.

Summary

Copy and complete this table to compare sexual and asexual reproduction.

Type of reproduction	Speed	Number of parents	Variation produced	Examples of where it takes place
sexual				
asexual				

H4 Sexual reproduction in animals

How do gametes join to make baby boys and girls?

In most species, after mating has taken place, the females give birth to the offspring. In sea-horses, the males give birth! The female sea-horse places **egg cells** into a pouch in the male. He adds **sperm cells** which **fuse** (join) with the egg cells. This process is called **fertilisation**. Each **fertilised egg cell** develops into a baby sea-horse.

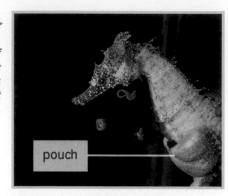

A

Each of these baby sea-horses is about 1 cm long.

pouch

 1 What is fertilisation?

Sperm cells and egg cells are known as sex cells or **gametes** and carry chromosomes from parents to offspring. Unlike **body cells**, gametes only have half the normal number of chromosomes. This is so that when they fuse, the fertilised egg cell contains the right number of chromosomes (and not double the number). Gametes are formed by a process called **meiosis**. Meiosis takes place in the testes in males and the ovaries in females.

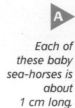 Human sperm cells are about 0.06 mm long.

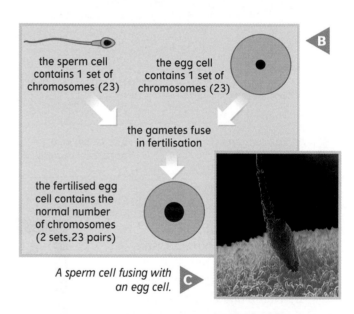

B

the sperm cell contains 1 set of chromosomes (23)

the egg cell contains 1 set of chromosomes (23)

the gametes fuse in fertilisation

the fertilised egg cell contains the normal number of chromosomes (2 sets, 23 pairs)

A sperm cell fusing with an egg cell. **C**

 2 a) How many chromosomes does a human gamete contain?
  b) How many chromosomes *in total* does a *fertilised* egg cell contain?

In humans, fertilisation occurs inside the woman. The fertilised egg cell contains a mixture of chromosomes (23 from each gamete). It will therefore have a mixture of genes and so it will grow into a baby with a set of characteristics that is different from either parent.

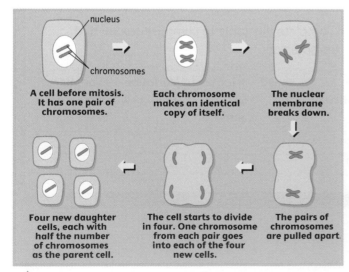

nucleus

chromosomes

A cell before mitosis. It has one pair of chromosomes.

Each chromosome makes an identical copy of itself.

The nuclear membrane breaks down.

Four new daughter cells, each with half the number of chromosomes as the parent cell.

The cell starts to divide in four. One chromosome from each pair goes into each of the four new cells.

The pairs of chromosomes are pulled apart.

D *Meiosis – forming gametes.*

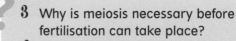 **3** Why is meiosis necessary before fertilisation can take place?
  4 Draw diagrams to show what happens when a cell with four chromosomes produces gametes.

5 What kind of cell division (mitosis or meiosis):
   a) produces sperm cells
   b) produces an adult from a fertilised egg cell
   c) produces new cells to repair wounds?

6 Look back at photograph B on page 48. Are these chromosomes from a man or a woman?

7 Why do brothers and sisters tend to look more alike than unrelated individuals?

One pair of chromosomes in the fertilised egg cell controls whether it will grow into a boy or a girl. These are called **sex chromosomes**. There are two types of sex chromosome – X and Y. Women have two X sex chromosomes and men have one X and one Y. Women are described as being XX and men as XY.

Half of a man's sperm cells contain an X sex chromosome, and the other half contain a Y sex chromosome. All egg cells contain an X sex chromosome. So, whether a baby is a boy or a girl depends only on the sperm cell.

8 Are your sex chromosomes XX or XY?

9 Look at diagram E. Draw a similar diagram to show how the gametes could produce a baby boy.

10 Name one way in which an egg cell is different from a normal body cell.

11 Explain why roughly 50% of children born are girls.

12 Identical twins are formed when the fertilised egg cell splits into two shortly after fertilisation. Non-identical twins are formed when two egg cells are fertilised by two separate sperm cells and grow in the womb at the same time. Explain why identical twins must be the same sex, but non-identical twins can be either the same or different sexes.

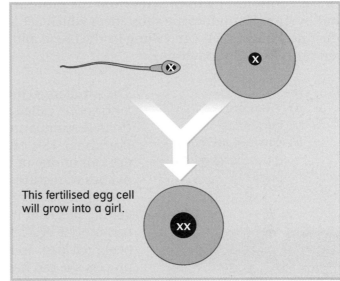

This fertilised egg cell will grow into a girl.

Summary

A Copy and complete the table to compare mitosis and meiosis in human cells.

Type of cell division	Where it takes place	Number of chromosomes in parent cell	Number of chromosomes in daughter cells	Are daughter cells identical to parent cell?
mitosis				
meiosis				

B Explain how the sex of a baby is inherited.

Fertility

How can a woman control her fertility?

Normally, women only give birth to one child at a time. Only once have eight *living* babies (octuplets) ever been born together. One died a week later, but the others are still alive. Their mother, Nkem Chukwu, became pregnant with so many babies as a result of **fertility treatment**.

 1 Why did Nkem Chukwu have so many children?

Each month a woman releases an egg cell from an **ovary**. This is controlled by **hormones** from the **pituitary gland** and ovaries. Hormones are substances which act like 'chemical messengers', travelling in the blood and 'telling' certain cells to do something.

 2 a) What are hormones?
b) How are hormones moved around the body?

The pituitary gland secretes a hormone called **FSH** (follicle stimulating hormone). FSH causes an egg cell in one of the ovaries to mature. If a woman is having trouble getting pregnant it may be because the egg cells are not being released. To help this process she can have injections of **fertility drugs** containing FSH.

Fertility treatment can cause more than one egg to be released at a time, so many egg cells are fertilised, and many babies start to grow.

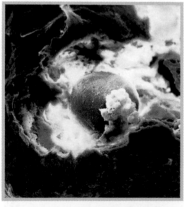

A An egg cell being released from an ovary. Magnification × 2130.

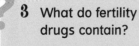 **3** What do fertility drugs contain?

4 Where is the pituitary gland?

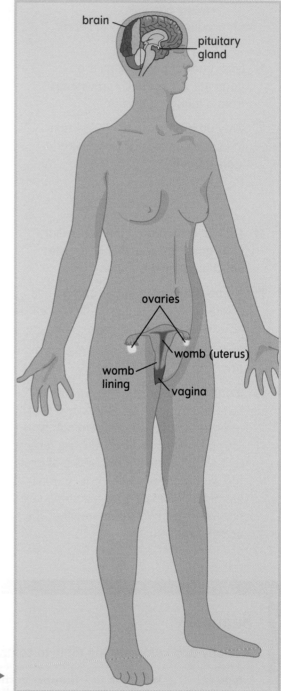

B

brain
pituitary gland
ovaries
womb (uterus)
womb lining
vagina

 Nearly 10 000 sets of twins are born naturally in the UK each year. Non-identical twins are the result of two egg cells being released at the same time. Identical twins are the result of a fertilised egg cell dividing, and the two new cells separating. Each cell grows into a baby.

The menstrual cycle

Several hormones are involved in controlling the **menstrual cycle**. FSH causes an egg cell to mature in one of the ovaries. FSH also **stimulates** (causes) the ovaries to produce the hormone **oestrogen**. Oestrogen causes the lining of the womb to get thicker. The thick womb lining contains many blood vessels to supply a growing baby with food and oxygen. Oestrogen **inhibits** (stops) the pituitary gland from producing any more FSH and stimulates the pituitary gland to produce another hormone called **LH** (luteinising hormone). LH stimulates the release of a mature egg cell from the ovary in the middle of the cycle. If the egg cell is not fertilised, the hormones stop being produced and the womb lining breaks down and passes out of the vagina. This is called a **period**. The cycle starts again with another egg cell getting ready to be released.

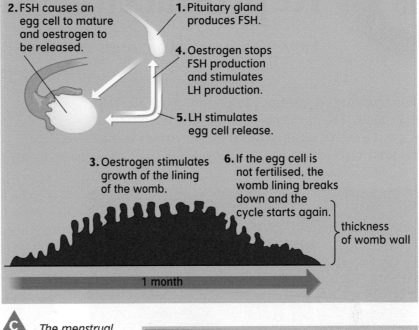

2. FSH causes an egg cell to mature and oestrogen to be released.

1. Pituitary gland produces FSH.

4. Oestrogen stops FSH production and stimulates LH production.

5. LH stimulates egg cell release.

3. Oestrogen stimulates growth of the lining of the womb.

6. If the egg cell is not fertilised, the womb lining breaks down and the cycle starts again.

thickness of womb wall

1 month

 The menstrual cycle.

Different methods of contraception. **D**

oral contraceptives

DELFEN

Contraception is used to prevent pregnancies. Some contraceptives come as pills which a woman can swallow. The pills contain oestrogen which inhibits FSH production so that no egg cells mature. This is called **oral** (by mouth) **contraception**.

Oral contraception works about 99% of the time. However, there can sometimes be problems. The pills:

● can cause headaches or sickness
● will not work if a woman forgets to take them – most types need to be taken every day.

Summary

Produce a leaflet to explain how a woman can control her fertility. Include the advantages and disadvantages of the different methods. Include the following words in your leaflet: contraception, FSH, hormone, LH, oestrogen, ovary, pituitary.

?

5 Which hormones controlling the menstrual cycle are produced by:
   a) the pituitary gland
   b) the ovaries?

6 What is the function of each of these hormones?

7 What do oral contraceptives do?

8 What might happen if a woman forgets to take them?

9 Fertility drugs can lead to multiple births. Explain how this can happen.

10 Explain how hormones control the release of egg cells. Present your answer as a flow chart.

Reproduction in plants

How can we make clones of plants?

The Quaking Aspen trees in picture A are all really one plant. The trunks are joined by underground roots. One tree has produced all the others using **asexual reproduction**.

1   A leaf is cut off a plant.

2   *Rooting powder contains a plant hormone which helps new roots to grow.*

3   *The plastic bag helps to keep the conditions around the leaf damp, otherwise it might dry up.*

4   *After a few weeks, new roots have grown. The leaf can now get water from the soil and the plastic bag is not needed any more. After a couple of months a new plant has grown.*

 C

? 1   What is asexual reproduction?

Asexual reproduction in plants

Many plants use asexual reproduction to make copies of themselves so that they can spread over a large area very quickly. Strawberry plants are another example. A stem called a 'runner' grows out of the parent plant. New plants grow at points along the runner.

runner

B   *A strawberry plant can reproduce asexually using runners.*

The new strawberry plants contain exactly the same genes as the parent plant. They are **clones**. Since clones of any organism contain identical genes, they are said to be **genetically identical**.

? 2   Explain why all the trees in picture A are the same.

Gardeners can make clones of plants by cutting off parts of a plant and growing new plants from them. This is called taking **cuttings**. Picture C shows how new plants are grown from African violet plants.

? 3   Write a short piece for a magazine explaining how to grow African violets from cuttings. Your article should contain step by step instructions and an explanation of why each step is necessary.

Growing plants from cuttings.

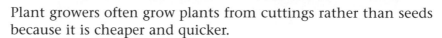

Parts of water hyacinth plants break off and grow into new plants. In a single summer, up to 60 000 clones can be produced from one plant. It is a serious pest because it blocks up rivers. **E**

P
How would you find out if it is only leaves that can be used for cuttings or whether other parts of plants will work just as well?

Plant growers often grow plants from cuttings rather than seeds because it is cheaper and quicker.

4 **a)** Why do plant growers grow new plants from cuttings?
   b) If a plant grower grows hundreds of plants from cuttings it is too fiddly to put plastic bags over each pot. How do you think a plant grower would keep the atmosphere damp?

Sexual reproduction in plants

Many plants have flowers. These produce male gametes (pollen grains) and female gametes (egg cells). Pollen grains are carried from one flower to another by insects or the wind. The pollen grains can then fuse with the egg cells and seeds are produced. The seeds grow into new plants. These plants will have a mixture of genes from two parents.

5 **a)** Which plants will show inherited variation, those grown from seeds or those grown from cuttings?
   b) Explain your answer to part a).

6 Why do you think strawberry plants reproduce both sexually and asexually?

7 Find out about another method of asexual reproduction in plants. State where you get your information from.

8 Why is it easier to clone plants than to clone humans?

Summary

You have been asked by a gardening magazine to write a piece about producing cloned plants. You will need to explain why plants formed by asexual reproduction are always the same, while plants formed from seeds show similarities and differences.

The discovery of genes

How was the idea of genes developed?

The *idea* of genes was first put forward by an Austrian Monk in 1865. His name was Gregor Mendel and he came up with his theory by looking at pea plants. Between 1856 and 1863 he grew nearly 30 000 pea plants in the monastery garden!

Mendel looked at different characteristics of the pea plants, one of which was their height. Some pea plants were naturally tall and some were naturally short.

He bred (crossed) these plants together, grew the seeds and looked at the characteristics of the new plants.

A   *Gregor Mendel (1822–1884).*

? 1 a) Who first put forward the idea of genes?
   b) What plant did he use in his investigations?

C   *One of Mendel's crossing experiments.*

B   *Some pea plants are naturally tall and others naturally short.*

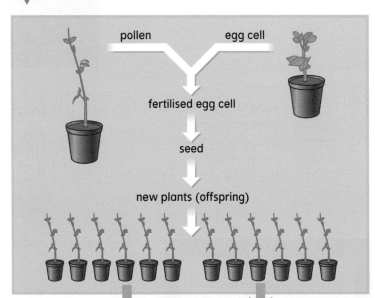

pollen   egg cell

fertilised egg cell

seed

new plants (offspring)

? 2 a) What is meant by 'crossing' plants?
   b) Does crossing involve sexual or asexual reproduction?

At the time, scientists thought that offspring got a 'blend' of characteristics from the parents. If this theory was right, then Mendel should have got medium height pea plants by crossing a tall plant with a short one. He didn't. He only got tall plants.

Mendel wondered where the 'shortness' characteristic had gone and whether he could get it back. So he crossed two of the new tall plants.

Mendel's next crossing experiment. D

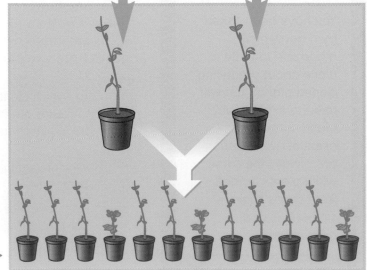

3 Look at diagram D.
   a) Did Mendel manage to get the short characteristic back again?
   b) What percentage of the pea plants were short?

Mendel decided that 'factors', each carrying the information for a certain characteristic, were passed from parents to offspring. He said that these 'factors' could not be changed and so the pea plants could either be tall or short depending on the 'factor' that they inherited. Pea plants could not have medium heights.

Walther Flemming (1843–1905) discovered chromosomes.

4 a) What did Mendel's 'factors' do?
   b) What do we call his 'factors' today?

 Wilhelm Johanssen (1857–1927) developed Mendel's ideas and invented the word 'gene'.

In Mendel's day, chromosomes had not been discovered and his work was ignored. Scientists could not understand how 'factors' could explain the large variation of some characteristics (like height in humans). Nor could they see how to use Mendel's theory to explain Darwin's theory of evolution (see page 78). They argued that if the factors could not change, then a species could not change (evolve) into other species over thousands of years.

Chromosomes were discovered in the 1880s and once they had been studied in more detail, scientists began to see how Mendel's 'factors' could work. By the early 1900s scientists were beginning to accept Mendel's ideas and the word **gene** was invented in 1909.

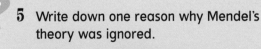 *James Watson (1928–) and Francis Crick (1916–) discovered the structure of DNA in 1953.*

5 Write down one reason why Mendel's theory was ignored.

6 What was Mendel's evidence that characteristics did not 'blend'?

7 There is a lot of variation in human height. What else, apart from genes, controls how tall you grow?

8 a) List the names of the scientists mentioned on these two pages and write down a brief sentence about what each one did.
   b) Find out about one other scientist and his or her work on the discovery of genes.

Summary

A TV programme is to be made about the work of Gregor Mendel. The producer has asked you to write down a list of the main points that should be covered. These should include why the importance of Mendel's work was not recognised until after his death.

People who do this sort of thing for a living are called television researchers.

Alleles

What are dominant and recessive alleles?

As a result of all his experiments, Mendel thought that the 'factors' controlling characteristics came in pairs. We now know that chromosomes come in pairs. Since each chromosome in a pair contains the same genes, there must be two genes for each characteristic.

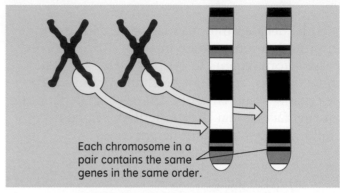

Each chromosome in a pair contains the same genes in the same order.

A *Most cells have two chromosomes of the same type, so there are two copies of each gene.*

1 Explain why normal body cells in organisms contain two genes for each characteristic.

Another characteristic of pea plants that has been used in the study of genes is the colour of the flowers. Pea plants have either red or white flowers. If red-flowered plants are bred with white-flowered plants all the offspring have red flowers; no white or pink or anything else. This is explained by the idea that some genes for the same characteristic (e.g. flower colour) contain slightly different instructions (e.g. white and red). Different versions of the same gene are called **alleles** (pronounced '*a-leels*'). If both chromosomes in a pair contain the same allele, the plant is **homozygous** for that characteristic. If the chromosomes in a pair contain different alleles, the plant is **heterozygous**.

B *Alleles are genes for the same characteristic that contain slightly different instructions.*

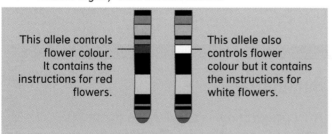

This allele controls flower colour. It contains the instructions for red flowers.

This allele also controls flower colour but it contains the instructions for white flowers.

Gametes contain only one of each type of chromosome. So each gamete will contain only one allele for flower colour.

2 What are alleles?

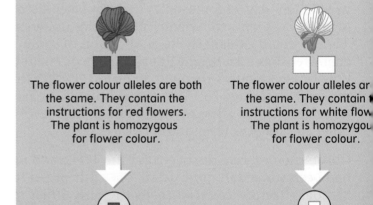

The flower colour alleles are both the same. They contain the instructions for red flowers. The plant is homozygous for flower colour.

The flower colour alleles ar the same. They contain instructions for white flow The plant is homozygou for flower colour.

All the pollen grains (male gametes) will get one copy of the red flower colour allele.

All the egg cells (female gametes) wi get one copy of the white flower colour alle

All the offspring have both alleles. However, all the flowers are This is because red is the dominant allele. The plant is heterozygous for flower colour.

C *The alleles of the gene for flower colour are red and white.*

3 a) What are the gametes produced by humans called?
b) What are the gametes produced by plants called?
c) Explain why pea plant gametes only have one type of allele for flower colour.

When the gametes fuse, the fertilised egg cell gets two alleles for flower colour. Every cell in the new plant will have two alleles, one from each parent. In diagram C, the offspring has one allele for white flowers and one for red flowers. The red flower allele is said to be **dominant**. It does not allow the white flower allele to work and so all the plants have red flowers. The white flower allele is said to be **recessive**.

In genetic diagrams we use letters to represent the alleles. The dominant allele has a capital letter and the recessive allele has a lower case version of the same letter. In this case R = red and r = white.

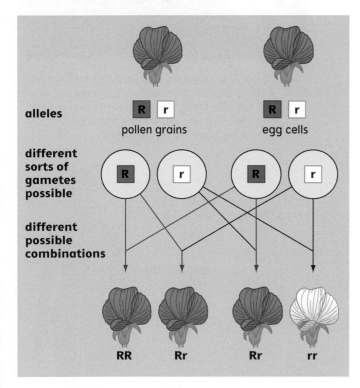

4 Look back at page 58. There are two alleles for pea plant height: tall and short.
  a) Which allele is dominant?
  b) Which allele is recessive?

Look at diagram D. If we take two of the plants which contain the two different alleles and cross them, we will get some plants with white flowers again.

The characteristics from recessive alleles are only seen if there are two copies of the recessive allele. The characteristics from dominant alleles are seen even if there is only one copy.

Leopards and black panthers are the same species. The black panther has two recessive alleles that make its fur black rather than spotted.

5 a) What is the dominant fur colour in leopards and panthers?
  b) What combination of alleles could the leopard have?

6 In what circumstances will the characteristics of a recessive allele be seen?

7 a) What will the colour of pea flowers be for the following pairs of alleles?
      RR   Rr   rr
  b) Which of these pairs of alleles are homozygous and which are heterozygous?
  c) What percentage of the pea flowers produced in diagram D are red?

8 The allele for tall pea plants is **T** and the allele for short plants is **t**.
  a) Draw a diagram, like diagram D, to show how Mendel got some short plants by crossing two tall ones.
  b) What is the ratio of tall plants to short plants?

Summary

Black hair colour is dominant to red. The allele for black is **B** and the allele for red hair is **b**.

Draw a diagram to show the possible hair colours of the children of two heterozygous black hair colour parents. Label your diagram with all the words in bold on these two pages.

H9 Inherited diseases

What are inherited diseases?

Some diseases that affect nerves cause the body to shake or jerk. From ancient times, until about 250 years ago, it was thought that people with these diseases were possessed by a demon. To try to cure the disease, holes were often cut into people's skulls, to try to release the demon!

 1 Name one symptom that might be caused by a nerve disease.

Huntington's disease

We now know much more about what causes diseases. **Huntington's disease** is caused by genes and is an example of a **genetic** or **inherited disease**. You can only get inherited diseases if your cells contain the alleles that cause them. You can't catch them.

 2 What is an allele?

3 a) What is an inherited disease?
b) Give one example.

Huntington's disease only affects people when they are about 40 years old. At this time nerves begin to be destroyed and the person's body starts to jerk uncontrollably.

 4 a) What is meant by the 'nervous system'?
b) Where are most nerves damaged by Huntington's disease?

A parent with Huntington's disease may pass it onto his or her children. It is a dominant allele and so even if a child only gets one copy of the allele, they will still get the disease. There is no cure for Huntington's disease.

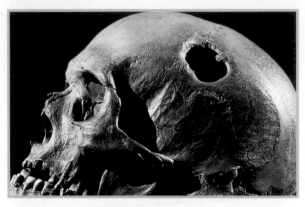

A The skull of someone who probably suffered from a nerve disease. This skull is 2500 years old. You can tell that the hole was cut while the person was still alive because it has smooth edges where the bone started to regrow.

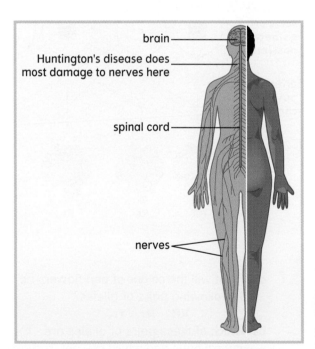

brain

Huntington's disease does most damage to nerves here

spinal cord

nerves

B The parts of the nervous system. The nerves in the nervous system are damaged by Huntington's disease.

 5 a) What is a dominant allele?
b) Do people with Huntington's disease need to be homozygous for the allele? Explain your answer.

Cystic fibrosis

This is an inherited disease that causes faulty cell membranes. Cells in the lungs produce too much of a sticky substance called mucus. This collects in the lungs and needs to be removed by special treatment (photograph C). There is no cure.

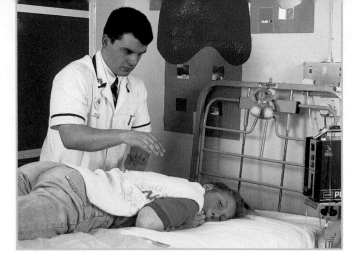

Treatment for cystic fibrosis. The person is hit gently on the back to help get rid of the mucus.

6 People with cystic fibrosis often have trouble breathing. Why do you think this is?

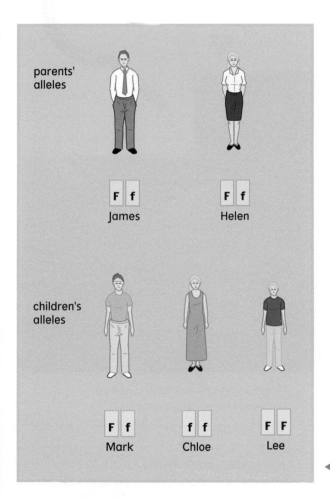

parents' alleles

F f
James

F f
Helen

children's alleles

F f
Mark

f f
Chloe

F F
Lee

D

Cystic fibrosis is caused by a recessive allele. People who have one copy of this allele are called **carriers**. They do not have the disease but they can pass the allele on to their children. If both parents have this recessive allele there is a chance that some of their children may get two copies of the allele. If this happens, a child will have cystic fibrosis.

7 Diagram D shows some pairs of alleles in a family. The small letter 'f' in a box shows the allele which causes cystic fibrosis.
   a) Explain why neither parent has cystic fibrosis.
   b) Which of their children have cystic fibrosis? Explain your answer.
   c) Which of their children are carriers of the disease?
   d) Are people with cystic fibrosis homozygous or heterozygous for the allele?
   e) Is a carrier of cystic fibrosis homozygous or heterozygous for the allele?

8 Why can Huntington's disease be passed on by only one parent?

9 Draw diagrams to show why:
   a) about 50% of children born to someone suffering from Huntington's disease get the disease
   b) about 25% of children born to a couple who are both carriers of cystic fibrosis get the disease.

Summary

Write brief notes to describe why you can't catch inherited diseases. In your notes, explain how it is possible that children may not inherit a genetic disease from their parents. Include the following words in your notes: carrier, dominant allele, recessive allele.

Sickle-cell anaemia

Why are sickle-cell anaemia alleles sometimes useful?

Some alleles that cause inherited diseases can actually help people. An example is the allele that causes **sickle-cell anaemia**. This disease causes faulty **haemoglobin** to be made. Haemoglobin is the substance found in red blood cells that allows them to carry oxygen. The faulty haemoglobin has two effects on red blood cells:

- it makes them less able to carry oxygen
- it makes them 'sickle-shaped'.

A

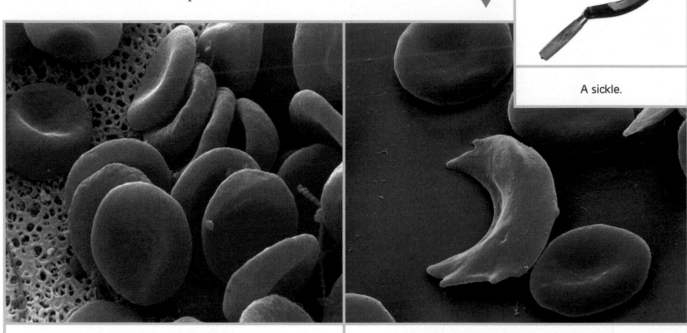

A sickle.

These are normal red blood cells.

These blood cells are from somebody who has sickle-cell anaemia.

 1 **a)** What does haemoglobin do?
b) What is the name of the disease that causes faulty haemoglobin?
c) How do you think the disease got the first part of its name?

A person needs two copies of the sickle-cell anaemia allele to get the disease. People with the disease suffer from **anaemia**. This is a condition when someone is always tired and short of breath. Sickle-cell anaemia is a very serious form of anaemia and often kills people. It is also very painful since the red blood cells stick together and get stuck in the blood vessels.

 2 Look at diagram B on the next page. The letter **s** in a box shows an allele that causes sickle-cell anaemia. The letter **S** shows a normal allele.
a) Who has sickle-cell anaemia?
b) Who is a carrier for sickle-cell anaemia?
c) Who could not pass the sickle-cell anaemia allele onto his/her children?
d) Who would always pass one copy of the sickle-cell allele onto his/her children?

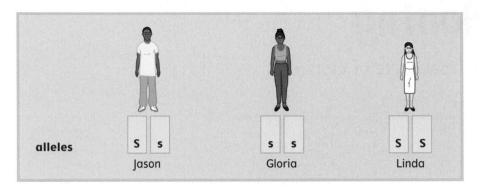

alleles	S	s	s	s	S	S
	Jason		Gloria		Linda	

 B

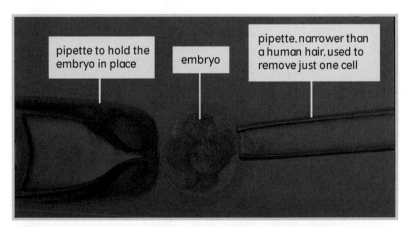
C Areas where malaria is found are coloured pink.

People who have one copy of the sickle-cell anaemia allele are carriers. Carriers only get a mild form of sickle-cell anaemia. However, carriers are less likely to get **malaria**, a very serious disease caused by a microbe which attacks red blood cells. Malaria often kills people. Being a carrier for sickle-cell anaemia can be an advantage if you live in an area where there is malaria.

Scientists can stop babies being born with some genetic diseases. Eggs are taken from a woman, fertilised with sperm, and allowed to develop into balls of eight cells (embryos). One cell is removed from each embryo and its genes are examined. Embryos that are found to be clear of alleles that cause genetic diseases are placed into the womb of the mother to develop into babies.

! Malaria kills between 1.5 and 2.7 million people every year.

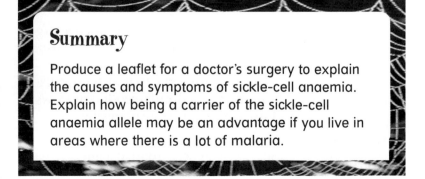

pipette to hold the embryo in place

embryo

pipette, narrower than a human hair, used to remove just one cell

D One cell from each embryo is removed and its genes are examined.

? 3 Look at map C.
  a) Name one area of the world where malaria is common.
  b) Imagine you live in this part of the world. Why might it be an advantage to be a carrier of sickle-cell anaemia?

4 Why do you think that people with sickle-cell anaemia feel short of breath?

5 Name one disease (other than sickle-cell anaemia) that kills many young people in Central Africa.

6 a) Explain how scientists can find out if an embryo contains alleles for a genetic disease.
  b) Write down three disease alleles that they might look for.

7 Look again at diagram B. Predict what alleles might be present in the children of:
  a) Jason and Gloria
  b) Jason and Linda
  c) Jason and Abigail, who has the alleles **Ss**.

Summary

Produce a leaflet for a doctor's surgery to explain the causes and symptoms of sickle-cell anaemia. Explain how being a carrier of the sickle-cell anaemia allele may be an advantage if you live in areas where there is a lot of malaria.

More cloning

How do farmers make use of cloning?

An individual cell from an embryo can be removed so that doctors can find out what alleles it carries. The rest of the embryo will grow and develop normally. This technique can also be used to make clones (exact copies) of animals. The cells in an embryo are split apart before they become specialised and each one is allowed to develop into a new embryo. The new embryos will all be identical and are put into the wombs of **host** mothers. This technique is called **embryo transplanting** or **embryo splitting**.

? **1** Embryos are often split when they contain eight cells. How many new cloned embryos could be made from an embryo like this?

2 Explain why all the new embryos made by embryo transplanting are identical.

! A British doctor, Paul Rainsbury, has proposed that human embryos should be split to create clones. One embryo would be frozen and used as a backup in case the first child dies.

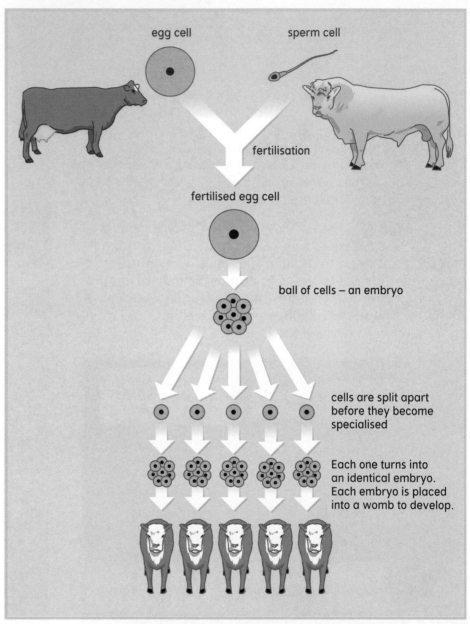

egg cell

sperm cell

fertilisation

fertilised egg cell

ball of cells – an embryo

cells are split apart before they become specialised

Each one turns into an identical embryo. Each embryo is placed into a womb to develop.

A

Embryo transplanting is used in farming since a large number of animals can be produced quickly. A farmer may want to breed from a cow that produces a lot of milk, in order to get more cows that also produce a lot of milk. Many more good milk-producing cows can be produced using embryo transplanting.

? **3** Why do farmers use embryo transplanting?

Farmers also use cloning to produce plants. Producing cloned plants by taking cuttings does not work very well on some species of plant and the small cuttings are at risk from diseases. **Tissue culture** is a way of producing thousands of cloned plants quickly, without the risk of disease.

A tiny piece of a plant (even a single cell) is taken and placed in a special solution or jelly. The cells grow into an embryo which grows into a new plant. Everything is kept very clean (**sterile**) so that the plants do not get diseases.

B *These plants were grown from single cells using tissue culture.*

In Malaysia, one oil palm which produced a lot of oil was used to make thousands of clones. **C**

?
4 List two disadvantages of taking cuttings.

5 Which method do you think will produce the most plants, tissue culture or taking cuttings? Explain your reasoning.

One problem of using so many clones is that a disease might kill them all. If they were all grown from seed, there would be more genetic variation and so some of them might be resistant and not get the disease.

?
6 Look at photograph C. What characteristic do all the cloned oil palms have?

7 Using cloned plants may cause problems. Explain why.

P Small pieces of cauliflower can be cloned using tissue culture. How do you think this could be done using this equipment?

D

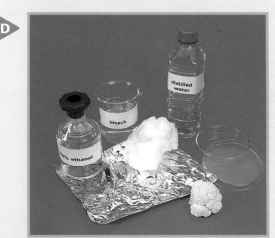

- How would you stop microbes growing in the jelly and ruining the experiment?

?
8 a) A farmer wants to breed from a good meat producing pig. Why will the farmer not necessarily get good meat producing pigs by embryo transplanting?

b) Find out about 'nuclear transfer'.

9 a) Explain why a cow born after being cloned may have different genes to its mother but identical genes to another calf.

b) Do you think it is right to use cloning and other techniques on farm animals? Give reasons for your views.

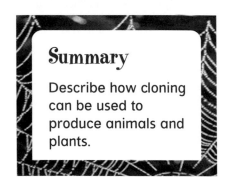

Summary

Describe how cloning can be used to produce animals and plants.

Genetic engineering

How is genetic engineering done?

The film Gattaca is set in 'the not too distant future'. In the film, scientists use **genetic engineering** to allow parents to choose what characteristics they want their children to have. At the moment, this cannot be done on humans, although genetic engineering is widely used on many organisms.

The organisms that are most commonly used for genetic engineering are bacteria. Genetically engineered bacteria produce a wide range of different products that humans use.

A *The tomatoes used in this puree have been genetically engineered to improve their flavour and shelf-life.*

 B *Products from genetically engineered bacteria.*

Product	Example of a use
Enzymes	Used in biological washing powders
Antibiotics	Used to treat diseases caused by other bacteria
Insulin	Used to treat people with diabetes
Human growth hormone	Used to treat people who lack this hormone and so do not grow very tall

?
1 What are the most common genetically engineered organisms?

2 List three products made using genetically engineered organisms.

A gene from an organism can be cut out of a chromosome using enzymes. The enzymes act a bit like tiny pairs of scissors. Bacteria naturally have small circles of DNA called **plasmids** which contain genes. The new gene can be joined into one of these plasmids using other enzymes. The plasmid is then put into a bacterium which copies the plasmid and reproduces. The bacteria have now been genetically engineered (sometimes said to be 'genetically modified').

Genes contain instructions on how to make a protein. The genetically engineered bacteria will make the protein that the new gene carries the instructions for. The bacteria are grown in huge tanks called fermenters and the useful protein is extracted. All the substances in table B are proteins made in this way.

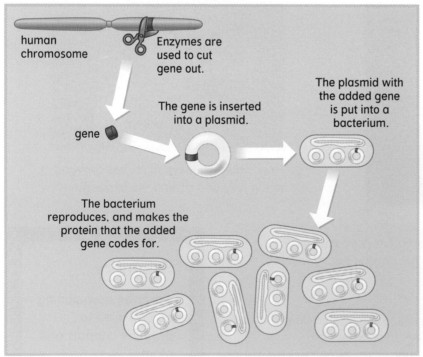

human chromosome

Enzymes are used to cut gene out.

gene

The gene is inserted into a plasmid.

The plasmid with the added gene is put into a bacterium.

The bacterium reproduces, and makes the protein that the added gene codes for.

Producing genetically engineered bacteria. **C**

 These tanks contain genetically engineered bacteria that produce the human hormone insulin.

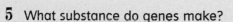 This mouse has been genetically engineered with genes from a jellyfish which make it glow.

3 How are genes cut out of chromosomes?

4 What are the cut out genes put into before they are put into bacteria?

Genes can also be put into plants and animals when they are embryos. This is more difficult to do and is often done using a virus. The virus is able to put genes into chromosomes. The virus itself has to be genetically engineered to stop it causing any diseases.

Carnations are usually pink, white or red. These ones have been genetically engineered to be purple.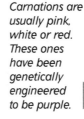

Genetic engineering can be used to modify crops to improve the yield. For example, it is possible to insert a gene into a plant to make the plant resistant to attack from pests or to help the plant convert nitrogen from the air into nitrates. Salmon have been genetically engineered to make them grow faster than normal salmon. Genetic engineering can also be used to help humans. There is a genetic disease, called ADA deficiency, that stops immune systems working. People with this disease can be treated by a form of genetic engineering called **gene therapy**. Their white blood cells have normal alleles added to them to allow them to work properly. Photographs E and F show some other things that have been genetically engineered.

P All of the examples of genetic engineering on these pages seem to be either interesting or good. However, many people are worried about genetically engineered things. Organise a debate in your class about genetic engineering. It might be about one particular example on these pages or just genetic engineering as a whole. Are you for or against it?

5 What substance do genes make?

6 What sort of substance is the hormone insulin? Explain your reasoning.

7 Why will a gene which helps a plant convert nitrogen from the air into nitrates increase the crop yield?

8 Are there any disadvantages in inserting genes which make plants resistant to attack from pests? Explain your answer.

9 Why does the film title 'Gattaca' only contain the letters G, A, T and C?

Summary

You have been asked to write a short article about genetic engineering for a newspaper. You need to explain what genetic engineering is and any benefits and drawbacks.

Selective breeding

How are new varieties produced without using genetic engineering?

Photograph A shows a quagga. Herds of these animals used to roam the plains of South Africa but were hunted to extinction in the 19th century. The last one died in Amsterdam Zoo on 12th August 1883.

It used to be thought that the quagga was a species. However, scientists took samples from the stuffed quagga in photograph A and looked at the genes of the animal. They discovered that it was not a species but a breed of plains zebra (photograph B).

A **breed** (or **variety**) is a group of animals or plants that look slightly different to other members of the species. For example, all dogs are the same species but there are nearly 150 different breeds.

A *A quagga.*

A plains zebra. **B**

1 Why did quaggas become extinct?

2 What is a breed?

Scientists in South Africa are now trying to recreate quaggas using **selective breeding** (sometimes called **artificial selection**). They took plains zebras from the wild that had the most characteristics in common with quaggas. They then mated these animals with each other. From the offspring, they took (or 'selected') only those which looked most like quaggas and mated them together. They hope that by doing this over and over again they will end up with animals that look like quaggas.

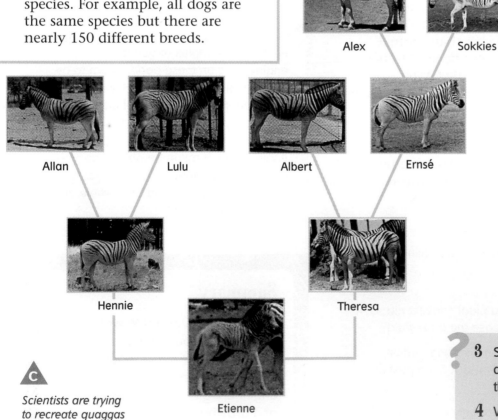

Alex Sokkies

Allan Lulu Albert Ernsé

Hennie Theresa

Etienne

C

Scientists are trying to recreate quaggas using selective breeding.

3 Scientists are trying to recreate the quagga. Name one characteristic that they are selecting for.

4 What is selective breeding sometimes called?

People have selectively bred plants and animals for thousands of years. Photograph E shows a mouflon sheep. It has been farmed for thousands of years but it has fatty meat and is more hairy than woolly. Over a long time, farmers have 'selected' for sheep which have leaner (less fatty) meat and which have woolly fleeces, like the ones in photograph F.

Farmers have increased milk production by selectively breeding from cows with the best characteristics. Breeding programs have been helped by **artificial insemination** – taking semen (fluid containing sperm) from a bull and inserting it into cows. Using this technique, the characteristics from a single bull can be passed on to many offspring.

E *A mouflon sheep.*

Modern day sheep. **F**

G

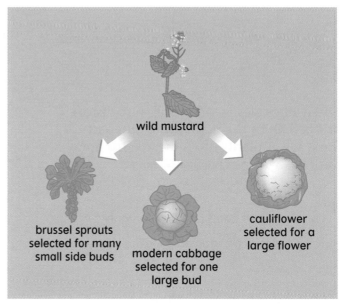

wild mustard

brussel sprouts selected for many small side buds

modern cabbage selected for one large bud

cauliflower selected for a large flower

5 Look at photographs E and F. Suggest three characteristics that have been selected for in modern sheep.

6 What are the advantages of using artificial insemination instead of a bull for selective breeding?

Plants have also been selectively bred. Diagram G shows which characteristics have been selected from wild mustard plants. Plants are also selected for their flavour, how well they cope with diseases (**disease resistance**) and how much food they produce for us (the **yield**).

! In the second century AD, the Chinese selectively bred the Pekinese dog to look like a small lion – the lion spirit of Buddha.

D

7 Which feature of wild mustard has been selected for in cauliflowers?

8 Suggest two things you would selectively breed for in:
a) chickens   **b)** roses   **c)** cows.

9 Doberman Pinscher dogs have part of their tails removed at a young age. This is called 'docking'. How would you selectively breed Dobermans that have naturally short tails?

10 Imagine quaggas were still alive today. Without looking at their genes, how could you show that they were a breed of plains zebra and not a separate species?

11 Explain why selective breeding can be slow and is not always successful.

Summary

Write notes to explain how new varieties of plants and animals can be produced without using genetic engineering.

Agricultural problems

What are the problems of selective breeding and cloning?

In 1970, in the United States, 1 billion dollars worth of maize plants were destroyed by a fungus disease called corn leaf blight. Eighty-five per cent of all the maize plants were **clones**, which produced a good yield but were not resistant to the fungus.

 1 What sort of organism causes corn leaf blight?

Since all clones are identical, one disease will kill all of them. Planting different varieties of plants often means that some varieties will survive a disease.

 2 Copy and complete this sentence:

Clones are organisms that . . .

A Decimation of maize plants by corn leaf blight.

Different varieties contain different alleles. Planting only one variety every year means that other varieties are not used and can become extinct. Their alleles will be lost and some of these alleles may be useful in the future.

Selective breeding also reduces the numbers of alleles available, since only certain characteristics are chosen. If conditions change, the lost alleles are no longer available to use for future selective breeding.

 3 a) Name two ways in which alleles can be lost from a species.
b) Why does it matter if alleles are lost from a species?

 B A Gloucester Old Spot pig.

 C A Large White pig.

Conditions can change because of a new disease, a change in the weather or a change in what people want. Until the Second World War, many people preferred pigs that produced a lot of fat. Pig fat (lard) was used a lot for cooking and the fatty meat did not go off very quickly. Pig breeds like the Gloucester Old Spot were very popular.

Today, people use vegetable oil for cooking because it is healthier, and almost everyone has a fridge. The most common breed of pig today is the Large White, since it grows rapidly to a large size and has lean (non-fatty) meat.

4 a) Why were Gloucester Old Spot pigs popular in the 1930s?
   b) Why is it a rare breed now?

5 What is the most common breed of pig today?

Rare breeds of farm animals are kept on **rare breeds farms** to stop them becoming extinct. Sperm from these animals can be stored deep-frozen in **sperm banks** for many years. Rare varieties of plants are stored in **gene banks** or 'seed banks'. This preserves alleles and means that we can use plants and animals with these alleles again if conditions change.

E Plant seeds or parts of plants are stored in seed or gene banks.

! During the Second World War, Leningrad (now St Petersburg) was under siege for 900 days. Many scientists died of starvation even though their laboratories were full of seeds and potatoes that they had collected for one of the world's first seed banks.

D Rare breeds of animals are kept on rare breeds farms. The photographs show a Long-horn cow and a Soay sheep.

Summary

Write notes for a TV programme to explain the problems of selective breeding and cloning.

6 a) Where are rare breeds of farm animals kept?
   b) How are different varieties of plants kept?
   c) Why is it important to keep rare breeds of animals and plants?

7 Why are the seeds in 'seed banks' kept cold?

8 At the beginning of the 1970s, 99% of all wheat plants grown in Canada were identical. Suggest why they now grow about 10 different varieties.

9 Zoos and rare breeds farms keep records showing the family trees of all their animals. Suggest why.

Natural selection

What is 'survival of the fittest'?

Photograph A shows a peppered moth. Like all organisms, peppered moths show **variation**. This is because different peppered moths have different alleles.

Many peppered moths are speckled and some are black. In Manchester in 1850, the black variety was very rare but by 1895, 98% of peppered moths were black.

1 a) What do we mean by the word 'variation'?
b) Why do organisms show variation?

2 What percentage of peppered moths were speckled in 1895 in Manchester?

A

During the last part of the 19th century many factories were built around cities. These churned out huge amounts of soot which made the buildings go black.

Buildings were often turned black due to soot from factory chimneys. **B**

Photograph C shows a speckled moth on a tree. You can hardly see it. However, birds could easily spot these moths on the blackened buildings and most of them were eaten. The black moths were much harder to spot and so more of them survived. They went on to reproduce and so their numbers increased.

3 a) In cities at the end of the 19th century, speckled moths were more likely to be eaten by birds. Why was this?

b) Why did the numbers of black moths in cities increase so much?

C *A speckled peppered moth on a tree.*

D *A speckled peppered moth on a black background.*

E *A black peppered moth on a black background.*

There are black squirrels around London. They were more common at the end of the 19th century.

 F

This increased survival of organisms with certain characteristics in nature is called **natural selection** or 'survival of the fittest'. Only the organisms that are most suited (**adapted**) to their surroundings will survive and reproduce. Their alleles will then be passed on to their offspring (the next generation).

P Design a game to demonstrate natural selection to young children. The children will represent birds. Different colours of pasta will represent caterpillars. The 'birds' have to hunt for caterpillars.

- Write a list of rules for your game.

- Write down what you would expect to happen and why.

 G

Disease and natural selection

Some members of a species will be killed by a disease while others will have alleles that allow them to survive. Those that are resistant to the disease will survive and produce resistant offspring.

Competition and natural selection

Organisms are in **competition** with each other for things that they need. Organisms that are better at getting hold of these things are more likely to survive. Only those organisms that survive will reproduce and pass on their alleles to the next generation. So the next generation will have a larger proportion of individuals with the characteristics most suited to their environment.

Summary

Many plants and animals produce large numbers of offspring. For example, a frog lays hundreds of eggs; a poppy plant makes thousands of seeds. Use the theory of natural selection to explain why only a few frog eggs and poppy seedlings survive and reproduce to make more frogs and poppies.

?

4 Copy and complete this sentence. Natural selection is often called 'survival of . . .'

5 Bacteria can cause many different diseases. Antibiotics can be given to patients to kill bacteria. However, doctors try not to prescribe too many antibiotics. Explain how natural selection can cause an increase in the number of bacteria resistant to a particular antibiotic.

6 a) List two things that plants might compete for.
    b) List two things that animals might compete for.

7 Explain what natural selection is.

8 Suggest why there were more black squirrels in London at the end of the 19th century than there are today.

9 Explain how humans reduce natural selection. (*Hint*: you may need to look back at page 72.)

10 Explain why variation is important in the process of natural selection.

75

Mutations

How are new alleles produced?

The African clawed frog in Photograph A was born with three back legs. This was caused by a **mutation**.

Organisms in the same species vary because they have different alleles. New alleles can be produced from existing ones by mutations. Mutations are sudden changes in an allele. A change may be very small but it can be enough to completely change the instructions carried on the allele. If we think of a gene as a sentence, even a small change can completely alter the meaning of the sentence. Look at cartoons B and C.

A

B 'Nits' are the eggs laid in human hair by animals called head lice.

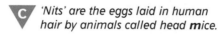

C 'Nits' are the eggs laid in human hair by animals called head mice.

1 Why do different members of the same species vary?

2 **a)** What is a mutation?
   b) What did the mutation in the African clawed frog cause?

3 What chemical molecule are genes are made of?

Some people are born with an extra finger caused by a mutation. Anne Boleyn, one of Henry VIII's wives, had an extra finger on her left hand.
D

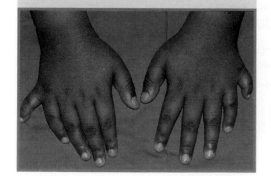

Mutations happen naturally, but the chance of one occurring is increased by:

- ionising radiation
- certain chemicals.

Ionising radiation

Radiation from radioactive substances, ultraviolet light and X-rays are all types of **ionising radiation**. They can produce reactive particles inside cells called ions. The ions damage the DNA that make up your alleles.

4 List two things that can cause mutations.

5 **a)** List three types of ionising radiation.
   b) What sort of particles does ionising radiation produce?

Scientists sometimes use radiation from radioactive substances to cause mutations. The fly on the left of photograph E was produced using this method. In rare cases new, useful alleles have been produced. For example, new varieties of plants with increased yields and resistance to disease. Some mutations that occur seem to have no effect at the time – they are neutral. However, some neutral mutations may be useful and increase the chances of survival of an organism if the environment changes.

Most mutations are harmful. If the mutation occurs in sex cells, the offspring may not develop properly or die at an early stage of development.

 E *The white eyes of the fly on the left are caused by a mutation.*

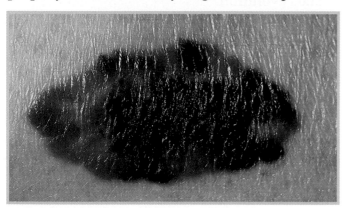

F *This type of skin cancer is called a melanoma.*

Mutations can also occur in body cells in the genes which control how quickly cells grow and divide. The cells start to multiply in an uncontrolled way. These cells may then invade other parts of the body. This is **cancer**. Ultraviolet light can cause mutations. People who sunbathe without sunscreens are at risk from skin cancer.

? **6** Why are people advised to put on sunscreen at the beach?

X-rays were discovered in 1895. At the beginning of the 20th century it became fashionable to have X-ray pictures taken – including family portraits! It was then discovered that people who had had a lot of X-rays taken got cancer. Today, the doses of X-rays used in hospitals are very low.

Chemicals

Certain chemicals can cause mutations. For instance, some of the chemicals in cigarette smoke cause lung cancer.

? **7** Why are women asked if they might be pregnant before they have any X-rays?

8 a) Are all mutations harmful?
b) Explain why a neutral mutation might become useful.

9 Mutated alleles in humans can be inherited. For each of these alleles, write down whether you think the mutation is inherited or has occurred during the person's life.
a) someone with blue eyes
b) someone with skin cancer
c) someone with cystic fibrosis

10 Smoking can cause lung cancer. Explain, in as much detail as you can, how this happens.

11 Mendel said that 'factors' or alleles could not change. Explain why this is not true and what effects such changes can have.

Summary

A What are the causes of mutations?

B Explain how a change in a single base in a strand of DNA could cause a mutation. (*Hint*: You may need to look back at pages 48 and 49.)

H17 Evolution: Theory

What is the theory of evolution?

Most scientists think that all life on Earth developed originally from bacteria living in the sea, like those shown in photograph A.

The first simple bacteria appeared on Earth about 3.8 billion years ago. Since that time many different species of animals and plants have existed. Scientists think that organisms gradually change from one species into other species over thousands of years. This gradual change is called **evolution**.

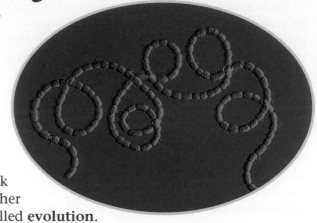

A *These are very primitive bacteria called cyanobacteria.*

1 What sort of organisms were the first to live on Earth?

2 What is the gradual changing of one species into another called?

Darwin's rather long-winded title for his book published in 1859.

B

THE ORIGIN OF SPECIES

BY MEANS OF NATURAL SELECTION

OR THE

PRESERVATION OF FAVOURED RACES IN THE STRUGGLE
FOR LIFE

By CHARLES DARWIN, M.A.,

LONDON:
JOHN MURRAY, ALREMARLE STREET
1859

Charles Darwin and Alfred Russel Wallace were the first scientists to work out *how* it happens. They said that over long periods of time, **natural selection** happens over and over again to produce new species.

3 **a)** What process causes evolution?
   b) Explain how this process can cause evolution to occur.

Elephants evolved from an animal the size of a pig, called *Moeritherium* (pronounced '*meer-uh-theer-ee-um*'), which lived about 55 million years ago. *Moeritherium* was **prey** for other animals. Like all animals, *Moeritherium* varied and the taller animals could more easily spot their **predators** and run away.

More of the taller animals survived and reproduced. Over thousands of years, the tallest animals became the most common. However, getting taller meant that the animals had to crouch down to drink and so were less likely to spot predators. Animals that happened to have a longer 'nose' and could use it to drink were at an advantage. So, over millions of years the tallest animals with the longest 'noses' (trunks) became the most common, because they were best adapted to survive in their environment.

C *Moeritherium was the ancestor of elephants.*

D *An African elephant.*

4 What animal did elephants evolve from?

5 Picture E shows a woolly mammoth. These animals also evolved from *Moeritherium*. Suggest why it was an advantage for them to evolve thick hair.

E

There are two species of elephant, the African and the Asian. Photograph F shows Asian elephants taking part in a race in Bangladesh!

F

6 Look at pictures D and F. Name one thing which varies between these two species.

Evolution is still occurring today. In very small organisms, like bacteria, it can happen very quickly. Antibiotics are medicines that kill bacteria. However, all bacteria vary and some of them, just by chance, will contain alleles which mean that they are not killed by a certain antibiotic. These **resistant** bacteria will then reproduce. This is a problem, since diseases like tuberculosis, which used to be easily treated using antibiotics, are now much more difficult to treat.

7 a) Why do you think evolution can take place very quickly in bacteria?
   b) What is the name for the process which causes changes in the alleles of the bacteria?

8 Explain why natural selection is making tuberculosis more difficult to treat.

9 Suggest another way, not mentioned on the page, that elephants have evolved so that they are not easy prey.

10 Look at picture B. Suggest what Darwin means by "The preservation of Favoured Races in the Struggle for Life".

11 a) Find out about Jean-Baptiste Lamarck's theory of evolution.
   b) How is his theory different from that of Darwin and Wallace?
   c) Are there any other theories which are used to explain evolution?

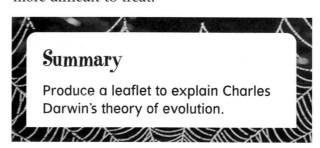

Summary

Produce a leaflet to explain Charles Darwin's theory of evolution.

Evolution: Evidence

How do fossils provide evidence for evolution?

In 1644, the Vice Chancellor of Cambridge University, Dr. John Lightfoot, claimed to have worked out when the world was created: Sunday September 12th, 3928 BC. According to him, humans were created at 9:00 am the following Friday.

Dr. John Lightfoot (1602–1675). **A**

When Darwin first suggested his theory of evolution, most people did not believe it because:

- many people believed that God created the world and all its species in six days
- they did not believe the Earth was old enough to allow such a slow process
- there were not many good collections of fossils.

It took many years before people started to accept the theory of evolution. Today, one of the best pieces of evidence for evolution is from **fossils** (the remains of dead plants and animals found in rocks). Since Darwin's time, scientists have found many more fossils.

? 1 Give two reasons why people did not believe Darwin's theory when he suggested it.

2 What can we use as evidence to support the theory today?

Scientists can work out how old rocks are. If fossils are found in a rock they can then work out how old the fossils are. The evolution of the horse is now well known thanks to fossils (see diagram C).

Hyracotherium was an animal about the size of a dog. It was well adapted to its marshy surroundings because it walked on four toes that were spread out, so it did not sink into the ground. It hid from predators in bushes growing in the marshes.

? 3 Look at diagram C. How tall was *Hyracotherium*?

4 How many toes did *Hyracotherium* walk on?

! The oldest rock is 4.4 billion years old.
The oldest fossil is 3.5 billion years old.

B *These fossil hunters work carefully to uncover dinosaur bones..*

Over millions of years, the marshy ground was replaced by drier grassland and there were fewer bushes to hide behind. Natural selection favoured animals that could run faster and get away from predators. Running on fewer toes is faster. Over millions of years natural selection favoured animals which had less toes touching the ground.

Organisms need to survive changes in their surroundings, new types of predators, new diseases or new competitors. Unless they change (evolve) to become better adapted to a new situation, the species may die out altogether (become **extinct**).

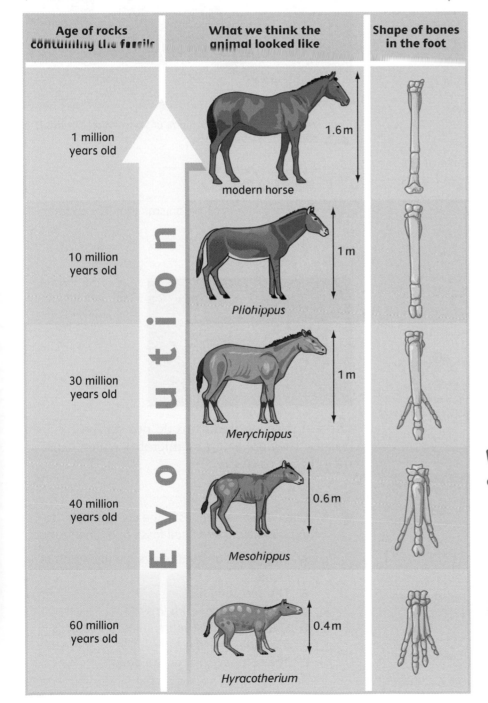

Age of rocks containing the fossils	What we think the animal looked like	Shape of bones in the foot
1 million years old	modern horse 1.6 m	
10 million years old	Pliohippus 1 m	
30 million years old	Merychippus 1 m	
40 million years old	Mesohippus 0.6 m	
60 million years old	Hyracotherium 0.4 m	

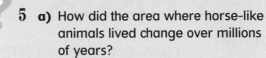

C

?

5 **a)** How did the area where horse-like animals lived change over millions of years?

b) How did the horse-like animals evolve to cope with this change?

6 Give four reasons why a species might become extinct.

7 Some people think that dinosaurs became extinct because new competitors evolved. What might these animals have competed for?

8 Modern horses are taller than their ancient ancestors. Suggest why.

9 When Darwin visited the Galapagos islands in 1835, he noticed that the finches (birds) had different shaped beaks according to the type of food they ate. Some had strong beaks to crack seeds, others had long thin beaks to pick up insects. He thought that they had all evolved from one type of finch.

a) Explain how this could have happened.

b) What evidence would scientists look for to support this theory?

!

Scientists think that 99% of all the species that have ever lived are now extinct.

Summary

What is the evidence for evolution? Use the modern horse as your example.

Fossils

How are fossils formed?

The logs in photograph A are made out of stone! They are a type of fossil and are millions of years old.

Fossils are the remains of ancient plants and animals, and are normally found in rock. Most fossils are of sea creatures because to make a fossil a dead organism needs to be covered quickly in something like mud or sand to prevent decay. Animals and plants which die on land are less likely to get covered up quickly in this way.

Fossils are formed in four main ways.

Turned to stone

This normally happens to the hard parts of an organism like bones and shells. The tree fossils in photograph A were also formed in this way. Diagram B shows how it can happen.

A These logs are actually made of stone. Wood like this is said to be 'petrified'.

? 1 What is a fossil?

2 Why are fossils of organisms that live on land quite rare?

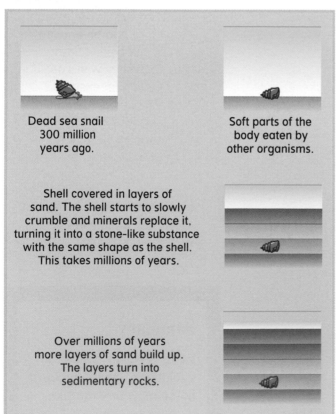

B

Dead sea snail 300 million years ago.

Soft parts of the body eaten by other organisms.

Shell covered in layers of sand. The shell starts to slowly crumble and minerals replace it, turning it into a stone-like substance with the same shape as the shell. This takes millions of years.

Over millions of years more layers of sand build up. The layers turn into sedimentary rocks.

C This fossilised sea snail is millions of years old.

The soft parts of organisms do not survive because they are eaten by microbes which cause them to rot or **decay**.

? 3 Copy these sentences in the correct order to explain how a sea snail fossil might be formed.

    A The layers of sand above the fossil turn to stone.

    B The sea snail dies.

    C The shell is covered in sand.

    D Over millions of years, minerals replace the shell.

    E The soft parts rot or are eaten.

Hard parts of animals are preserved

Shells and bones can sometimes remain as they are. This often happens to shells if they are covered in other bits of shell.

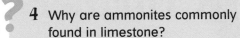

4 Why are ammonites commonly found in limestone?

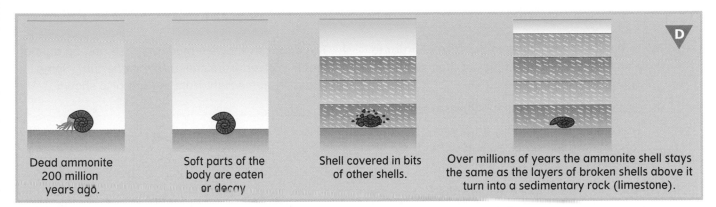

Dead ammonite 200 million years ago.

Soft parts of the body are eaten or decay

Shell covered in bits of other shells.

Over millions of years the ammonite shell stays the same as the layers of broken shells above it turn into a sedimentary rock (limestone).

D

 E *These ammonites are 200 million years old.*

Traces of animals or plants

Sometimes fossilised footprints or other traces of plants and animals are found. Look at photograph H. A dinosaur left this footprint in soft mud millions of years ago. The mud baked hard in the Sun and was then covered by more mud which also baked hard. Over millions of years the layers of baked mud turned into mudstone. Peeling off the other layers of rock has revealed the footprints.

A dinosaur footprint. H

Whole organisms are preserved

Most microbes need oxygen, warmth and water to survive. If one of these is missing, no decay will happen and so a whole organism might be preserved.

Occasionally, the soft parts of plants and animals do become fossilised because they happen to fall into an area where decay happens very, very slowly. This can happen in a bog, where it is too acidic for most microbes to live.

 F *This man was buried under ice for 5000 years.*

 G *These leaves became fossilised because they fell into a bog.*

5 Look at photograph F. Why did this man's body not decay?

6 Explain how an animal burrow could be fossilised.

7 Suggest why plant fossils are much rarer than animal fossils.

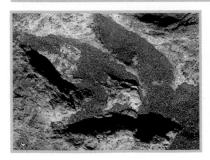

Summary

Briefly summarise the four ways in which fossils can be formed.

1 a) Write out these sentences in the correct order to explain how cells make copies of themselves.

- The cell splits into two.
- Copies are made of all 46 chromosomes.
- There are now two cells, each with a nucleus containing a full set of chromosomes.
- The nucleus splits into two. (3)

b) What is this type of cell division called? (1)

c) What is the name of the process by which egg cells are formed? (1)

d) Name *one* organism that has 46 chromosomes in the nucleus of each body cell. (1)

e) How many chromosomes are present in the egg cells of this organism? (1)

2 Strawberry plants reproduce using strawberries and runners.

a) Which part of the plant allows it to reproduce asexually? (1)

b) The new plants grow. Which plants will be identical to the parent plant, those produced sexually or those produced asexually? Explain your answer. (2)

3 A gardener bred a sweet pea plant which had purple flowers with a sweet pea plant with white flowers. All the new plants had purple flowers.

a) Before Mendel suggested his theory, people thought that offspring inherited a 'blend' of characteristics from their parents. How do the results of the gardener's crossing suggest that 'blending' does not happen? (1)

b) Which flower colour was dominant? (1)

c) What percentage of the offspring of a cross between two heterozygous purple flowered plants will have white flowers? Show your working. (1)

d) A company called Florigene has recently produced a purple carnation. Carnations are normally red, pink or white. How do you think they have produced the purple carnation? (1)

4 The diagram shows a modern horse and an animal that it evolved from called *Hyracotherium*. Some bones from the right front leg are also shown.

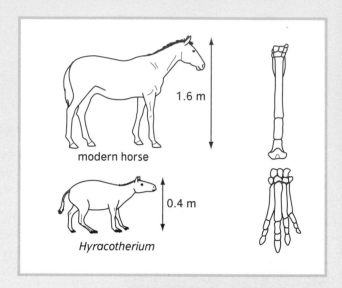

modern horse
1.6 m
0.4 m
Hyracotherium

a) *Hyracotherium* lived in marshes. How was it adapted to live in this environment? (1)

b) Why would a modern horse not be well adapted to living in marshes? (1)

c) Apart from the bones in the leg, describe *one* other way in which the modern horse is different from *Hyracotherium*. (1)

d) What is the advantage for the modern horse of the change you described in part c? (1)

e) Evolution occurs by 'natural selection'. Explain what natural selection is. (2)

5 In embryo transplanting, a fertilised egg cell is allowed to develop into a ball of cells (an embryo). The embryo is then split apart and each cell grows into a new embryo. These embryos are placed into the wombs of 'host' animals to develop.

a) Each of the offspring produced using embryo transplanting is a 'clone'. What is a clone? (1)

b) Name *one* advantage of this process for a farmer. (1)

c) Name *one* disadvantage of this process. (1)

6 Look at the three family trees below. There is an inherited disease in each of the families.

a) What is an inherited disease? (1)

b) One of the family trees shows a disease that only affects one sex. Which one? (1)

c) Which family tree shows a disease which is caused by a dominant allele? (1)

d) In family tree B, only one person has an inherited disease. Explain how this person could get the disease if neither of her parents had the disease. (2)

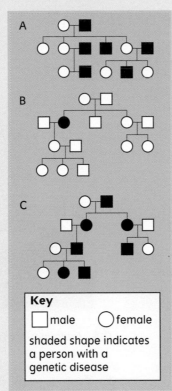

Key

□ male   ○ female

shaded shape indicates a person with a genetic disease

7 Some people can roll their tongues. Other people cannot. The allele that allows tongue rolling is called '**R**'. It is dominant over the allele that does not allow tongue rolling – '**r**'.

a) Copy the diagram and add in the letters '**R**' or '**r**' to show the different alleles that the gametes of these two people will contain. (2)

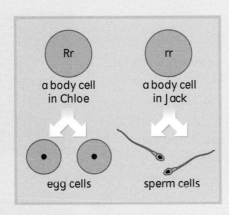

a body cell in Chloe   a body cell in Jack

egg cells   sperm cells

b) Continue your diagram to show what alleles a fertilised egg would contain if each of the egg cells joined with each of the sperm cells. (2)

c) What percentage of their children would you expect to be unable to roll their tongues? (1)

8 Explain why there are not more fossils and why this was a problem for early evolution theories. (3)

9 The diagram shows the female reproductive system.

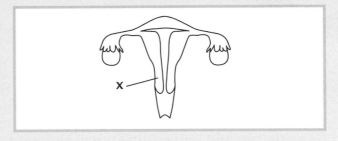

a) What is the name of the part where egg cells are released from? (1)

b) What is the name of the part where the baby develops? (1)

c) The part labelled X gets alternately thicker and thinner in a monthly cycle. What is the name of this cycle? (1)

d) This cycle is controlled by chemicals. What are these chemicals called? (1)

e) In which *two* places are these chemicals made? (2)

f) Name the chemical that can be used to increase the number of egg cells that are released. (1)

g) Name the chemical that can be used as an oral contraceptive. (1)

10 The diagram shows part of a DNA molecule.

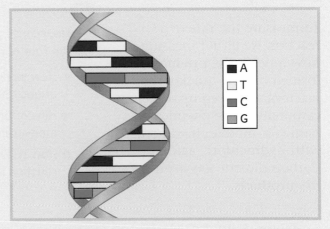

■ A
□ T
■ C
■ G

Mutations can happen because of changes to DNA.

a) Name *two* possible causes for an increase in the normal rate of mutations. (2)

b) Explain how a change in a DNA molecule can cause a cell to code for a different protein. (3)

11

Rates of reaction

What do we mean by the 'rate of reaction'?

Chemical reactions happen at different speeds. Some are very slow, like rusting, which can take years. When a nail rusts, the iron (or steel) reacts very slowly with oxygen (from the air) and water. Other reactions are very fast, like explosions. They are over very quickly.

! The most powerful explosive in the world is code-named CL20. When it explodes, the shock wave travels at 34 000 km/h!

? 1 Give examples of three chemical reactions which occur at different rates and place them in order of increasing speed.

A Explosions are very fast reactions.

Measuring the rate of reaction

A chemical reaction goes at different speeds until it has finished. A reaction usually starts off quicker and then slows down. The speed of a reaction is called the **rate of reaction**. There are different ways of measuring the rate of reaction. If the reaction gives off a gas, then you can trap it in a measuring cylinder.

? 2 In an explosion, is more gas likely to be produced in the first 5 seconds or the last 5 seconds?

To measure the rate of a reaction we either measure how quickly the products are formed or how quickly the reactants are used up. Calcium carbonate is the chemical name for marble. It will react with hydrochloric acid. Carbon dioxide gas is one of the **products**.

P How could you measure the rate of reaction?

● How will you measure the volume of gas given off?

● How often will you take measurements?

● How will you know when the reaction has finished?

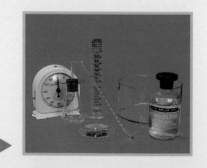

B

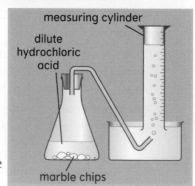

C

measuring cylinder

dilute hydrochloric acid

marble chips

calcium + hydrochloric → calcium + carbon + water
carbonate   acid   chloride   dioxide

$$CaCO_3 \; + \quad 2HCl \quad \longrightarrow \quad CaCl_2 \; + \; CO_2 \; + \; H_2O$$

⎵ reactants   products ⎵

The gas is collected in a measuring cylinder filled with water. It pushes the water out so it is easy to measure the volume of gas. The volume of gas in the measuring cylinder is measured every 10 seconds until the reaction is over.

Table D and graph E show the results.

Time (seconds)	Volume of gas (cm³)
0	0
10	35
20	53
30	65
40	73
50	73
60	73

3 Write a balanced symbol equation for the reaction of sodium carbonate (Na_2CO_3) with sulphuric acid (H_2SO_4).

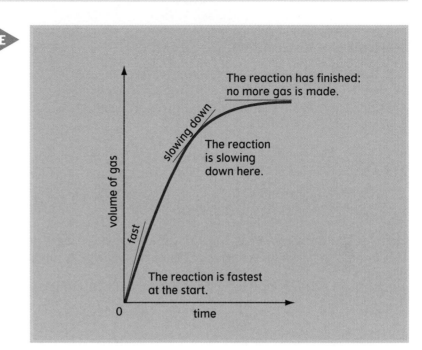

The reaction has finished: no more gas is made.

slowing down

The reaction is slowing down here.

volume of gas

fast

The reaction is fastest at the start.

0   time

4 Why do you think the reaction in graph E stops?

5 How can you tell from the graph that the reaction has finished?

The **mean rate** of a reaction is calculated by dividing the change in the products (or reactants) by the time taken for the change to occur.

In reactions which produce a gas, the mean rate can be calculated by dividing the volume of gas produced by the time taken to produce the gas. For example, the mean rate of this reaction in the first 20 seconds can be calculated as shown below:

$$\text{mean rate} = \frac{\text{change in reactants or products}}{\text{time}}$$

$$= \frac{53 \text{ (cm}^3)}{20 \text{ (s)}} = 2.65 \text{ cm}^3/\text{s}$$

The graph is steepest at the beginning. This means that the rate of reaction is fastest at the beginning of the reaction. When the slope goes horizontal (flat), the reaction is over. One, or both of the reactants has been used up.

6 Look at the results in table D.
  a) Plot a graph of the results.
  b) What was the volume of gas made at the end of the reaction?
  c) How long did the reaction take to finish?

7 Use the table of results and your graph from question 6 to calculate the mean rate of this reaction in cm³/s:
  a) in the first 15 seconds
  b) in the second 15 seconds (between 15 and 30 seconds).

8 Try to explain why the reaction is fastest at the start.

Summary

Write a short summary of these two pages in your own words (maximum 100 words). Include the meaning of the term 'rate of reaction', and explain how reaction rates can be measured.

12

Measuring rate of reaction - 1

How else can the rate of reaction be measured?

Method 1 – Volume of gas given off

You have already seen how gas can be trapped by pushing water out of a measuring cylinder. Another way of measuring the volume of a gas is to use a syringe.

 1   Name two units used to measure the volume of a gas.

P   How can you measure the rate of reaction using a gas syringe?

● How often will you take measurements?

● How will you know when the reaction has finished?

 A

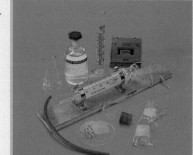

In the reaction below a gas is given off and pushes the syringe out. The faster the gas is given off, the faster the syringe is pushed out.

magnesium + hydrochloric acid ⟶ magnesium chloride + hydrogen

$$Mg + 2HCl \longrightarrow MgCl_2 + H_2$$

B

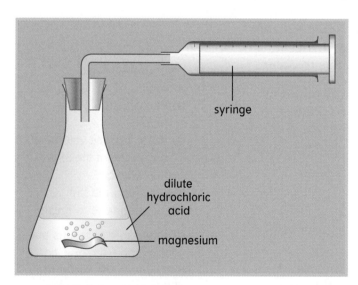

syringe

dilute hydrochloric acid

magnesium

The reaction finishes because one of the reactants has been used up. The graph is very steep at the beginning. This means that the reaction is going fastest at the start.

 2   How can you tell when the reaction has finished?

3   Use graph C to calculate the mean rate of this reaction (in cm^3/s) between:
   a) 0 and 30 seconds
   b) 0 and 60 seconds.

Here is a graph of the results from the experiment.

C

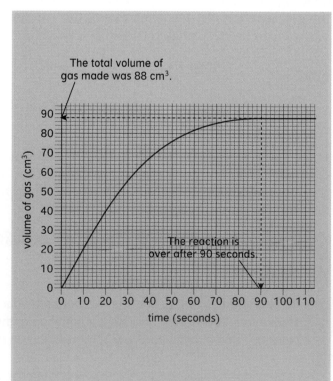

The total volume of gas made was 88 cm^3.

The reaction is over after 90 seconds.

volume of gas (cm^3) vs time (seconds)

Method 2 – Mass of gas given off

We can measure the rate of reaction in a different way by measuring the mass of gas given off.

We don't actually measure the mass of gas given off, but we can work it out. The gas escapes from the flask and so the flask loses mass (gets lighter). If the flask loses 1.5 g in mass, then 1.5 g of gas must have been given off. If the flask loses 3.7 g in mass, then 3.7 g of gas must have been given off. The faster the gas is given off, the faster the flask loses mass. The faster the flask loses mass, the faster the rate of reaction. This method of measuring the rate of reaction is sometimes called the 'loss in mass' method.

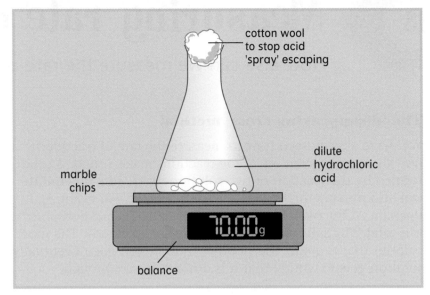

cotton wool to stop acid 'spray' escaping

dilute hydrochloric acid

marble chips

70.00 g

balance

D

P Calcium carbonate reacts with hydrochloric acid. How could you measure the rate of this reaction using the 'loss in mass' method?

- What measurements will you take?
- What will you need cotton wool for?

4 Explain why the flask in this experiment loses mass.

5 Write a balanced symbol equation to show how calcium and sulphuric acid (H_2SO_4) react to form calcium sulphate ($CaSO_4$) and hydrogen.

6 A student added some marble chips to acid and measured the mass every minute. Here are the results from the experiment:

Time (min)	0	1	2	3	4	5
Mass (g)	130.13	129.98	129.95	129.91	129.85	129.74
Loss in mass (g)						

Time (min)	6	7	8	9	10	11
Mass (g)	129.69	129.66	129.63	129.61	129.6	129.6
Loss in mass (g)						

a) Copy and complete the table by working out the values for 'loss in mass'.

b) Plot the results on a graph, with time on the horizontal axis.

c) Use the graph and data to calculate the mean rate of reaction in g/s during:
   i) the first 2 minutes **ii)** the second 2 minutes.

d) Explain what happens to the rate of reaction with time.

Summary

Your friend has asked you to explain how you can measure rates of reaction by experiment.

Briefly describe two ways of measuring the rate of a reaction when one of the products is a gas. Explain how you could calculate the rate of reaction. Include a balanced symbol equation for the reaction in your explanation.

13

Measuring rate of reaction - 2

How else can we measure the rate of reaction?

The 'disappearing cross' method

You have already seen how to measure the rate of reaction by how quickly a gas is given off. Some reactions make a solid. A solid formed by the reaction of two solutions is called a **precipitate**. You can also measure how quickly a solid is made. For example, in diagram A, the two chemicals react together to make sulphur, which is a solid. The sulphur makes the solution go cloudy. The more sulphur that is made, the cloudier the solution goes. Eventually, the solution gets so cloudy that it is difficult to see through.

? **1** What makes the solution turn cloudy?

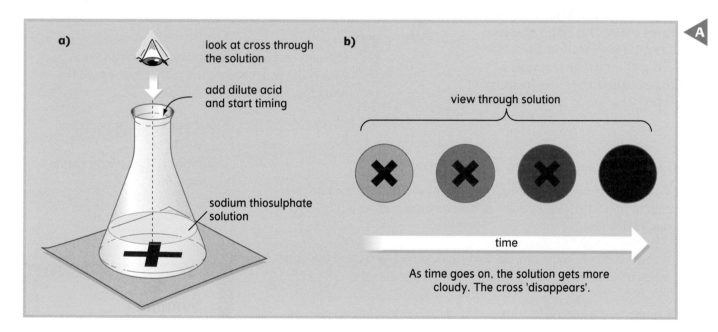

a) look at cross through the solution

add dilute acid and start timing

sodium thiosulphate solution

b) view through solution

time

As time goes on, the solution gets more cloudy. The cross 'disappears'.

A

sodium thiosulphate + hydrochloric acid → sodium chloride + sulphur + sulphur dioxide + water

$$Na_2S_2O_3(aq) + 2HCl(aq) \rightarrow 2NaCl(aq) + S(s) + SO_2(g) + H_2O(l)$$

This experiment is sometimes called the 'disappearing cross' experiment. Timing how long it takes the cross to disappear can be used to measure the rate of reaction. The faster the cross disappears, the faster the reaction.

? **2** The reaction shown in diagram A could be described as a precipitation. Explain what is meant by a precipitation reaction and name the precipitate in this reaction.

P How could you measure how quickly a solid is formed in a reaction?

● How will you decide when the reaction has finished?

B

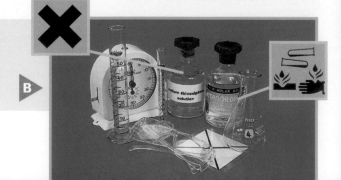

Hazard symbols

In many experiments, the chemicals that you use can be harmful and dangerous. There are special symbols on the bottles to warn you of the dangers. You must take great care when handling chemicals because they can do real harm to you or someone else. You may have seen some of these hazard symbols on the sides of bottles at school or on cleaning products used at home.

D *Toxic* chemicals can cause death if swallowed, breathed in, or allowed to absorb through the skin.

C *Highly flammable.* The petrol in this tanker will catch fire easily.

E *Harmful* substances are like toxic substances but less dangerous. Substances which are *irritants* are not corrosive but can cause skin to go red or blister.

F *Oxidising* substances, like hydrogen peroxide, provide a source of oxygen which allows other things to burn fiercely.

G *Corrosive* substances, like battery acid, attack and destroy living tissues like eyes and skin.

?

3   What problems can irritants cause?

4   **a)** What can happen to chemicals that are highly flammable?
    b) Name any chemical that is flammable.

5   A new chemical, 'dramicon' can be used to clean car engines. It has these properties:
    - it burns easily
    - it helps other chemicals to burn
    - if you spill it on your skin, it causes an itchy rash all over your body.

    a) Draw and name the hazard symbols that should be on a bottle of 'dramicon'.
    b) Write down a list of safety instructions for people who are going to use the chemical.

Summary

Write a set of practical instructions to allow someone to measure the rate of reaction using the disappearing cross method. Make sure you include appropriate safety precautions.

91

Effect of concentration

How does changing the concentration affect the rate of reaction?

A **solution** is formed when a **soluble** substance, like salt, sugar or copper sulphate, dissolves in a liquid like water. The solid that dissolves is called the **solute** and the liquid is called the **solvent**.

If a lot of solute is dissolved in a small volume of solvent, the solution is very **concentrated**. The greater the amount of solute dissolved in the same volume of solvent, the more concentrated the solution. A **dilute** solution contains less particles of solute in the same volume of solvent.

Look at diagram A. The volume of water in each beaker is the same. If more and more copper sulphate is added to the same volume of water, the **concentration** of the solution increases. This means that the solution with the highest concentration is beaker 3.

A

 1 Describe the difference between a concentrated and a dilute solution.

Changing the concentration

Look at this experiment. The concentration of acid is changed each time.

The *total* volume of acid and water is kept the same each time (50 cm³) to make it a **fair test**. Also, the same mass of marble chips is used and the chips are similar sizes. For example, it would not be a fair test if in one experiment you used large chips, and then in another you used smaller chips. Remember, you are only changing one thing – the concentration of acid. Everything else must be kept the same.

B

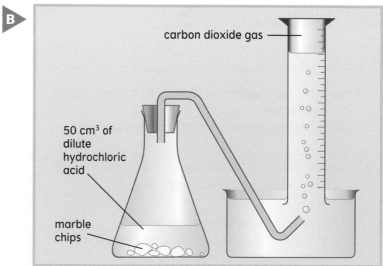

 2 Look at diagram B. What two things must be kept the same to make it a fair test?

Here are the results from the experiment:

Solution	Volume of acid (cm³)	Volume of water (cm³)	Time to collect 20 cm³ of gas (s)
V	10	40	255
W	20	30	132
X	30	20	70
Y	40	10	51
Z	50	0	42

Solution V is the least concentrated (most **dilute**). Moving from V to Z, the solutions get more concentrated. Solution Z is the most concentrated and gives the fastest reaction. As the concentration increases, the rate of reaction increases.

P How could you investigate the effect of concentration on the rate of reaction?

● How will you change the concentration of the acid?

● How will you make it a fair test?

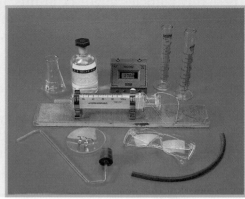

3 Use the information in table C to explain why solution **Z** produces the gas more quickly than solution **V**.

4 Look at the results in table C.

a) Plot a graph of the volume of acid used in cm³ (horizontal axis) against time to collect 20 cm³ of gas in seconds (vertical axis).

b) Use your graph to find the time to collect 20 cm³ of gas using these volumes of acid:

i) 15 cm³ ii) 35 cm³ iii) 25 cm³.

c) Use the data to calculate the average rate of the reaction for:

i) solution **W** ii) solution **Y**.

d) Describe how changing the concentration of the acid affects the speed of the reaction.

Summary

Imagine your friend has missed today's lesson and to help him/her catch up, you have been asked write a brief answer to the topic question at the top of page 92. Answer the question in your own words, including a definition of the words in bold on these two pages.

5 A student made five solutions of copper sulphate that had different concentrations. She made them by dissolving different amounts of copper sulphate in different volumes of water.

Solution M = 2 g dissolved in 500 cm³ of water.

Solution N = 2 g dissolved in 5000 cm³ of water.

Solution P = 4 g dissolved in 1000 cm³ of water.

Solution Q = 3 g dissolved in 250 cm³ of water.

Solution R = 4 g dissolved in 1500 cm³ of water.

a) Which two are actually the same concentration?
b) Put the solutions in order, with the most concentrated first.

6 A student has been given a solution of copper sulphate. Describe how the student could make up a solution which was 1/10th as concentrated as the original solution.

15

Collision theory

Why does increasing the concentration speed up a reaction?

All substances are made up of tiny **particles**. These tiny particles might be **atoms**, **ions** or **molecules**. (Molecules are made up of atoms that are joined together.) For a chemical reaction to take place, the reactant particles must bang into each other. They must **collide**. If they bang into each other hard enough, they will react.

This idea is called the **collision theory**. It states that a reaction will only take place if the reacting particles bump into each other with enough energy (i.e. crash into each other hard enough).

 1 What must happen to particles for a reaction to happen?

Explaining the effect of concentration

When marbles chips react with acid, you can make the reaction go faster by increasing the concentration of the acid. We can use the collision theory to explain why the reaction is faster when the concentration is increased.

In beaker B there are more acid particles in the same volume of liquid. It is more concentrated. The acid particles are more crowded. This means that there is a greater chance of acid particles colliding with particles on the surface of the marble. There are more collisions in a certain time and so the rate of reaction increases.

 **2** Look at beaker B. Use the collision theory to explain what would happen to the rate of the reaction if there were even more particles of acid in the same volume.

3 Use the collision theory to explain why magnesium burns faster in pure oxygen than in air.

Increasing the concentration increases the number of collisions and so increases the rate of reaction.

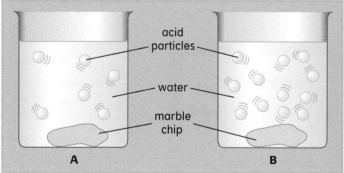

A *A hard collision!* **B**

acid particles

water

marble chip

A B

It's a bit like dancers on a dance floor. When a good track is played, more people get up to dance and the dance floor becomes crowded. The concentration of people on the dance floor increases and there is more chance of bumping into someone! There are more collisions.

4 Describe another situation where concentration affects the speed of a reaction.

 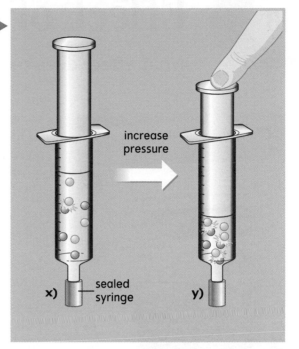

x) | sealed syringe | y)

increase pressure

Gas reactions

Look at the syringe in diagram D. There are two gases inside reacting with each other. If the end is sealed you can increase the pressure inside the syringe by pushing the plunger. By pushing the plunger down, the particles of gas get squashed together and are now in a smaller volume. This means the concentration has increased and so the rate of reaction increases.

Increasing the pressure of a gas increases the number of collisions and so increases the rate of reaction.

5 How could you increase the rate of reaction between gases?

6 Two students are studying the effect of concentration on the rate of reaction. They use magnesium reacting with hydrochloric acid. Hydrogen gas and magnesium chloride ($MgCl_2$) are made in the reaction and all the magnesium is used up. Three different concentrations of acid were used: A, B and C.

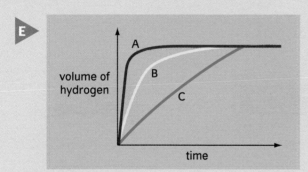

E

volume of hydrogen

A

B

C

time

a) Write word and balanced symbol equations for this reaction.
b) Describe two factors which would need to be kept the same to make it a fair test.
c) Explain how you know that acid **A** is the most concentrated. Use the collision theory in your answer.

7 a) Sketch the graphs from question 6 into your book.
b) Draw on your graph a line for acid with a concentration less than A, but higher than B. Label your line 'D'.

Summary

Someone who doesn't know anything about how chemical reactions occur has asked you to explain the following:

A Why a more concentrated acid will react faster with marble chips than a dilute acid.

B Why the pressure of the gases used in the reactions in industrial processes is often increased.

Write down what you would say for each. Include the following words in your answer:

collision, particles, concentrated, energy, dilute, pressure.

16

Effect of temperature

What effect does temperature have on the rate of reaction?

We keep food in a fridge to stop it 'going off'. Some substances in food react with oxygen in the air to make the food go off or turn 'rancid'. Microbes also make food go off. Even food kept in a fridge will eventually go off, but the low temperature slows down the reactions that turn the food rancid.

If lowering the temperature slows down the rate of reaction, then increasing the temperature should increase the rate of reaction.

Look at the experiment below. A student was timing how long it took to collect 20 cm³ of gas.

At 25 °C, it took 2 minutes to collect 20 cm³ of gas. When the temperature was increased to 35 °C, it only took 1 minute to collect the gas. The reaction was faster.

A

B

P How could you investigate the effect of temperature on the rate of reaction?

- How many different temperatures will you choose?

- What will be the lowest and highest temperatures you will choose?

- How will you know when the reaction has finished?

C

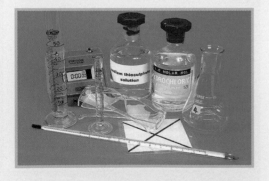

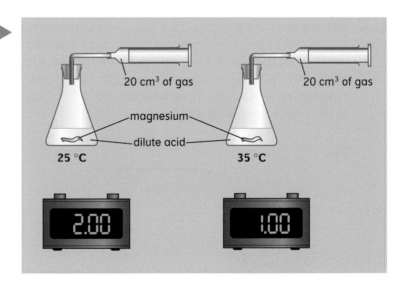

20 cm³ of gas   20 cm³ of gas

magnesium

dilute acid

25 °C   **35 °C**

2.00   1.00

Explaining the effect of temperature

Particles move around faster when you heat them, so there is more chance of them bumping into each other. This means there are more collisions in a certain time and the rate of reaction increases. It's a bit like the dancers on the dance floor again. If they dance very fast, they are more likely to bump into each other.

There is another reason why the rate of reaction increases when the temperature increases. Some particles don't have enough kinetic energy to react when they collide with other particles. There is a minimum (least) amount of energy that particles need to react, called the **activation energy**.

? 1 Describe two other real life situations where temperature affects the speed of a reaction.

Graph D shows the main energy changes which occur during a reaction. At a certain temperature, the particles have different kinetic energies. Therefore only some of the particles can react when they collide. At higher temperatures, the particles have more energy and bang into each other harder. This means that the collisions are more likely to produce a reaction, because more particles will have reached the activation energy.

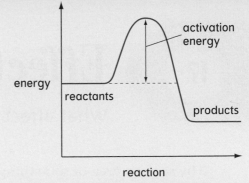

A reaction will only take place if the energy of the reacting particles is equal to or greater than the activation energy.

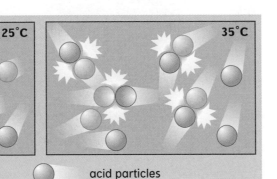

magnesium particles   acid particles

Look at the experiment in diagram B. Graph F shows the results.

When the temperature is higher, the reaction is faster, so the 20 cm^3 of gas is made faster.

When the temperature is increased, the rate of reaction increases for two reasons.

- *The particles move faster and collide more often.*
- *More particles will have the activation energy needed to react.*

2 What is activation energy?

3 Give two reasons why food 'goes off' more slowly at lower temperatures.

4 Explain why leaving the gas tap open in the lab does not cause an explosion until there is a spark.

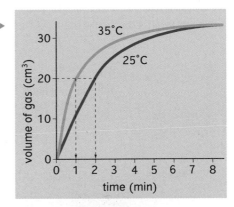

Summary

Copy and complete each of the sentences below to answer the topic question at the top of page 96.

For a reaction to take place the reacting particles must …

The kinetic (movement) energy of the particles increases …

This explains the effect of temperature as the higher the temperature the …

Therefore as temperature increases the rate of reaction …

5 Look at graph F.

   a) How long do you think it would take to make 20 cm^3 of gas if the temperature was 45 °C?

   b) Sketch the graph in diagram F. Draw a line on your graph to show the rate of reaction at 45 °C.

   c) Draw a line on your graph to show the rate of reaction at 15 °C.

Effect of surface area

What effect does surface area have on the rate of reaction?

The **surface area** of something measures how much surface is exposed. Imagine cooking a potato in oil. The outside of the potato is in contact with the hot oil. You can make the potato cook faster by cutting it up into smaller pieces (chips!). This is because more surface is exposed to the hot oil when the potato is cut up. By cutting the potato into chips, the surface area becomes larger. If the chips are cut into crisps, the surface area becomes even larger!

It is the same with chemical reactions. Look at the experiment in diagram B. The experiment is carried out twice – first with large marble chips and then with small marble chips. The small chips have a larger surface area. The total mass of chips is kept the same (5 g) to make it a fair test. The volume of acid must also be kept the same in each experiment.

1 A cube with each side 2 cm long is cut in half.
  a) What was the total surface area of the uncut cube?
  b) What is the increase in surface area when it is cut in half?
  c) What is the percentage increase in surface area?

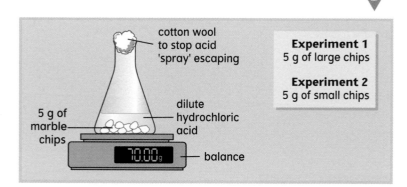

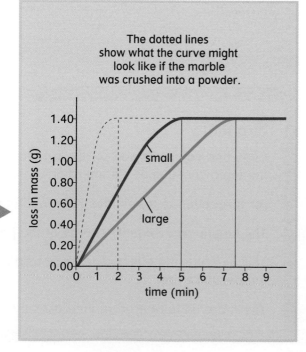

The dotted lines show what the curve might look like if the marble was crushed into a powder.

2 Look at the experiment in diagram B. What two things must be kept the same to make it a fair test?

After all the results have been collected, a graph can be drawn. This is shown in graph C.

3 a) How long did the reaction take with large chips?
  b) How long did the reaction take with small chips?
  c) How long would the reaction take if the chips were crushed into a powder?

P

How could you investigate the effect of surface area on rate of reaction?

- How will you change the surface area of the marble chips?
- What will you need to do to make it a fair test?
- How will you measure the rate of reaction?

D

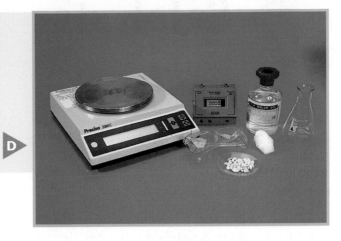

Explaining the effect of surface area

When the marble chips are broken into small pieces, the surface area is bigger. There are more particles on the surface for the acid particles to collide and react with, so the reaction is faster. When the surface area is increased, the rate of reaction increases because there are more collisions.

E

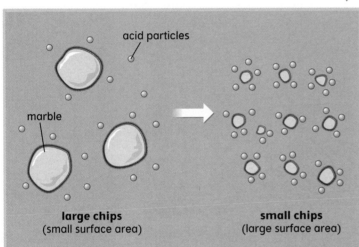

large chips
(small surface area)

small chips
(large surface area)

The smaller the pieces of a solid reactant, the bigger its surface area and the faster the rate of reaction as more collisions take place between reacting particles.

?

4 Describe one real-life situation where the size of the solid pieces affects the rate of a reaction. (*Hint*: think about how different solids burn.)

5 Explain why the fine flour dust in a flour mill sometimes explodes.

!

Coal dust can cause explosions in mines, if it catches fire. The surface area of the dust is very large and so, if it is ignited, the reaction is so fast it causes an explosion. This can also happen with substances like flour. In 1878 a flour mill in Minneapolis exploded when the flour dust caught fire. It killed 18 people and flattened nearby buildings.

Summary

Write a short note to describe what experiment B tells us about rates of reaction. Include the following in your note:

- a labelled diagram
- a graph of results
- an explanation of the effect of changing the size of the pieces of marble.

18

Catalysts

What is a catalyst?

Some chemical reactions are very slow. This is sometimes useful. For example, iron rusts very slowly and food rots slowly. We would not want iron bridges to rust away quickly or for our food to go off quickly!

But there are some reactions that we might want to speed up. A **catalyst** is a substance that speeds up a chemical reaction. Catalysts are used a lot in factories which make chemicals. Modern cars use platinum as a catalyst in the exhaust. This part of the exhaust is called a **catalytic converter**. Its job is to quickly turn poisonous gases into less harmful ones.

Look at the experiment in diagram B. Hydrogen peroxide breaks down slowly to make water and oxygen:

hydrogen peroxide $\longrightarrow$ water + oxygen

$$2H_2O_2 \longrightarrow 2H_2O + O_2$$

A catalyst (manganese (IV) oxide) is added to the second test tube. The reaction is much faster with the catalyst. The catalyst is still there at the end of the reaction and does not get used up. It can be used over and over again.

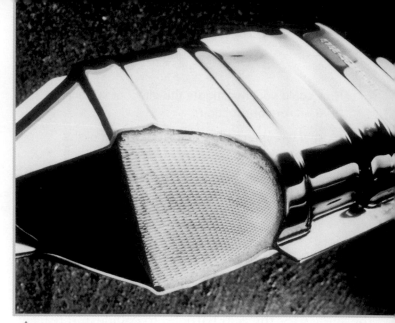

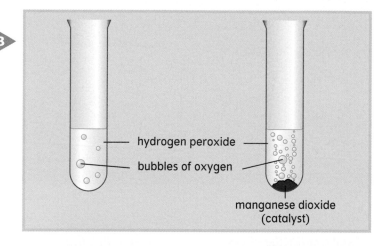

A *The inside of a catalytic converter in a car.*

1 Catalytic converters are found in the exhaust systems of all modern cars.
  a) What is the name of the catalyst used in catalytic converters?
  b) What do catalytic converters do?

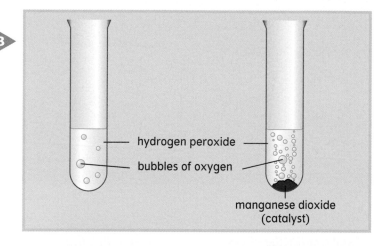

B hydrogen peroxide

bubbles of oxygen

manganese dioxide (catalyst)

2 Experiment B is about the use of a catalyst in a chemical reaction.
  a) Name two factors which should be kept the same to make this a fair test.
  b) How could you measure which of the reactions was fastest?
3 Why do industrial processes which use a catalyst not need to buy a new supply of catalyst very often?

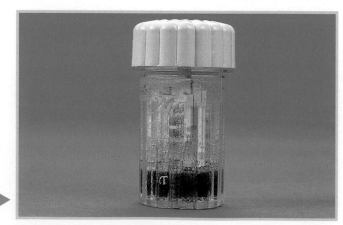

Hydrogen peroxide solution sterilises these contact lenses. But you might forget to rinse the lenses before putting them back in your eyes. A catalyst at the bottom of the container quickly breaks down hydrogen peroxide into water and oxygen.

C

P How could you investigate the effect of different catalysts?

● How will you make it a fair test?

● How will you decide which is the best? **D**

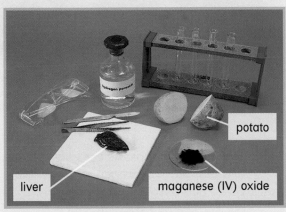

potato

liver

maganese (IV) oxide

Catalysts in industry

Catalysts are important for speeding up chemical reactions in industry. This saves a lot of money because the factory does not need to operate for as long to produce the same amount of chemicals. There are lots of different types of catalyst. Different reactions need different catalysts.

E *Iron is the catalyst used to make ammonia. Ammonia is an important chemical for making fertilisers.*

F *Platinum is the catalyst used to make nitric acid. Nitric acid is another important chemical used to make fertilisers.*

G *Nickel is the catalyst used to make margarine.*

Summary

Draw a concept map for catalysts. Start your map like this:

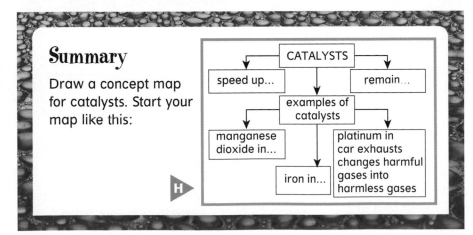

H

```
              CATALYSTS
        ↓        ↓        ↓
   speed up...       remain...
              ↓
         examples of
          catalysts
        ↓             ↓
   manganese      platinum in
   dioxide in...  car exhausts
                  changes harmful
              ↓   gases into
         iron in...  harmless gases
```

?

4 Industrial catalysts can be expensive to buy. Explain how the use of catalysts in industrial reactions can make the processes more profitable.

5 Why are many catalysts made into small pellets or crushed into powders?

19

Enzymes

What are enzymes?

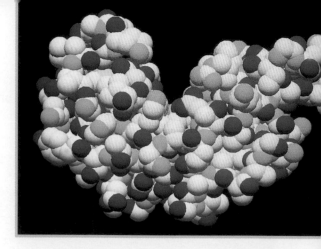

All living things are made from cells. There are chemical reactions going on inside every cell, keeping them alive. The chemical reactions have to be speeded up by catalysts made by the cell. These catalysts are called **enzymes**. Enzymes are catalysts from living things. Sometimes they are called 'biological catalysts'.

A A computer model of a molecule of the enzyme lysozyme. This enzyme is found in certain body fluids and can break down bacterial cell walls.

Look at the experiment in diagram B. Hydrogen peroxide breaks down slowly into water and oxygen.

$$\text{hydrogen peroxide} \longrightarrow \text{water} + \text{oxygen}$$
$$2H_2O_2 \longrightarrow 2H_2O + O_2$$

Liver has enzymes in it that speed up the reaction.

B

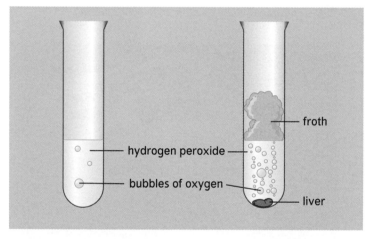
- froth
- hydrogen peroxide
- bubbles of oxygen
- liver

The bombardier beetle uses an enzyme to break down hydrogen peroxide into water and oxygen. It happens so quickly, like an explosion, that it frightens away any predators. **C**

 1   Explain what an enzyme is and name one example.

Effect of temperature

The chemical reactions in cells actually happen faster when it is warm rather than hot. Enzymes are large protein molecules and they are affected by temperature. If it is too hot (above 45 °C), they are damaged or **denatured**. When an enzyme is denatured its shape changes and it will not work. Biological washing powders contain enzymes. The enzymes in the washing powder break down stains. They work best at about 40 °C. The temperature that an enzyme works best at is called its **optimum temperature**.

The rate of reaction of enzymes breaking down stains on dirty clothes is affected by temperature. **D**

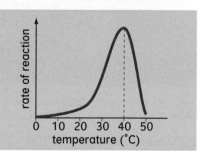
rate of reaction
temperature (°C)
0 10 20 30 40 50

2   Graph D shows the rate of reaction for the enzyme used in biological washing powders.
a) What is the optimum temperature for this enzyme?
b) What is the purpose of the enzyme in biological washing powders?
c) What would happen if this washing powder was used to wash clothes at 70 °C? Briefly explain your answer.

How could you study the effect of temperature on enzymes?

- Think how you could destroy the enzymes in the liver.
- How will you know if the enzymes have stopped working?
- How will you make it a fair test?

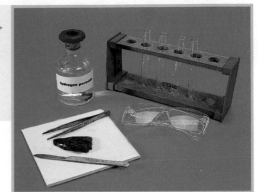

Effect of pH

Enzymes can be affected by how much acid or alkali is present. Remember, pH is a measure of how acidic or alkaline a substance is. Enzymes have an **optimum pH** at which they work best. Like changes in temperature, changes in pH can denature an enzyme so that it cannot work efficiently.

?

3 Graph F shows how two different enzymes, X and Y, are affected by changes in pH.
   a) What is the optimum pH for each of these enzymes?
   b) Which of the enzymes works best in alkaline conditions?

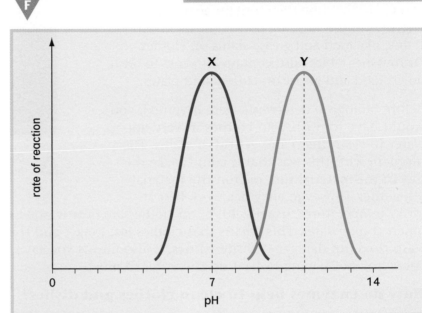

P

Protease breaks down proteins into smaller molecules. How could you investigate the effect of pH on protease?

- How will you change the pH to see what effect it has?

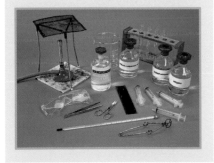

?

4 When you are ill you sometimes get a high temperature. If your body temperature goes too high, you can die. Explain why a high body temperature is dangerous. (*Hint*: look at the first paragraph of this topic.)

5 Enzymes are catalysts for chemical reactions. Explain why catalysts are vital to life.

6 The enzyme amylase (found in our mouths, pH 7) helps break down starch. Why does this enzyme not work in our stomachs (pH 2)?

Summary

Imagine you have been asked to give a talk to the rest of the class on enzymes. Design a poster to explain what enzymes are, and how changing conditions affect how they work. Include definitions of the words in bold on these pages and also graphs which show optimum pH and temperature.

Uses of enzymes

How are enzymes useful to us?

Enzymes have many uses and are used at home and in industry.

Enzymes in the home

Some washing powders are called 'biological detergents' because they contain enzymes. The enzymes in the washing powder break down stains, like food and grease stains on clothes. Dishwasher tablets also contain enzymes to break down food and grease on cutlery and plates.

Before biological detergents were invented, you would have to wash your clothes in very hot water to clean them and get rid of stains. The problem with this was that it could make the dye in the material run, or ruin the material altogether. However, enzymes work best at lower temperatures, usually 40 °C, so clothes are now washed in much cooler water. This means that clothes last longer and the wash does not damage delicate fabrics. It also means you save energy by not having to heat up the water so much.

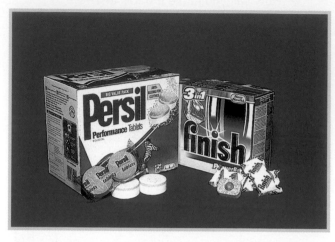

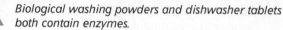 **A** Biological washing powders and dishwasher tablets both contain enzymes.

How do enzymes help to clean clothes and dishes?

Most foods contain **proteins** and **fats**, which are insoluble. Also, stains like sweat contain protein. Protein and fat molecules are very big and they stick to clothes and dishes. To clean the clothes and dishes, the large molecules have to be broken down into smaller molecules. This is called **digestion**. The smaller molecules are soluble and so dissolve in the wash.

 B

A biological detergent has protein-digesting enzymes in it called **proteases**. It also contains fat-digesting enzymes called **lipases**.

Enzymes in industry

Using enzymes in industry means that lower temperatures and pressures can be used for the reactions. This means that a company does not have to buy expensive equipment that also uses a lot of energy. This saves money.

One problem in the 1970s was that workers in washing-powder factories developed allergies to the enzymes and came out in a rash. The problem was solved in the factories, but some people using washing powders at home still get rashes and allergies from the enzymes.

?

1 Name two enzymes which are used in biological washing powders.

2 How do enzymes help to clean clothes?

3 What are the main advantages of using a biological washing powder?

4 What process in the body is similar to the action of enzymes in washing powder?

Enzymes in the food industry

Enzymes are used in industry to make all sorts of foods. Table C shows the uses of some of these enzymes.

Type of enzyme	Proteases	Carbohydrases	Isomerases
Use	To 'pre-digest' the protein in some baby foods.	To turn starch syrup into sugar syrup for making chocolates, cakes and other food products.	To turn glucose syrup into fructose syrup, which is used in slimming foods. Fructose and glucose are both sugars.
Why is it used?	The baby may not be able to digest all the protein itself.	Sugar syrup is sweet and makes the food 'taste nice'.	Fructose is twice as sweet as glucose. This means it can be used in smaller quantities in slimming foods.

Advantages of using enzymes

Enzymes can speed up industrial processes and make them more profitable. To use enzymes in industry they need to be stabilised (so they keep working for a long time) and held in place on unreactive beads. Alginate beads are often used to trap and stabilise enzymes so that the reactants in the process can be fed in at one end of the chemical plant, and the products can be continually removed at the other end, 24 hours a day. This is called a **continuous process** and it is more efficient than a **batch process**, where reactants are mixed together and the products have to be separated from the reaction mixture when the reaction is complete.

Summary

A TV company is making a programme about the food industry. They need a short introduction to the programme, including examples, to describe the main advantages and disadvantages of the use of enzymes in industry. Write the script for this introduction.

5 Describe one advantage and one disadvantage of using enzymes in industry.

6 A fat-digesting enzyme found in a fungus can be used in washing powders. It can act at low temperatures. The enzyme breaks down after a few days into carbon dioxide, nitrogen and water.
 a) Why is the fungus useful for making washing powder?
 b) Why do you think the enzyme is 'environmentally friendly'?

7 Compare the use of continuous and batch processes in the chemical industry by describing one advantage and one disadvantage of each process.

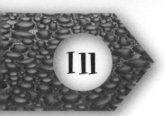 **111**

Enzymes and food
How else can enzymes be useful to us?

Our bodies need enzymes to speed up chemical reactions in our cells and to help digest our food. We can also use enzymes to make some foods and drinks.

 1 Write down three examples of foods or drinks that can be made with the help of enzymes.

 A *Enzymes are used to make all these things.*

Yeast is a fungus. Enzymes in the yeast cells can turn sugars into carbon dioxide and alcohol. This process is called **fermentation**.

 2 What is fermentation?

B

C *Yeast cells; magnification × 1300.*

Making beer and wine

Beer and wine contain **alcohol** and are made by fermentation. Look at diagram B. The yeast cells are fermenting the glucose solution. Since fermentation is a chemical reaction we can write it as a word equation:

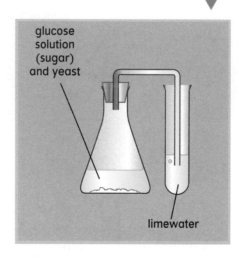
glucose solution (sugar) and yeast

limewater

$$\text{glucose} \longrightarrow \text{carbon dioxide} + \text{ethanol}$$
$$(C_6H_{12}O_6) \qquad\qquad\qquad\qquad (C_2H_5OH)$$
(a type of sugar) \qquad\qquad\qquad\qquad (a type of alcohol)

Limewater is used to test for carbon dioxide. If you breathe out through a straw into a test tube of limewater it will turn milky (cloudy). This is because you breathe out carbon dioxide, made in respiration. If the limewater turns milky in diagram B, then carbon dioxide has been made and we know that fermentation has taken place.

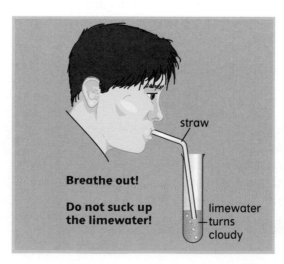 **D**

straw

Breathe out!

Do not suck up the limewater!

limewater turns cloudy

 3 Write a balanced symbol equation for the fermentation of glucose ($C_6H_{12}O_6$).

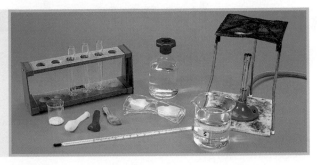

How could you find out which temperature yeast works fastest at?

- How will you trap the carbon dioxide?
- How will you know which is the best temperature?
- How will you make it a fair test?

E

Making bread

F

Yeast has also been used for thousands of years by people all around the world, to make bread. Yeast is added to the dough mixture. The dough is warmed so that the enzymes in the yeast can work properly. It slowly makes bubbles of carbon dioxide. These bubbles of carbon dioxide make the dough rise. The bread can then be baked in a hot oven.

! The ancient Egyptians found out that yeast makes bread rise around 4000 BC!

G *Straining yogurt makes it thicker.*

Using microbes to make food

Microbes are very small living things, usually only one cell big. Yeast and bacteria are both microbes. We have seen how the enzymes in yeast are used to make food and drink.

Making yoghurt

People have made yoghurt for thousands of years. Yoghurt is made from milk, which contains a sugar called **lactose**. There are bacteria in milk. Enzymes in the bacteria change lactose into **lactic acid**. The lactic acid makes the milk curdle and turn thick.

4 Explain how each of the following happens.
   a) The dough that is used to make bread rises when warmed.
   b) Milk can change into yoghurt.

5 What is the lactose in milk changed into to make yoghurt?

6 Naan bread, pitta bread and chapattis are all 'flat' breads. They have not risen like other breads. What is the difference between the way they are made and the way ordinary bread is made?

7 When the enzyme catalase is added to hydrogen peroxide, a gas is produced. A pupil thought that the gas could be oxygen, hydrogen, nitrogen or carbon dioxide. Describe how the pupil could test for each of these gases to find out which gas was produced in the reaction.

Summary

Imagine that you are in charge of a large factory that makes lots of different foods and drinks. Write an information leaflet for visitors to the factory, about the enzymes that are used in your factory.

Include the following words in your leaflet: bread, bacteria, yeast, carbon dioxide, glucose, yoghurt, enzyme, fermentation.

Energy transfer

What is energy transfer?

There are many different types of energy: chemical energy, heat energy, light energy, sound energy, kinetic (movement) energy and electrical energy.

When a chemical reaction takes place, energy is **transferred**. This means it moves from one place to another. When it transfers, it also changes into a different type of energy.

 1 Write down six different types of energy.

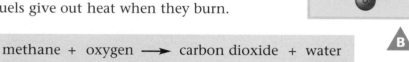

A

The chemical energy stored in these fireworks is transferred to light, heat, kinetic and sound energy.

During all chemical reactions **bonds** are broken and new bonds are formed. Energy has to be put in to break bonds and energy is given out when new bonds are formed.

When methane burns it gives out heat. All fuels give out heat when they burn.

methane + oxygen ⟶ carbon dioxide + water
CH_4 + $2O_2$ ⟶ CO_2 + $2H_2O$

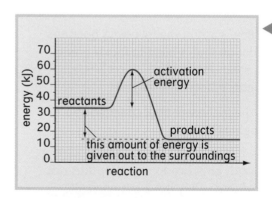

C *Energy graph for an exothermic reaction.*

  2 Use graph C to answer the following questions about an exothermic reaction.
   a) How much energy is needed to break the bonds in the reactants?
   b) How much energy is given out when the new bonds are formed?
   c) What is the overall energy change in this reaction?
   d) Where has this energy gone?

Exothermic reactions

In the reaction shown in diagram B the amount of energy given out when the new bonds are formed is greater than the energy put in to break the original bonds. This type of change is called an **exothermic reaction**. Exothermic reactions give out heat energy to their surroundings. This makes the surroundings feel hot.

Graph C shows the energy changes, measured in kilojoules (kJ), involved in an exothermic reaction.

Endothermic reactions

In some reactions the energy needed to break the original bonds is greater than the energy given out when the new bonds are formed. These reactions take in energy from the surroundings and are called **endothermic reactions**. Graph D shows the energy changes involved in an endothermic reaction. As the overall energy change takes in energy, the surroundings get colder.

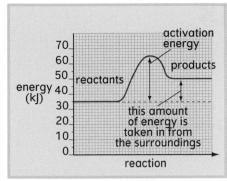

D *Energy graph for an endothermic reaction.*

P How could you tell whether a reaction was endothermic or exothermic? **E**

● What measurements will you take?

● How will you make it a fair test?

● How will you know which reactions are exothermic and which are endothermic?

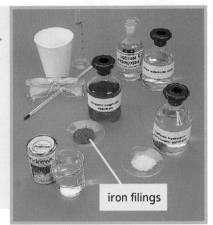

iron filings

F

? **3** Use graph D to answer the following questions about an endothermic reaction.

   a) What is the overall energy change in this reaction?

   b) Where has this energy come from?

Temperature changes in reactions

Look at diagram F. It shows an exothermic reaction and an endothermic reaction. The surroundings could be air, a test tube or water that chemicals have dissolved in, or even your leg!

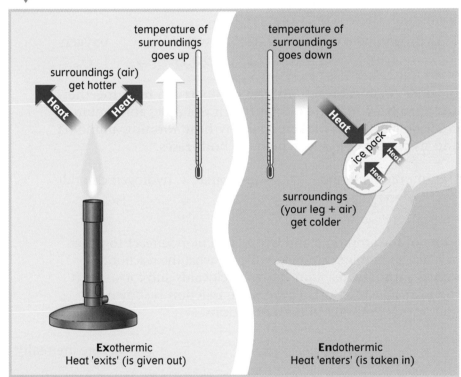

? **4** Diagram B shows what happens when methane burns.

   a) Describe the bonds that have to be broken and formed during this reaction.

   b) Explain why the combustion of methane is exothermic.

5 A catalyst speeds up a reaction by lowering the activation energy. However, it does not alter the overall energy change of the reaction.

   a) Make a sketch of graph C. Add a dotted line to your graph to represent the energy change when a catalyst is used.

   b) Explain, in terms of the collision theory, why lowering the activation energy speeds up the rate of a reaction.

Summary

Design a poster to explain how exothermic and endothermic reactions occur and affect their surroundings. Your poster should include suitable graphs with a few words of explanation.

Reversible reactions

What is a reversible reaction?

A chemical reaction starts off with reactants. The reactants react together to make the products.

reactants $\longrightarrow$ products

For example, when an acid neutralises an alkali:

hydrochloric + sodium $\longrightarrow$ sodium + water
acid   hydroxide   chloride

$$HCl + NaOH \longrightarrow NaCl + H_2O$$

Sometimes there is only one reactant:

hydrogen peroxide $\longrightarrow$ water + oxygen

$$2H_2O_2 \longrightarrow 2H_2O + O_2$$

In some chemical reactions, the products can react together and turn back into the reactants. For example, ammonium chloride (a solid) is broken down by heat, forming ammonia and hydrogen chloride, which are both gases.

ammonium chloride $\rightleftharpoons$ ammonia + hydrogen chloride

$$NH_4Cl \rightleftharpoons NH_3 + HCl$$

Some of the ammonia and hydrogen chloride react together to make ammonium chloride, which is what the reaction started with! The reaction can go backwards and forwards. It is a reversible reaction. A **reversible reaction** is shown by half arrows pointing in both directions.

$$A + B \rightleftharpoons C + D$$

? **1** With the aid of a catalyst, sulphur dioxide and oxygen react in a reversible reaction to produce sulphur trioxide (SO_3). Using the correct symbols, write a word and a balanced symbol equation for this reaction.

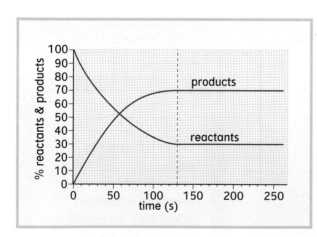
A

There are really two reactions going on:

$$A + B \longrightarrow C + D$$
$$C + D \longrightarrow A + B$$

A reversible reaction can never produce 100% products because some of the products will always change back into the reactants. Look at graph A. It shows how the rates of the forward and backward reactions change as a reversible reaction takes place.

As the forward reaction slows down the backward reaction speeds up until they happen at exactly the same rate. After this point is reached the percentage of reactant and product in the mixture will not change. This is called the **equilibrium position**. In the example shown in the graph, equilibrium is reached at 70% products and 30% reactants.

? **2** Explain, using your own words, how an equilibrium position is reached in a reversible reaction.

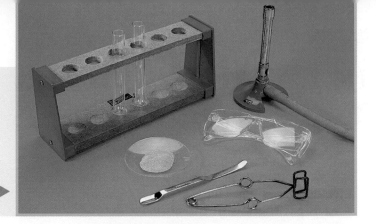

P How could you investigate a reversible reaction?

- Blue copper sulphate crystals can be changed into white powder by heating.
- How do you turn the white powder back into blue crystals (the backward reaction)?

C

Test for water

Copper sulphate crystals normally contain water as well as copper sulphate. They are called **hydrated** copper sulphate and are blue.

If hydrated copper sulphate is heated, it loses water and turns into **anhydrous** copper sulphate powder which is white.

When water is added to anhydrous copper sulphate it turns from white back to blue, forming the blue hydrated copper sulphate crystals again. The reaction is reversible. (In the equation below heat is in brackets because it is not a chemical.)

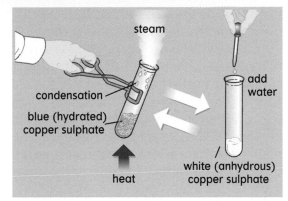

steam

condensation

blue (hydrated) copper sulphate

heat

add water

white (anhydrous) copper sulphate

D

hydrated copper sulphate (blue crystals) (+ heat energy) $\rightleftharpoons$ anhydrous copper sulphate (white powder) + water

$CuSO_4.5H_2O$ (+ heat energy) $\rightleftharpoons$ $CuSO_4$ + $5H_2O$

You can use this to test for water. White anhydrous copper sulphate turns blue if water is present.

Energy changes in reversible reactions

If a reversible reaction is exothermic in one direction, it will be endothermic in the other direction. In the example used above:

- In the *forward reaction* energy is taken in, so this is an endothermic reaction.
- In the *backward reaction* energy is given out, so this is an exothermic reaction.

The same amount of energy is transferred in each case.

Summary

Answer the topic question at the top of page 110. Include a balanced symbol equation for one example of a reversible reaction. Make sure you explain each of the words and phrases in bold on these two pages.

?

3 a) In the reaction of hydrated copper sulphate shown above is the forward reaction exothermic or endothermic?

b) Would energy be given out or taken in when water is added to anhydrous copper sulphate?

c) Explain your answer to b).

4 Equilibrium can only be established in a **closed system** where none of the reactants or products are lost. If calcium carbonate is heated, the following decomposition reaction occurs:

$CaCO_3(s) \longrightarrow CaO(s) + CO_2(g)$

Explain why equilibrium cannot be established if this reaction is carried out in an open test tube.

Nitrogen – a very useful gas!

What is nitrogen used for?

The air around us is made up of a mixture of different gases. Pie chart A shows how much of each gas there is in the air.

Plants need nitrogen, which they use to make proteins for growth. Even though the air is nearly 80% nitrogen, plants cannot use this nitrogen. Plants get their nitrogen from compounds called **nitrates** in the soil. Special bacteria living in the soil can turn the nitrogen in the air into nitrates. Nitrates are dissolved in water in the soil and the plants get them when they absorb water through their roots.

Nitrogen can be used to make lots of useful chemicals, like **fertilisers**. Fertilisers are made from nitrates. Using fertilisers adds nitrates to the soil. Fertilisers are used by farmers to increase the **yield** of crops (to get the crops to grow better and produce more food or other useful materials).

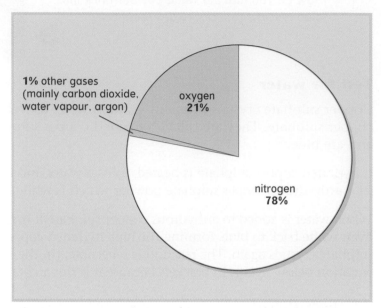

1% other gases (mainly carbon dioxide, water vapour, argon)

oxygen 21%

nitrogen 78%

A

B Farmers add fertiliser to the soil. The fertiliser gives crops nitrogen, which they need for growth.

? 1 Many fertilisers contain soluble compounds of nitrogen, including ammonium nitrate, ammonium sulphate, potassium nitrate and ammonium phosphate.
   a) What do you think happens to plants that don't get enough nitrogen?
   b) Why should the compounds used in fertilisers be soluble?
   c) Name the element present in both ammonium and nitrate ions.

? 2 Nitrogen is a very unreactive element. Making nitrates means breaking the strong bonds in the nitrogen molecules. Do you think this reaction is exothermic or endothermic?

! Lightning can turn nitrogen in the air into nitric acid. Nitric acid falls to the ground and ends up as nitrates in the soil.

Crops take nitrates from the soil as they grow. When they are harvested, the crops are cut down and taken away. They are not allowed to rot back into the soil. This means there are less nitrates in the soil. Farmers have to add fertilisers to replace the missing nitrates.

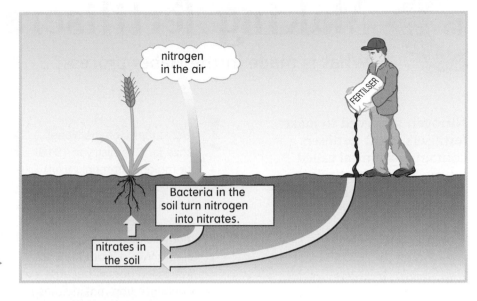

Two ways that a plant can get nitrates. **C**

The 'pros and cons' of using fertilisers **D**

There are advantages of using fertilisers but also disadvantages. Diagram D compares the advantages and disadvantages.

3 Explain why farmers have to use fertilisers on their land, while wild plants grow well, year after year without any added nitrates.

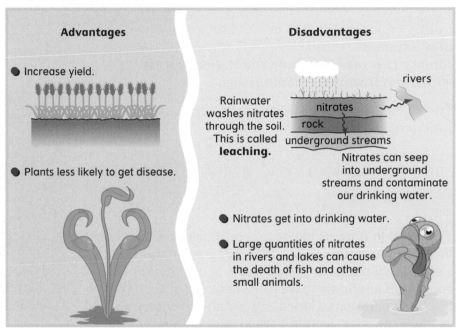

Summary

Design a leaflet to be handed out at garden centres. Your leaflet should explain what fertilisers are and why they are needed. You will also need to explain to gardeners why they should not use too much fertiliser.

4 Many years ago farmers used to 'rotate' their crops. They would leave one of their fields without a crop and grow clover instead. Clover roots contain lots of bacteria, which turn nitrogen into nitrates. The clover was ploughed into the field before planting the seeds for a new crop.

Explain why this was a good idea.

5 In nature, plants take nitrogen compounds from the soil to make protein. Animals eat the plants and use the protein in their bodies. The nitrogen compounds are returned to the soil when the plants and animals die and decay. This is called the nitrogen cycle. Draw a diagram to illustrate this cycle and explain why fertilisers are not needed in nature.

Making fertilisers – part 1

What is made in the Haber process?

Nitrogen is needed to make fertilisers. Most fertilisers contain a chemical called **ammonium nitrate**. Two chemicals are needed to make ammonium nitrate:

● ammonia
● nitric acid.

Both these chemicals contain nitrogen.

In this topic we will look at how ammonia is made.
Ammonia is made by using the **Haber process** which was invented by Fritz Haber.

Two chemicals are needed to make ammonia – nitrogen and hydrogen.

Fritz Haber won the Nobel Prize for Chemistry in 1918 for making ammonia from nitrogen and hydrogen. But he also made poisonous gases, which were used to kill many soldiers in the trenches during World War One. His wife killed herself because he would not stop making these poisonous gases.

A

These British soldiers were blinded by poisonous gases. B

$$\text{nitrogen} + \text{hydrogen} \rightleftharpoons \text{ammonia (+ heat)}$$
$$N_2 + 3H_2 \rightleftharpoons 2NH_3 \text{ (+ heat)}$$

The reaction is reversible, so an **equilibrium** is established in the reaction. This means that in the apparatus there is a mixture of reactants and products at equilibrium. The amount of ammonia made (the yield) depends on the reaction conditions. Conditions are always chosen to produce the most economic yield of ammonia:

● catalyst: iron
● temperature: 450 °C
● pressure: about 200 atmospheres.

C

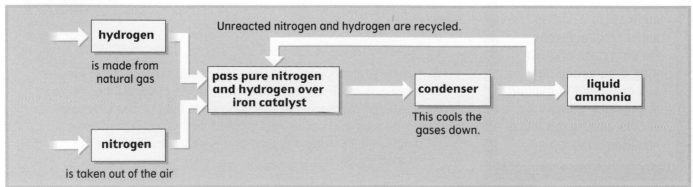

hydrogen

is made from natural gas

nitrogen

is taken out of the air

Unreacted nitrogen and hydrogen are recycled.

pass pure nitrogen and hydrogen over iron catalyst

condenser

This cools the gases down.

liquid ammonia

1 Look at diagram C.
   a) Name the raw materials used as a source of the nitrogen and hydrogen used in the Haber process.
   b) What is the purpose of the iron catalyst?
   c) How is the ammonia removed from the reaction mixture?
   d) Explain why the process does not need to allow the reaction to come to equilibrium. (*Hint*: What happens to the unreacted nitrogen and hydrogen?)

 Part of the Haber plant at Billingham in North East England.

Whatever you do to the conditions of a reaction in equilibrium, the equilibrium position will move in the opposite direction. So, increasing the temperature will move the equilibrium in the endothermic direction, cooling the surroundings down. Increasing the pressure will move the equilibrium in the direction which forms less gas molecules, thus reducing the pressure. These ideas explain why the Haber process conditions are chosen.

- The reaction which makes ammonia is exothermic, so a low temperature would mean more ammonia is made. However, if the temperature is too low then the reaction is too slow. Therefore a temperature of 450 °C is used.
- The reaction which makes ammonia causes a reduction in the number of gas molecules, so a high pressure would mean more ammonia is made. However, very high pressures are dangerous and expensive. Therefore a pressure of 200 atmospheres is used.

These conditions produce a yield of about 15% ammonia. However, none of the reactants are wasted. As the ammonia is formed it is removed, and the unreacted nitrogen and hydrogen are **recycled**.

Making ammonia uses up huge amounts of energy – about 1% of the world's energy production. But a new catalyst recently discovered in Germany means that less pressure is needed and so less energy is used up.

2 Methane can be formed by the reversible reaction:
   $$CO(g) + 3H_2(g) \rightleftharpoons CH_4(g) + H_2O(g) \text{ (+ heat)}$$
   a) Is the reverse reaction forming carbon monoxide and hydrogen exothermic or endothermic?
   b) Briefly explain your answer to a).
   c) Explain how the yield of methane would change if the temperature was increased.
   d) Explain how the yield of methane would change if the pressure was increased.

3 Hydrogen iodide can be formed by the following reversible reaction:
   $$H_2(g) + I_2(g) \rightleftharpoons 2HI(g)$$
   a) If the yield of hydrogen iodide is higher at lower temperatures, what does this tell us about the reaction forming it?
   b) Explain how the yield of hydrogen iodide would change if the gas pressure was increased.

Summary

Imagine that you were Fritz Haber in 1918, trying to win the Nobel prize for chemistry. Write a report for the awards committee making sure you explain:
- a formula equation for the reaction
- a flow diagram for the process
- a list of the conditions used
- an explanation of why each condition is chosen.

Making fertilisers – part 2

How is ammonium nitrate fertiliser made?

Two chemicals are needed to make ammonium nitrate:

- ammonia (made in the Haber process)
- nitric acid (made from ammonia).

Some of the ammonia from the Haber process can be used to make the nitric acid needed.

? **1** Why is a catalyst needed and why is it made hot?

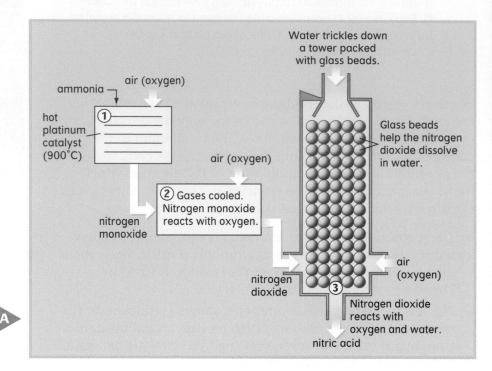

Water trickles down a tower packed with glass beads.

ammonia

air (oxygen)

hot platinum catalyst (900°C)

①

air (oxygen)

② Gases cooled. Nitrogen monoxide reacts with oxygen.

nitrogen monoxide

Glass beads help the nitrogen dioxide dissolve in water.

nitrogen dioxide

③

air (oxygen)

Nitrogen dioxide reacts with oxygen and water.

nitric acid

A

Making nitric acid

There are three stages to the process, shown in diagram A.

1 The ammonia is oxidised.

A hot platinum catalyst is needed to speed up the reaction.

$$\text{ammonia} + \text{oxygen} \longrightarrow \text{nitrogen monoxide} + \text{steam}$$
$$4NH_3 + 5O_2 \longrightarrow 4NO + 6H_2O$$

2 The nitrogen monoxide is cooled and then reacted with oxygen to make nitrogen dioxide.

$$\text{nitrogen monoxide} + \text{oxygen} \longrightarrow \text{nitrogen dioxide}$$
$$2NO + O_2 \longrightarrow 2NO_2$$

3 The nitrogen dioxide reacts with oxygen and water to make nitric acid.

$$\text{nitrogen dioxide} + \text{oxygen} + \text{water} \longrightarrow \text{nitric acid}$$
$$4NO_2 + O_2 + 2H_2O \longrightarrow 4HNO_3$$

Nitric acid can be used to make lots of chemicals. Most of the nitric acid made is used to make fertiliser.

! About 3.5 million tonnes of nitric acid are made in the UK every year.

? **2** What catalyst is used to make nitric acid?

B *The nitric acid plant at Billingham. It uses ammonia so it is built next to the Haber plant.*

Making ammonium nitrate fertiliser

Ammonium nitrate is a salt. It is made in a **neutralisation** reaction between ammonia and nitric acid. Diagram D shows how this is done.

Ammonium nitrate crystals.

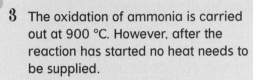

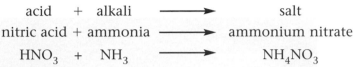

acid + alkali ⟶ salt

nitric acid + ammonia ⟶ ammonium nitrate

HNO_3 + NH_3 ⟶ NH_4NO_3

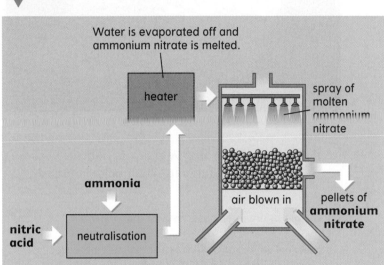

Water is evaporated off and ammonium nitrate is melted.

heater

spray of molten ammonium nitrate

ammonia

air blown in

pellets of **ammonium nitrate**

nitric acid

neutralisation

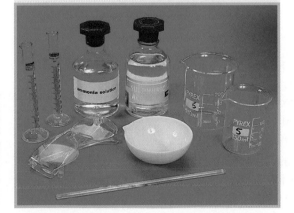

P How could you make ammonium sulphate fertiliser? **E**

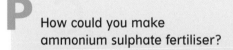

3 The oxidation of ammonia is carried out at 900 °C. However, after the reaction has started no heat needs to be supplied.
  a) Is this reaction exothermic or endothermic?
  b) Explain your answer to part a).

4 In stage 3 of the manufacture of nitric acid, water is trickled down a tower packed with glass beads.
  a) Explain how the glass beads help the nitrogen dioxide to dissolve in the water.
  b) Why is air also added to the tower?

5 Ammonium nitrate is formed by reacting an acid and an alkali.
  a) What type of chemical reaction takes place to make ammonium nitrate?
  b) Write word equations for the reactions of ammonia with:
    i) sulphuric acid
    ii) hydrochloric acid.

6 Jane says that you only need ammonia to make fertiliser.
  a) Why does Jane think this?
  b) Explain why she is wrong.

Summary

Draw a concept map for the manufacture of fertilisers like ammonium nitrate. Start your map like this:

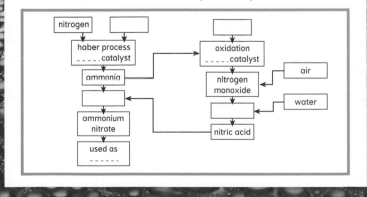

nitrogen

haber process
_ _ _ _ .catalyst

ammonia

ammonium nitrate

used as
_ _ _ _ _ _

oxidation
_ _ _ _ .catalyst

air

nitrogen monoxide

water

nitric acid

117

Masses and moles

How are atoms and molecules compared and measured?

All chemicals are made of atoms. The mass of an atom is too small to measure.

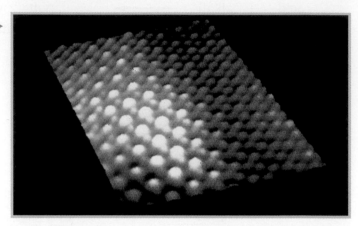

These palladium atom are magnified × 4.5 million. A

 The mass of a nitrogen atom is about 0.00000000000000000000000023 g!

Working with such small numbers would be too difficult. So, it is easier to give each atom a number on a scale and see how heavy they are compared to each other. This number is called the **relative atomic mass**.

The relative atomic mass can be called **R.A.M.** for short and it has a symbol, A_r. The lightest atom is hydrogen, so it is given a relative atomic mass of 1. Carbon is 12 times heavier than a hydrogen atom, so it is given a R.A.M. of 12.

Each element in the Periodic Table has a symbol with two numbers. The relative atomic mass is the bigger number. From diagram B you can see that carbon atoms are three times heavier than helium atoms.

Relative formula mass

The chemical formula for water is H_2O. If the relative atomic masses of the atoms in water are added together, you get the **relative formula mass**. It can be called **R.F.M.** for short and has the symbol M_r. The R.F.M. for water is 18.

Worked example

A What is the R.F.M. of ammonium nitrate (NH_4NO_3)?

(R.A.M.s: H = 1, N = 14, O = 16)

2 nitrogen	=	2 × 14	=	28
4 hydrogen	=	4 × 1	=	4
3 oxygen	=	3 × 16	=	48
				80

So the relative formula mass of ammonium nitrate (NH_4NO_3) is 80.

 1 Why is it easier to give atoms a relative atomic mass than to use their actual masses?

Carbon atoms are three times heavier than helium atoms. B

relative atomic mass (R.A.M.) sometimes just called the mass number (number of protons and neutrons)

^4_2He $^{12}_6C$

atomic number (number of protons in the atom)

 2 Use the Periodic Table on page 246 to find the relative atomic mass of:
   a) oxygen
   b) sulphur
   c) magnesium.

3 Use the Periodic Table on page 246 to answer this question. How many times heavier than an oxygen atom is a sulphur atom?

4 Work out the relative formula masses for these compounds:
   a) carbon dioxide – CO_2
   b) ammonia – NH_3
   c) nitric acid – HNO_3
   d) magnesium sulphate – $MgSO_4$.

Moles

Atoms and molecules are far too small to weigh, so chemists often use a quantity called the **mole** in calculations. A mole is simply a quantity – like a dozen. In fact a mole is actually 6×10^{23} of something.

One mole of an element is its relative atomic mass (A_r) measured in grams. One mole of a compound is its relative formula mass (M_r) measured in grams.

Moles are not just furry animals.

Worked examples

B What is the mass of 1 mole of sodium?

A_r for sodium   = 23
So 1 mole of sodium   = 23 g

C What is the mass of 5 moles of sodium carbonate?

Formula for sodium carbonate	=	Na_2CO_3
2 sodium $= 2 \times 23$	=	46
1 carbon	=	12
3 oxygen $= 3 \times 16$	=	48
total	=	106

So M_r for sodium carbonate   = 106
And 1 mole of sodium carbonate = 106 g

So 5 moles of sodium carbonate   = 5×106
                                          = 530 g

Calculations using moles

Chemists use the mole to work out the amounts of chemicals in a reaction. The first stage in these calculations is to work out the balanced symbol equation for the reaction. The numbers in front of the formulae in these equations tell us the number of moles of each substance. Therefore, given a certain mass of reactant or product, other quantities can be worked out.

Worked example

D What mass of water would be produced by the complete combustion of 50 g of pentane? (C = 12, O = 16, H =1)

Balanced symbol equation:
$$C_5H_{12} + 8O_2 \longrightarrow 5CO_2 + 6H_2O$$

The equation can be used to find the ratio in moles of the substances in the question.

From the equation the mole ratio is:
1 mole $C_5H_{12} \longrightarrow$ 6 moles H_2O
We can now calculate the ratio in grams:

M_r of $C_5H_{12} = (12 \times 5) + (1 \times 12)$	= 72
1 mole of C_5H_{12}	= 72 g
M_r of $H_2O = (2 \times 1) + (1 \times 16)$	= 18
1 mole of H_2O	= 18 g
6 moles of $H_2O = 6 \times 18$	= 108 g

The ratio in grams:
72 g of $C_5H_{12} \longrightarrow$ 108 g of H_2O

Solve by simple proportion:
1 g of $C_5H_{12} \longrightarrow$ 108/72 = 1.5 g of H_2O
50 g of $C_5H_{12} \longrightarrow$ 50 $\times$ 1.5 = 75 g of H_2O

So 50 g of pentane produces 75 g of water when burned.

?

5 Using the Periodic Table on page 246 to help you, calculate the mass of 1 mole of:
   a) aluminium – Al   **b)** uranium – U
   c) water – H_2O **d)** zinc nitrate – $Zn(NO_3)_2$.

6 What mass of water would be produced by complete combustion of 20 g of ethane (C_2H_6)?

7 Work out the R.F.M.s of:
   a) aluminium sulphate – $Al_2(SO_4)_3$
   b) lead nitrate – $Pb(NO_3)_2$.

Summary

Write out definitions of the terms 'relative atomic mass', 'relative formula mass' and 'mole'. Explain how these are used to calculate the amounts of reactants or products in a reaction. You could design a flowchart of steps to follow for this type of calculation.

More moles

How can we use moles to do calculations?

You have seen how to calculate the masses of reactants and products using moles. However, moles can also be used to calculate volumes of gas given off, and when considering half equations in electrolysis.

Calculating volumes of gas

It is also possible to calculate the volume of gas produced in a chemical reaction, if the volume of one mole of the gas is known.

Worked example

A What volume of oxygen would be produced by decomposing 10 g of hydrogen peroxide?
(The volume of one mole of a gas is 24 litres. O = 16, H = 1)

Balanced symbol equation:
$$2H_2O_2 \longrightarrow 2H_2O + O_2$$

The equation can be used to find the ratio in moles of the substances in the question. From the equation the mole ratio is:
2 moles $H_2O_2 \longrightarrow$ 1 mole O_2

We can now calculate the ratio in grams and litres.

M_r of $H_2O_2 = (2 \times 1) + (2 \times 16)$ = 34
1 mole of H_2O_2 = 34 g
2 moles of H_2O_2 = 68 g
Volume of 1 mole of O_2 = 24 l
Ratio in grams and litres:
68 g of $H_2O_2 \longrightarrow$ 24 l of O_2
Solve by simple proportion:
1 g of $H_2O_2 \longrightarrow$ 24/68 = 0.353 l of O_2
10 g of $H_2O \longrightarrow 10 \times 0.353 = 3.53$ l of O_2

So 3.53 litres of oxygen is made from 10 g of hydrogen peroxide.

Calculations involving electrolysis

Half equations can be used to find the mole ratio of the products formed during electrolysis. For example, during the electrolysis of copper chloride solution the following reactions occur:

At the negative electrode:
$Cu^{2+}(aq) + 2e \longrightarrow Cu(s)$ Copper ions form copper metal.

At the positive electrode:
$2Cl^-(aq) \longrightarrow Cl_2(g) + 2e$ Chloride ions form chlorine gas.

As two electrons are lost and gained these can be added together and the electrons cancelled out.

1 What mass of water is produced by burning 6 g of hydrogen according to the following equation?

$$2H_2 + O_2 \longrightarrow 2H_2O$$

(H = 1, O = 16)

2 What mass of iron would be produced by the reduction of 80 kg of iron oxide using carbon as the reducing agent? The equation for the reaction is:

$$2Fe_2O_3 + 3C \longrightarrow 4Fe + 3CO_2$$

(Fe = 56, C = 12, O = 16)

3 What volume of hydrogen would be produced by reacting 1 g of magnesium with excess hydrochloric acid? The balanced formula equation for the reaction is:

$$Mg + 2HCl \longrightarrow MgCl_2 + H_2$$

(In this example the volume of 1 mole of a gas is 24 litres.
Mg = 24, H = 1)

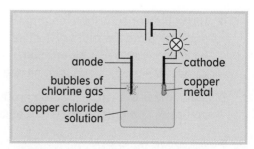

anode
bubbles of chlorine gas
copper chloride solution
cathode
copper metal

Given the half equations for an electrolysis reaction and the amount of one of the products formed, we can calculate the amount of the other product.

Worked examples

B Aluminium is produced by the electrolysis of molten aluminium oxide. During this electrolysis the following reactions occur:

at the negative electrode: $Al^{3+} + 3e^- \longrightarrow Al$
at the positive electrode: $2O^{2-} \longrightarrow O_2 + 4e^-$

An aluminium plant produces 500 kg of aluminium per hour by electrolysis. What mass of oxygen would be produced in the same time? (Al = 23, O = 16)

To balance the electrons, multiply the first half equation by 4 and the second one by 3:

$$4Al^{3+} + 12e^- \longrightarrow Al$$
$$6O^{2-} \longrightarrow 3O_2 + 12e^-$$

This gives 12 electrons on each side which can then be cancelled.

The combined equation is:
$$4Al^{3+} + 6O^{2-} \longrightarrow 4Al + 3O_2$$
(electrons cancelled)

The mole ratio of products is then:
4 moles of Al $\longrightarrow$ 3 moles of O_2

We can now calculate the ratio in grams:

A_r of Al $\quad\quad\quad\quad$ = 27
1 mole of Al $\quad\quad\quad$ = 27 g
4 moles of Al = 4 × 27 $\quad$ = 108 g
M_r of O_2 = 2 × 16 = 32
1 mole of O_2 $\quad\quad\quad$ = 32 g
3 moles of O_2 = 3 × 32 $\quad$ = 96 g
Ratio in grams:
108 g of Al $\longrightarrow$ 96 g of O_2
Solve by simple proportion:
1 g of Al $\quad\longrightarrow$ 96/108 = 0.889 g of O_2
500 kg of Al $\longrightarrow$ 500 × 1000 × 0.889 = 444 500 g of O_2

So 444.5 kg of oxygen is formed per hour.

Aluminium is manufactured by the electrolysis of molten aluminium oxide.

4 What volume of oxygen gas would be produced when 100 g of aluminium is formed during the electrolysis of molten aluminium oxide? (Note: 1 mole of any gas is 24 litres and the half equations are the same as in worked example B.)

5 What mass of hydrogen peroxide would be needed to produce 1 litre of oxygen gas? (Use the same conditions and decomposition equation given in worked example A.)

Summary

There are three different types of calculations that involve moles. Explain what each type of equation allows you to find out about a chemical reaction.

Formulae and percentage mass

How do you calculate percentage mass and formulae?

Farmers may want to know how much nitrogen there is in different fertilisers to see which one contains the most. They need to be able to calculate the **percentage mass** of nitrogen in the fertilisers.

A

 You can work out the percentage mass of an element in a compound if you know:

- the relative atomic mass of the element (A_r)
- the number of atoms of the element in the formula of the compound (n)
- the relative formula mass of the compound (M_r)

$$\text{percentage mass of an element in a compound} = \frac{\text{R.A.M.} \times \text{number of atoms (of that element)}}{\text{R.F.M.}} \times 100$$

The equation can be shortened to:

$$\% \text{ mass} = \frac{A_r \times n}{M_r} \times 100$$

Worked example

A Calculate the percentage of sodium in sodium sulphate (Na_2SO_4).

First work out the relative formula mass (M_r):

2 sodium = 2×23 = 46
1 sulphur = 1×32 = 32
4 oxygen = 4×16 = 64
                              142

Now put the numbers into the equation:

$$\% \text{ mass} = \frac{A_r \times n}{M_r} \times 100$$

$$\% \text{ mass} = \frac{23 \times 2}{142} \times 100 = 32.4\%$$

So, the percentage mass of sodium in sodium sulphate is 32.4%.

1 Find the percentage mass of oxygen in magnesium oxide MgO.

2 Find the percentage mass of nitrogen in ammonia NH_3.

3 Find out the percentage mass of sodium in sodium carbonate – Na_2CO_3.

4 Find out the percentage mass of sulphur in sulphuric acid – H_2SO_4.

Working out formulae

The percentage of an element in a compound can be found by measuring its mass. We can use this information to work out the simplest ratio of atoms or ions in a compound. This was how the formulae of compounds were originally worked out. The simplest ratio of atoms or ions in a compound is called the compound's **empirical formula**. The total number of atoms or ions in a compound is called its **molecular formula**.

Compound	Molecular formula	Empirical formula
water	H_2O	H_2O
ethene	C_2H_4	CH_2
hydrogen peroxide	H_2O_2	HO

 Examples of molecular formulae and empirical formulae.

Worked example

Calculate the empirical formula of the oxide of iron that contains 70% of iron combined with 30% of oxygen.

The stages involved in finding the empirical formula are as follows:

1	Elements' symbols	Fe	O
2	% of element	70	30
3	R.A.M. of elements	56	16
	Ratio = %/R.A.M	70/56	30/16
		= 1.25	= 1.875
4	Convert to whole number ratio (divide each by the smallest)	1.25/1.25 = 1	1.875/1.25 = 1.5
	(multiply to get whole numbers – in this case by 2)	= 2	= 3

Therefore the Formula is Fe_2O_3

Summary

Explain how to calculate the percentage by mass of an element in a compound and an empirical formula. Include an appropriate example of each type of calculation.

5 Find the empirical formula for the sulphide of lead which contains 76% lead and 24% sulphur.

6 Find the empirical formula for the hydrocarbon which contains 86% carbon and 14% hydrogen.

7 Find out which one of these fertilisers has the highest percentage mass of nitrogen.
   a) ammonium sulphate – $(NH_4)_2SO_4$
   b) ammonium nitrate – NH_4NO_3
   c) urea – $CO(NH_4)_2$. (*Hint*: $(NH_4)_2$ means two lots of NH_4 in the compound.)

8 What is the percentage content by mass of each element in glucose $(C_6H_{12}O_6)$?

9 What is the empirical formula of the compound that contains 40% carbon, 53% oxygen and 7% hydrogen?

Further questions

1 James is investigating the reaction between zinc and hydrochloric acid.

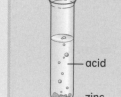

acid

zinc

a) Write down *four* ways James could increase the rate of reaction. (4)

b) If the test tube becomes warm during the experiment what kind of chemical reaction is occurring? (1)

2 Use the reaction profile shown below to answer the following questions.

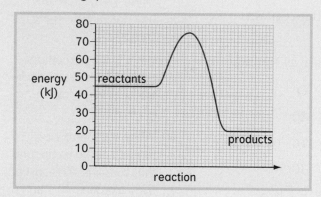

a) What is the overall energy change for this reaction? (1)

b) Is the forward reaction exothermic or endothermic? (1)

c) What is the activation energy for the forward reaction? (1)

3 Find the percentage composition for each element in the following compounds.

a) copper sulphate – $CuSO_4$ (3)

b) ethanol – C_2H_5OH. (3)

4 What is the empirical formula of the compound that contains 40% sulphur and 60% oxygen? (3)

5 The reaction of sodium carbonate (Na_2CO_3) and hydrochloric acid (HCl) can be followed by measuring the volume of gas produced with time.

a) Write a balanced symbol equation for this reaction. (2)

b) A group of pupils wished to investigate the affect of temperature on the rate of this reaction. They set up an experiment to measure how the volume of gas formed changed with time. The experiment was first carried out at 20 °C and then repeated at 40 °C.

   i) Name *two* things they would need to keep the same to make the investigation fair. (2)

   ii) Draw a labelled diagram of the experimental set up. (2)

   iii) Using the same axes, draw line graphs to show the volume of gas produced against time for these two reactions. No graph paper is required, but name the axes, units and each of the graphs. (3)

6 The following industrial reaction is endothermic.

$$H_2(g) + CO_2(g) \rightleftharpoons H_2(g) + CO(g)$$

The reaction is carried out at 1000 °C with the help of a platinum catalyst.

a) Write a word equation for this reaction. (2)

b) What is the meaning of the double arrow ($\rightleftharpoons$) symbol? (1)

c) What is the purpose of the platinum catalyst? (1)

d) Why is a high temperature used? (2)

e) Explain the effect of increasing pressure on the amount of hydrogen and carbon monoxide in the equilibrium mixture. (2)

7 Calculate the mass of the following.

a) one mole of $MgCl_2$ (2)

b) four moles of $CaCO_3$ (2)

c) 0.5 moles of carbon monoxide (CO) (2)

d) 10 moles of boron sulphide (B_2S_3) (2)

8 Explain the effect of temperature on the rate of a reaction, in terms of the kinetic energy of the reacting particles, collisions occurring and the activation energy for the reaction. (3)

9 Marble chips (calcium carbonate) react with dilute hydrochloric acid as shown in this equation:

$$CaCO_3 + 2HCl \longrightarrow CaCl_2 + H_2O + CO_2$$

The rate at which this reaction takes place can be studied by measuring the amount of carbon dioxide gas produced. The graphs below show the results of four experiments, 1 to 4. In each experiment, the amount of marble chips, the volume and the concentration of the acid were kept the same. The temperature of the acid was changed each time. Small marble chips were used for the experiment.

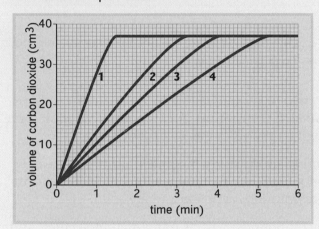

a) Which graph, 1 to 4, shows the results for the highest temperature? Explain fully how you know. (2)

b) Explain what happens to the particles in a reaction when they are heated and why this speeds up the reaction. (2)

c) i) What was the total volume of gas made in each experiment? (1)

   ii) Why was it the same volume for each experiment? (1)

   iii) How could you increase the volume of gas made in each experiment? (1)

10 Magnesium reacts with sulphuric acid as shown below:

$$Mg + H_2SO_4 \longrightarrow MgSO_4 + H_2$$

What mass of magnesium sulphate would be produced by reacting 100 g of magnesium with excess dilute sulphuric acid? (3)

11 The table below shows the results from the reaction between marble chips with (A) 20 cm³ of dilute hydrochloric acid and (B) 10 cm³ of dilute hydrochloric acid + 10 cm³ of water.

Time (min)	Total mass of carbon dioxide produced (g)	
	(A) 20 cm³ dilute HCl	(B) 10 cm³ dilute HCl + 10 cm³ H₂O
0	0.00	0.00
1	0.54	0.27
2	0.71	0.35
3	0.78	0.38
4	0.80	0.40
5	0.80	0.40

a) Plot *two* graphs on the same grid (time along the bottom). Label the first graph (A) and the second graph (B). (3)

b) Sketch, on the same grid, the curve you might have expected for the reaction (A) if it was carried out at a higher temperature. Label this curve (C). (1)

c) Sketch, on the same grid, the curve you might have expected for reaction (B) if the marble chips had been ground into a powder. Label this curve (D). (1)

d) Explain your answer to part c). (1)

12 Both manganese dioxide and catalase, a natural substance which can be found in liver, can be used to speed up the decomposition of hydrogen peroxide into water and oxygen. In each case the substances can be recovered unchanged when the reaction is over.

a) Write a balanced symbol equation for the decomposition of hydrogen peroxide. (2)

b) What kind of substances are manganese dioxide and catalase? (2)

c) i) Describe how you could compare the action of each of these substances on the decomposition of the hydrogen peroxide. (2)

   ii) Draw a labelled diagram of the apparatus you would use to carry out the investigation. (2)

d) Explain how raising the temperature would affect the rate of decomposition of the hydrogen peroxide when using manganese dioxide and when using catalase. (2)

Elements and compounds

What are different materials made from?

Carbon dioxide is an invisible gas, and water is a clear liquid. Green plants like grass can turn these substances (with a few other things) into new leaves and roots. A cow can turn grass into milk and beef.

These changes are possible because everything is made from **atoms**. Atoms are very tiny particles. There are about 100 different kinds of atoms, which can join together in different ways to form millions of different substances.

A substance containing just one kind of atom is called an **element**. Some elements, such as helium, exist as individual atoms. Other elements, like oxygen, exist as two atoms joined together to form a **molecule**. In elements that are solid at room temperature, millions of atoms are joined together in a **giant structure**.

B

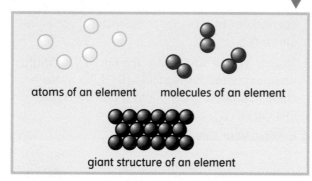

atoms of an element   molecules of an element

giant structure of an element

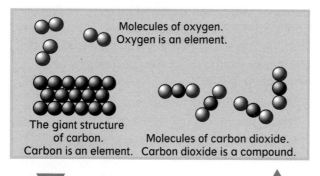

Molecules of oxygen.
Oxygen is an element.

The giant structure of carbon.
Carbon is an element.

Molecules of carbon dioxide.
Carbon dioxide is a compound.

D

? 1 Explain the differences between an atom, a molecule and a giant structure.

When two or more *different* kinds of atom combine, they form a **compound**. A compound can look quite different to the elements it is made from.

Sodium is a soft, shiny metal. Chlorine is a green, poisonous gas. When they react together they form sodium chloride, which is a white solid.

Some compounds exist as individual molecules, and some exist as giant structures.

? 2 What is the difference between an element and a compound?
3 Name one compound that exists as:
   a) molecules
   b) a giant structure.

C

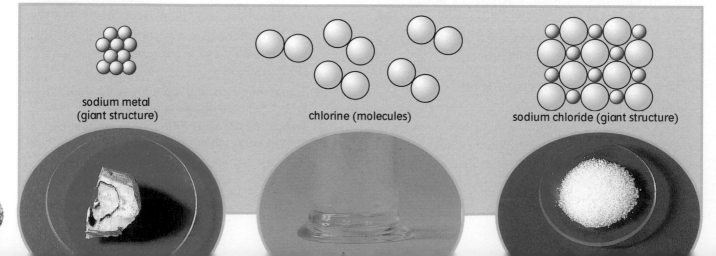

sodium metal
(giant structure)

chlorine (molecules)

sodium chloride (giant structure)

A compound is only formed when two or more different kinds of atoms **react** together. Oxygen and hydrogen can be mixed together, but they do not form a compound until they react.

4 What is the difference between a mixture and a compound?

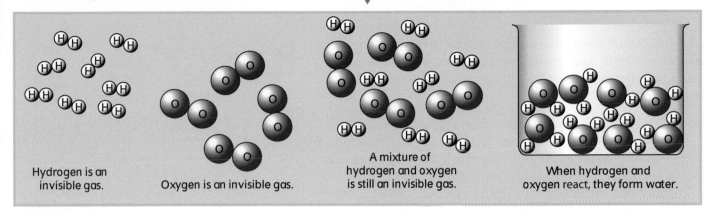

Hydrogen is an invisible gas.

Oxygen is an invisible gas.

A mixture of hydrogen and oxygen is still an invisible gas.

When hydrogen and oxygen react, they form water.

A reaction can be described using a **word equation**. The arrow shows that the **reactants** change into the **products**.

hydrogen + oxygen ⟶ water

(reactants)   (product)

Each element has its own **symbol**. The symbols for the elements are a kind of shorthand, because they make it easier to write down equations for reactions. However, symbols are also important as a kind of international language. Chemists in different countries may have different names for elements, but they always use the same symbol for the element.

> ❗ The most common compound in the Universe is water.

> ❗ The symbol for tungsten is W, from the German name wolfram, and the symbol for mercury is Hg from the Greek word hydrargyros.

Summary

Write sentences in your own words to explain the meanings of all the words in bold on these two pages.

5 Write a word equation for the reaction between carbon and oxygen.

6 German chemists use the symbol O for an element they call sauerstoff.
  a) What do we call this element?
  b) Explain why it is important that all chemists use the same set of symbols.

7 Draw particle diagrams to represent these elements. Include the correct symbol on each atom you draw. (*Hint*: you may need to look at the Periodic Table on page 246.)
  a) sulphur (solid – giant structure)
  b) fluorine (gas – molecules of two atoms)
  c) neon (gas – atoms)
  d) iodine (liquid – molecules of two atoms)
  e) iron (solid – giant structure)

8 Nitrogen is an invisible gas. Hydrogen and nitrogen react together to form ammonia.
  a) Write a word equation for this reaction. Show which chemicals are the reactants and which are the products.
  b) Show the reaction in a particle drawing.
  c) Ammonia is a gas. Do you think it exists as molecules or a giant structure?

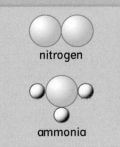

nitrogen

ammonia

Formulae

How do we know which atoms are in a compound?

The names of some compounds make it easy to tell which atoms are in it. One **molecule** of hydrogen chloride is made from one atom of hydrogen and one atom of chlorine.

Some compounds do not have such useful names. The name 'water' does not tell you anything about which atoms are in water. A better way of describing a compound is to use a **formula**. A formula shows which atoms are in a molecule of a compound (or in a molecule of an element), and how many atoms of each kind there are.

 1 What does the formula for a compound tell you?

The formula for water is H_2O_1.

> This number means that there is one oxygen atom.

> This number means that there are two hydrogen atoms. The number is always written after the symbol.

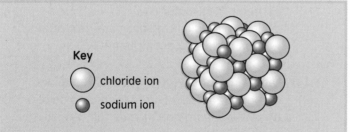

Key

○ chloride ion

● sodium ion

B

Sodium chloride.

No one bothers to write the small number 1s in formulae, so we write the formula as H_2O.

Things are not quite so simple for compounds that exist as giant structures. Sodium chloride, for instance, exists as a giant structure which can have millions of **ions**. An ion is an atom with a charge. There is one sodium ion for every chloride ion in sodium chloride. The formula for a crystal of sodium chloride could be written as $Na_{50}Cl_{50}$, $Na_{1000}Cl_{1000}$, or with even bigger numbers, depending on the size of the crystal. For compounds like this, we use the formula to show us the **ratio** of the different elements in the compound.

2 The formula for methane is CH_4.
  a) Which two kinds of atom are in methane?
  b) How many of each kind of atom are there in a molecule of methane?

3 Write down the formula for each of the compounds in diagram C.

4 If there are a million chloride ions in a piece of sodium chloride, how many sodium ions are there?

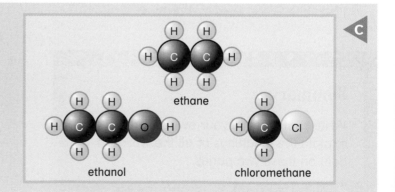

C

ethane

ethanol

chloromethane

A

one molecule of hydrogen chloride

We show the state of an element or compound by putting 's', 'l' or 'g' in brackets after the formula. These are called **state symbols**.

Mg(s) shows us that magnesium is a solid.

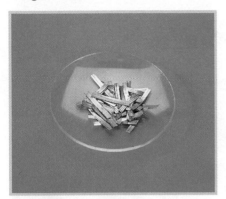

$H_2O(l)$ shows us that water is a liquid.

$Br_2(g)$ shows us that bromine is a gas.

 The letters 'aq' stand for aqueous, which is Latin for 'dissolved in water'.

We can also show when a chemical is dissolved in water, by putting (aq) after the formula. NaCl(aq) is salty water!

Some elements have a formula as well. In most elements and compounds that are gases at room temperature, the atoms form molecules. Oxygen, nitrogen and hydrogen all form molecules with two atoms joined together. The formula for hydrogen is $H_2(g)$.

We can use formulae instead of words to show what happens in a reaction.

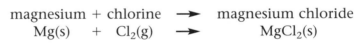

$$\text{magnesium} + \text{chlorine} \longrightarrow \text{magnesium chloride}$$
$$Mg(s) + Cl_2(g) \longrightarrow MgCl_2(s)$$

5 Write down the formula for:
  a) oxygen gas
  b) nitrogen gas.

Summary

Design an A4 poster to summarise everything that the formula of a compound can tell you about the compound. Include at least two different examples.

6 Which elements are in these compounds, and how many atoms of each element are there?
  a) ammonia (NH_3)
  b) chloroethane (CH_3CH_2Cl)
  c) methanoic acid (HCO_2H)

7 This is the equation for the reaction between sulphuric acid and magnesium.

$$\text{sulphuric acid} + \text{magnesium} \longrightarrow \text{magnesium sulphate} + \text{hydrogen}$$
$$H_2SO_4(aq) + Mg(s) \longrightarrow MgSO_4(aq) + H_2(g)$$

  a) For each substance in the reaction, write down:
    i) which atoms or ions are in it, and how many there are
    ii) what state it is in.
  b) What would you see if you watched this reaction?
    (*Hint*: look at the state symbol for hydrogen.)

8 The compounds below all form giant structures. If a piece of each compound has 300 oxide ions in it, work out how many ions of the other element are present.
  a) magnesium oxide (MgO)   **b)** silicon oxide (SiO_2)   **c)** aluminium oxide (Al_2O_3)

Balancing equations

How do we know how much of a chemical is needed?

When you bake a cake or make biscuits, you follow a recipe that tells you how much of each ingredient to use. In the same way, chemists who make new materials need to know how much of each chemical to use to get the right reaction. They need to work out a **balanced equation** for the reaction.

When a chemical reaction happens, there are always the same number of atoms there at the beginning and at the end. Only the arrangement of the atoms has changed.

A

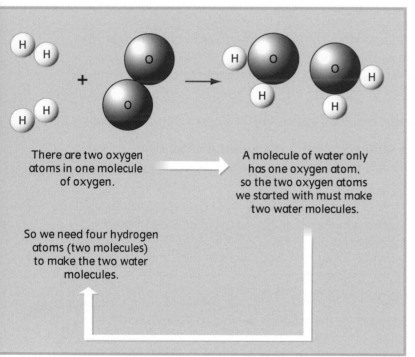

There are two oxygen atoms in one molecule of oxygen.

A molecule of water only has one oxygen atom, so the two oxygen atoms we started with must make two water molecules.

So we need four hydrogen atoms (two molecules) to make the two water molecules.

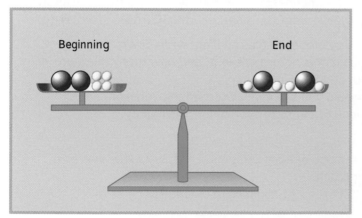

Beginning   End

B

Picture B shows what happens when hydrogen and oxygen react to form water.

We show that two molecules of something are needed by putting a 2 in *front* of the formula.

$$2H_2(g) \quad + \quad O_2(g) \quad \longrightarrow \quad 2H_2O(l)$$

This equation is **balanced**. It shows how many molecules of each substance react together.

C

 1 Why do we need to balance equations?

If you could find the mass of hydrogen and oxygen that reacted, their total mass would be the same as the mass of water that forms. In any reaction, the total mass of the reactants is always equal to the total mass of the products.

2 If 46 g of sodium react with 70 g of chlorine, what mass of sodium chloride will be formed?

3 If 32 g of oxygen react with hydrogen to make 36 g water, what mass of hydrogen was used?

You can balance an equation by counting the number of atoms of each element on each side of the equation.

For instance, carbon burns in hydrogen to form methane.

$$C(s) \ + \ H_2(g) \ \longrightarrow \ CH_4(g)$$
$$1\ C \qquad 2\ H \qquad \qquad 1\ C,\ 4\ H$$

There are more hydrogen atoms on the right than on the left of the equation, so it is not balanced. When carbon burns in hydrogen, the compound formed *always* has four hydrogen atoms for each carbon atom. We cannot balance the equation by writing CH_2 as the product on the right, because that would be a completely different substance (and in this case, it is a substance that does not exist!). So here we must have started with two molecules of hydrogen for each carbon atom. We show this by writing a 2 in front of the symbol for the hydrogen molecule on the left-hand side. This number multiplies everything in the formula after it, so $2H_2$ means two lots of H_2, which is four atoms of hydrogen.

$$C(s) \ + \ 2H_2(g) \ \longrightarrow \ CH_4(g)$$
$$1\ C \qquad 4\ H \qquad \qquad 1\ C,\ 4\ H$$

Now the equation is balanced.

Remember:

- you can only add whole molecules
- you cannot change the formula of a compound!

Summary

Someone who does not know much about chemistry asks you why equations have to be balanced. Write down what you would say, and explain the rules for balancing a chemical equation.

P Copper reacts with oxygen to form copper oxide (CO). How could you find out what mass of oxygen reacts with a certain mass of copper?

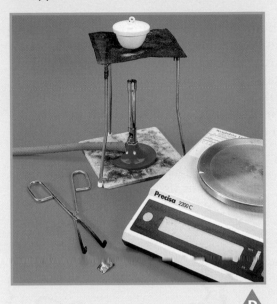

D

4 Write symbol equations for these reactions, and balance them:
 a) hydrogen + chlorine
  → hydrogen chloride
 b) hydrochloric acid (HCl(aq)) + calcium (Ca(s)) → calcium chloride (CaCl$_2$(aq)) + hydrogen.

5 When magnesium is added to sulphuric acid, the mass of the mixture at the end of the reaction is less than the mass at the beginning. Explain why you think this happens. (*Hint*: look at the equation for the reaction in question 7 on page 129.)

6 Copy these symbol equations and balance them.
 a) $N_2(g) + H_2(g) \longrightarrow NH_3(g)$
 b) $C_2H_6(g) + O_2(g) \longrightarrow CO_2(g) + H_2O(l)$
 c) $CO_2(g) + H_2O(l) \longrightarrow C_6H_{12}O_6(aq) + O_2(g)$

7 Find out what the reaction in question 6c is called.

Ideas about atoms

How have ideas about atoms changed?

Chemists use ideas about atoms to develop new materials. There have been lots of different ideas about what materials are made from. Some of these ideas were linked to people's religions. The earliest scientific ideas came from thinkers in Greece, around 2500 years ago.

? 1 Look at picture A. Write down the four 'elements' that some Greeks thought the world was made from.

B The first ideas about atoms came from Leucippus, and his pupil Democritus.

People who investigated chemicals and chemical changes were called alchemists. They tried different ways of treating chemicals to try to make new substances. They were usually trying to turn ordinary metals into gold, or to discover a chemical that would let people live forever. They did not use theories to work out how to make new substances.

? 3 Why were most people not interested in ideas about atoms?

4 What were most alchemists trying to make?

A Empedocles' idea.

? 2 What did Leucippus and Democritus think everything was made of?

Another very famous scientist called Aristotle believed the ideas about earth, air, fire and water. Most scientists thought that Aristotle was right.

Not many people bothered to think about atoms. The people who actually used chemistry thousands of years ago were the perfume and dye makers, and metal workers, and they did not need theories to help them.

In the 1650s, an English scientist called Robert Boyle did some experiments on gases. He did not just try to make new substances, but made lots of careful measurements. He thought that the results of his experiments could be explained if air was made of separate particles.

5 What was Boyle's idea about gases?

Robert Boyle in his laboratory with his assistant.

In 1785, the French chemist Louis-Joseph Proust discovered that all compounds had simple, fixed ratios of different elements in them, measured by mass. For instance, a compound could contain three times as much of one element as another, but never 3.2 times as much, or 2.8 times as much.

Our modern ideas about atoms started with an English scientist called John Dalton. He agreed with Boyle's idea that gases were made of tiny particles. He thought that if all substances were made of particles, and each element was made of a different kind of particle with a different mass, this would explain Proust's discovery.

E *John Dalton collecting gas from a marsh.*

Dalton's theory was accepted by most scientists because it could explain what happened in experiments. There were still some scientists who were not convinced about atoms until Einstein proved that atoms existed in 1905.

6 Why did most scientists believe Dalton's ideas about atoms?

7 How are our modern ideas about atoms different to the ancient Greeks' ideas?

Summary

Draw a table to summarise the changing ideas about atoms. You could start your table like this:

Scientist	Idea	Why it was or wasn't accepted

Atomic structure

What are atoms made from?

New and useful materials are being invented all the time. Medicines or drugs can be designed to target specific diseases, and materials for building cars or aeroplanes can be developed that are stronger or lighter than before. New materials and medicines can be designed to have particular properties because scientists know a lot about how different elements behave and react with one another. The way different elements react depends on the particles that make up their atoms.

Atoms are made up of three different kinds of particles, called **protons**, **neutrons** and **electrons**.

The masses of these particles are very tiny, so we do not use units like grams. We say that protons and neutrons both have a mass of 1. Electrons are even smaller. They do have a mass, but it is so small that we can ignore it. We say that electrons have a **negligible** mass.

Protons and electrons have **electric charges**. Protons have a **positive** (+) charge, and electrons have a **negative** (–) charge. Neutrons are 'neutral'; they have no charge. Atoms always have the same number of protons and electrons, so the charges cancel each other out. Atoms have no overall electrical charge.

All elements are made from these three kinds of particles. Each atom in an element has the same number of protons. A different element will have a different number of protons in its atoms. The number of protons in an atom is called its **atomic number**, or **proton number**.

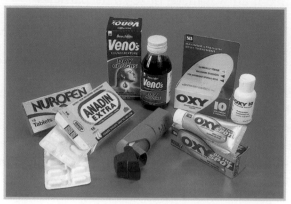

A These medicines were all developed using knowledge about atoms and how they join up.

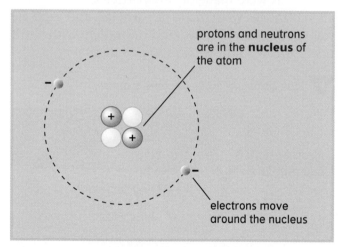

protons and neutrons are in the **nucleus** of the atom

electrons move around the nucleus

B The structure of a helium atom.

C

	Mass	Charge
proton	1	+1
neutron	1	0
electron	negligible	−1

 1 a) Write down two ways in which protons and neutrons are similar.
   b) Write down one way in which protons and neutrons are different.

2 a) Write down one way in which protons and electrons are similar.
   b) Write down three ways in which protons and electrons are different.

3 What does the atomic number of an element tell you about the number of electrons in an atom of the element? Explain your answer.

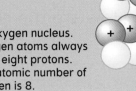

A hydrogen nucleus. Hydrogen atoms always have just one proton in the nucleus. The atomic number of hydrogen is 1.

A carbon nucleus. Carbon atoms always have six protons. The atomic number of carbon is 6.

An oxygen nucleus. Oxygen atoms always have eight protons. The atomic number of oxygen is 8.

The mass of an atom depends on the number of protons and neutrons. The total number of protons and neutrons in an atom is called its **mass number**. Look at picture D. Carbon has six protons and six neutrons, so it has a mass number of 12. Mass number is sometimes called relative atomic mass (see topic I17 for more details).

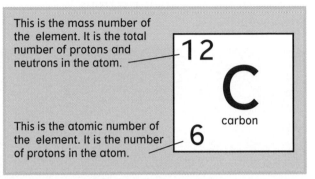

This is the mass number of the element. It is the total number of protons and neutrons in the atom.

12
C
6
carbon

This is the atomic number of the element. It is the number of protons in the atom.

 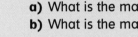

4 Look at picture D.
   a) What is the mass number of oxygen?
   b) What is the mass number of hydrogen?

 This is the way that information about elements is shown on the Periodic Table.

The nuclei of two isotopes of carbon.

Sometimes atoms of an element have different numbers of neutrons. Picture F shows two different carbon atoms. They are both carbon, because they both have six protons in the nucleus. These two atoms are **isotopes** of carbon. Isotopes are atoms of the same element that have different numbers of neutrons. Most elements have different isotopes.

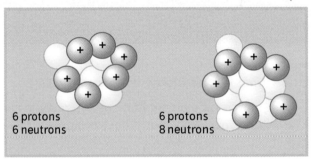

6 protons
6 neutrons

6 protons
8 neutrons

5 What are isotopes of an element?

6 The element sodium can be shown like this:

23
Na
sodium
11

   a) What is the atomic number of sodium?
   b) How many protons does a sodium atom have in its nucleus?
   c) What is the mass number of sodium?
   d) How many neutrons does a sodium atom have?
   e) How many electrons does a sodium atom have?

7 Explain, in as much detail as you can, why many Periodic Tables show chlorine with a mass number of 35.5.

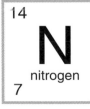

Summary

A Copy table C and add a column to show where in the atom each type of particle is found.

B Nitrogen is often shown on Periodic Tables like this:

Explain what this tells us about nitrogen atoms.

14
N
nitrogen
7

Electronic structure

How are the electrons arranged inside an atom?

Some elements are very reactive, and some hardly react at all. Elements behave differently because of the way their electrons are arranged.

Calcium reacts very quickly with weak acid.

 Neon does not react in these lighting tubes, even though it is so hot that it is glowing

Electrons have a negative charge, and protons have a positive charge. An atom normally has the same number of protons and electrons, so it has no overall charge.

 1 What kind of charge do electrons have?

2 Boron is an element that has five protons in its nucleus. How many electrons does it have?

Lithium has three protons and three electrons. Two of the electrons are close to the nucleus, and the third one is further away. These different locations for electrons are called **energy levels**, or **shells**. The inner shell can only hold two electrons.

Helium has two protons and two neutrons in its nucleus. It has two electrons moving around the nucleus.

Hydrogen has just one proton. One electron moves around it.

A hydrogen atom.

A helium atom.

A lithium atom.

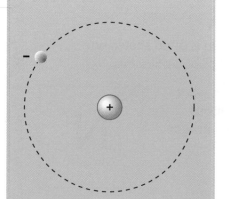

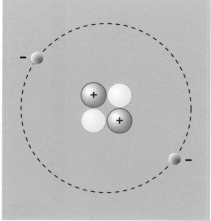

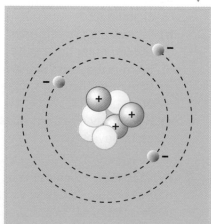

The second shell can hold eight electrons. When the second shell is full, the third shell starts to fill up. The third shell can also hold eight electrons. The inner shells always fill up first. Atoms with higher atomic numbers have even more energy levels or shells.

You can think of electrons as boxes that have to be put onto shelves. Each shelf (or shell) can only hold a certain number of boxes (or electrons).

3 How many electrons will fit into:
  a) the inner shell
  b) the second shell
  c) the third shell?

2,1

2,8,1

When we are thinking about electrons, we usually draw each electron as a cross, and show the whole nucleus as a circle.

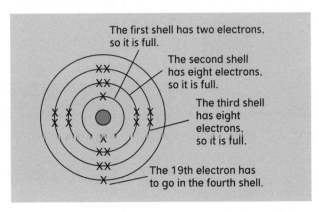

The first shell has two electrons, so it is full.

The second shell has eight electrons, so it is full.

The third shell has eight electrons, so it is full.

The 19th electron has to go in the fourth shell.

A potassium atom.

We can show the electronic structures of all the elements by drawing diagrams like diagram G. Some elements have nearly 100 electrons, so these diagrams could get very big! An easier way of showing the **electronic structure** is to write the number of electrons in each shell. We can write the electronic structure of potassium as 2,8,8,1.

4 Look at diagram G.
  a) Make a neat copy of the diagram for potassium.
  b) Write the electronic structure for potassium in numbers.

5 Sulphur has an atomic number of 16.
  a) How many electrons does an atom of sulphur have?
  b) Draw a diagram to show how the electrons are arranged.
  c) Write the electronic structure for sulphur in numbers.

6 Li, Na, Mg and Al are metals; O, F, Cl and He are non-metals.
  a) Write the electronic structures of each of these elements.
  b) How could you use the electronic structure of an element to decide if it is a metal or a non-metal?

Summary

Draw a concept map to summarise the information on these pages and in Topic J5. You can use the suggestion below to get you started, or you can think of your own starting point.

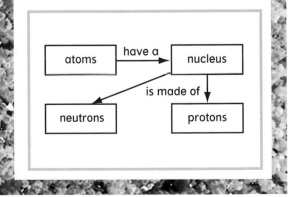

The Periodic Table

What does the Periodic Table tell us about different elements?

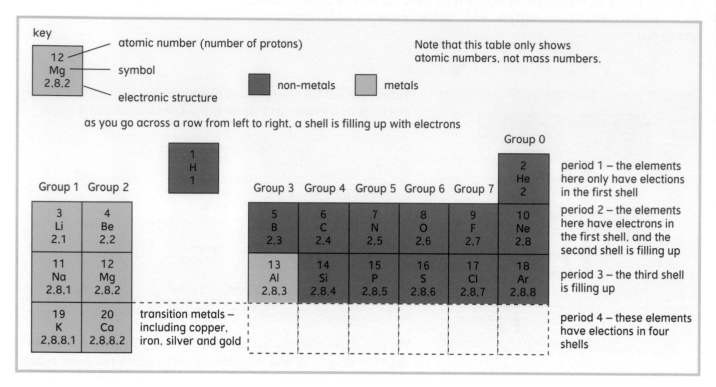

key

12
Mg
2,8,2

atomic number (number of protons)

symbol

electronic structure

non-metals   metals

Note that this table only shows atomic numbers, not mass numbers.

as you go across a row from left to right, a shell is filling up with electrons

Group 0

Group 1	Group 2					Group 3	Group 4	Group 5	Group 6	Group 7	

period 1 – the elements here only have elections in the first shell

1
H
1

2
He
2

period 2 – the elements here have electrons in the first shell, and the second shell is filling up

3 Li 2,1	4 Be 2,2					5 B 2,3	6 C 2,4	7 N 2,5	8 O 2,6	9 F 2,7	10 Ne 2,8
11 Na 2,8,1	12 Mg 2,8,2					13 Al 2,8,3	14 Si 2,8,4	15 P 2,8,5	16 S 2,8,6	17 Cl 2,8,7	18 Ar 2,8,8
19 K 2,8,8,1	20 Ca 2,8,8,2	transition metals – including copper, iron, silver and gold									

period 3 – the third shell is filling up

period 4 – these elements have elections in four shells

The elements are arranged in the Periodic Table in order of their atomic numbers.

Part of the Periodic Table (the whole table is shown on page 246).

1 Look at Table A.
  a) If you know which period of the Periodic Table an element is in, what does that tell you about its electronic structure?
  b) If you know how far across a row an element is, what does that tell you about its electronic structure?

The position of an element in the Periodic Table can also tell us something about how the element reacts. Look at table A again. You can see that the elements in a **group** have the same number of electrons in the outer shell. Only the electrons in the outer shell of an atom will take part in chemical reactions. Because all the elements in a group have a similar arrangement of electrons, they usually have similar properties and reactions to each other. They also form compounds with similar formulae.

2 Look at Table A. Why do lithium and sodium have similar reactions?

3 Describe *in words* the electronic structure of the outer shells of the elements in Groups 1, 2, 7 and 0.

4 Argon is not a reactive element. It is very difficult to make it react with anything.
  a) What can you predict about the reactions of neon? Explain your answer.
  b) If you know how argon reacts, what can you predict about the reactions of chlorine? Explain your answer.

Some properties change as you go down a group. For instance, elements at the top of a group may have lower melting and boiling points than ones at the bottom, or the reactivity of the elements may change.

The elements can be split up into **metals** and **non-metals**. Look at the large Periodic Table on page 246. Over three quarters of the elements are metals, and these are shown on the left-hand side of the Periodic Table. The non-metals are shown on the right-hand side of the Periodic Table.

B The melting points of the Group 7 elements get higher as you go down the Periodic Table.

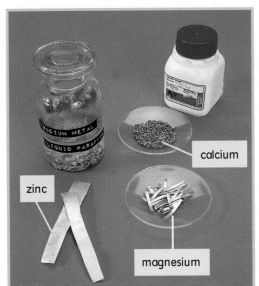

C Metals.

Some elements, like boron and silicon, are called semi-metals, because they have some properties of metals, and some properties of non-metals.

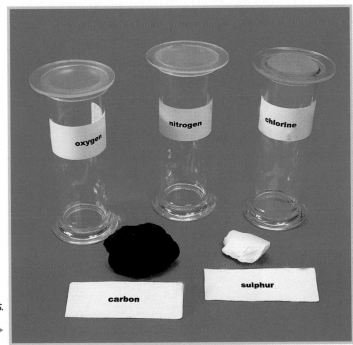

Non-metals.

D

Summary

Write a paragraph in your own words to answer the topic question at the top of page 138. Include as much information as you can.

5 What is the difference between metals and non-metals in terms of their electronic structures?

6 If you were drawing a Periodic Table, there are several places you could put hydrogen.
   a) Explain why you might want to put it at the top of Group 1.
   b) Explain why you might want to put it at the top of Group 7.
   c) Why do you think it is usually shown on its own?

Looking for patterns

How was the Periodic Table discovered?

One way that scientists can learn more about the world is to look for patterns, and then try to explain *why* these patterns exist.

Johan Döbereiner was one of the first scientists to look for patterns of properties in the elements. He noticed that chlorine, bromine and iodine had similar properties. He noticed two other triads (or groups of three), but he could not find a pattern in any more of the elements.

1 Would a modern-day chemist agree with Döbereiner's triads? (*Hint*: you may need to look at the Periodic Table on page 246.)

In 1864, John Newlands decided to put all the elements in order of the masses of atoms (mass numbers). When he did this he found that the elements could be divided into groups, with every 8th element having similar properties. He called this the Law of Octaves.

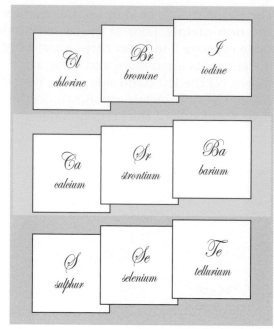

A Döbereiner's triads.

1	H	F	Cl	Co & Ni	Br	Pd	I	Pt & Ir
2	Li	Na	K	Cu	Rb	Ag	Cs	Tl
3	G	Mg	Ca	Zn	Sr	Bd	Ba & V	Pb
4	Bo	Al	Cr	Y	Ce & La	U	Ta	Th
5	C	Si	Ti	In	Zr	Sn	W	Hg
6	N	P	Mn	As	Di & Mo	Sb	Nb	Bi
7	O	S	Fe	Se	Ro & Ru	Te	Au	Os

B Newlands' octaves. Not all the symbols are the same as the modern symbols. The colours show which elements are grouped together in the modern Periodic Table.

Most scientists took no notice of Newlands' ideas, because his law did not work for all the elements. This was partly because the mass numbers of some elements had not been measured correctly, and partly because he had not allowed for any new elements that might be discovered.

2 Look at Table B, and look at the Periodic Table on page 246. Describe two ways that Newlands' table is different to our modern Periodic Table.

3 Why didn't scientists agree with Newlands' ideas?

A Russian scientist called Dmitri Mendeleev arranged the elements in something like their 'modern' order in 1869. Mendeleev arranged the elements in order of their mass numbers, but he also looked at their properties. If the order of mass numbers put elements in the wrong place for their properties, he ignored the masses. He also left gaps in the table where there was no element that fitted the pattern. He predicted the mass numbers and other properties of these 'missing elements'.

 Dmitri Mendeleev.

? **4** Mendeleev did two things to make his elements 'fit' into his table. What were they?

The Periodic Table was useful because it could be used to *predict* the properties of undiscovered elements. In 1874, a French scientist called Paul-Emile Lecoq discovered gallium, one of the 'missing' elements, and found that it had properties very similar to the properties predicted by Mendeleev.

It was not until the structure of the atom was discovered in 1910 that scientists realised that Mendeleev's order for the elements depended on atomic number (the number of protons in the nucleus) rather than mass number. Today, the Periodic Table is a useful way of summarising the structure of atoms.

A compound of gallium is used in some solar cells.

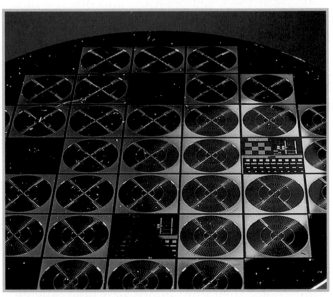

? **5** Why did scientists start to think that Mendeleev's Periodic Table was useful?

6 What do scientists use to decide the order of elements in the modern Periodic Table?

7 Look at the Periodic Table on page 246. Which pairs of elements are in the 'wrong' place according to their mass numbers?

8 Explain why Döbereiner's triads and Newlands' octaves were not very useful to scientists.

Summary

Write two sentences for each scientist mentioned on these pages, explaining what patterns they suggested and why their ideas were (or were not) accepted.

Metals and non-metals

Why are metals and non-metals different?

Metals and non-metals have very different **properties**.

Metals:

- have high melting and boiling points (all except mercury are solid at room temperature)
- are strong, and can be bent or hammered into shape without breaking
- are good conductors of heat and electricity.

Non-metals:

- have low melting and boiling points (nine are gases at room temperature, and one is a liquid)
- are brittle and crumbly when solid
- are poor conductors of heat and electricity.

A *Copper is a metal.*

B *Sulphur is a non-metal.*

Diamond and graphite are unusual non-metals. They are both made of pure carbon, but diamond is very hard and graphite conducts electricity!

1 a) Write down three properties of metals.
b) Write down three properties of non-metals.

Metals and non-metals are different because of their electronic structures. The electrons in an atom's outer shell form **bonds** that hold different atoms together. Different electronic structures mean that different kinds of bonds are formed. Atoms of metal elements have only a few electrons in their outer shell. Atoms of non-metal elements have outer shells that are full, or nearly full.

2 Why do metals and non-metals have different properties?

Group 0

The elements in Group 0 are non-metals. They are all gases at room temperature. It is very hard to make them react with anything. We say they are very **unreactive**. They are sometimes called the **noble gases**.

Atoms of Group 0 elements all have full outer shells of electrons. When an atom has a full outer shell, it tends to stay that way. If atoms had feelings, you could say that they 'liked' to have a full outer shell. Elements that do not have full outer shells react with other atoms to get full shells.

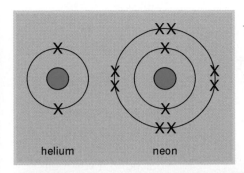

C

Atoms of the elements in Group 0 all have full outer shells.

helium   neon

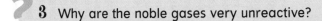

 3 Why are the noble gases very unreactive?

The noble gases are useful because they do not react.

Helium is much less dense than air. It is used in balloons. The only other gas that can be used in balloons is hydrogen, and that is dangerous because it burns very easily.

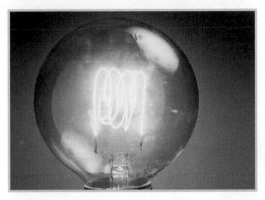

D

Argon is used inside light bulbs to stop the hot filament reacting with anything

E

Helium is used inside this weather balloon.

4 Why are noble gases used inside light bulbs?

5 Why is helium used in balloons instead of hydrogen?

6 Look at picture F, which shows the electron shells of three different elements. For each element, say whether it is a metal or a noble gas. Explain your answers.

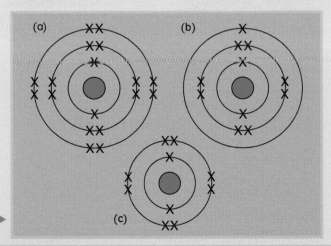

(a)   (b)

(c)

F

7 Aluminium atoms have one more electron than atoms of magnesium. Some of the properties of aluminium and magnesium are very similar. Argon atoms have one more electron than chlorine atoms, but the properties of argon and chlorine are very different. Explain why this is so.

Summary

A Draw a table to summarise the differences between metals and non-metals. You could start your table like this:

Property	Metals	Non-metals
melting points	high	
boiling points		

B What is different about the electronic structures of noble gases compared to other non-metals?

C How does this explain the properties and uses of the noble gases?

143

Metallic bonding
How can we explain the properties of metals?

People have been using metals for thousands of years, to make tools, jewellery and even weapons. Picture A shows some of the properties of metals, and why these properties are important. Metals have these properties because of the way their atoms are held together.

A

malleable - metals can be hammered into shape.

ductile - metals can be pulled into wires.

metals are strong

Gallium is a metal with a melting point of 30 °C. If you hold a piece in your hand it will melt!

1 Write down four properties of metals.

B Metals conduct heat and electricity.

Lithium atoms form lithium ions by losing one electron. Lithium ions have a full outer shell of electrons. **C**

All metals have only a few electrons in their outer shells. Metal atoms need to lose electrons if they are to have full outer shells (like the electronic structure of a noble gas).

An atom normally has the same number of protons and electrons. The positive charges on the protons are balanced by the negative charges on the electrons. If a metal atom loses some electrons it will have a positive charge, because there are no longer enough electrons to balance out the protons. An atom that has lost (or gained) electrons is called an **ion**.

When you are writing out the electronic structure of an ion you put brackets around the numbers and write the charge outside the brackets, for example $[2,8]^{2+}$.

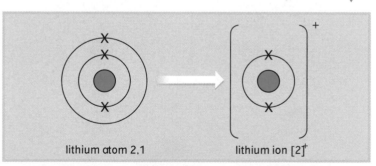

lithium atom 2,1   lithium ion $[2]^+$

2 Write down the electronic structures of each of these elements, and write out the structure of the ion each one would form. The first one has been done for you.
a) magnesium: atom = 2,8,2, ion = $[2,8]^{2+}$
b) sodium
c) aluminium
d) calcium

In a piece of metal, all the metal atoms lose their outer electrons. The electrons move around between the metal ions. The negative electrons attract the positive metal ions, and hold them together in a regular arrangement called a **giant structure**. There are strong forces holding all the ions in place.

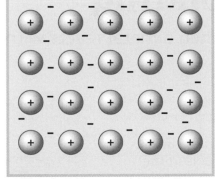

D *In a metal the ions are arranged in a regular pattern.*

3 Why are the ions in a metal held together?

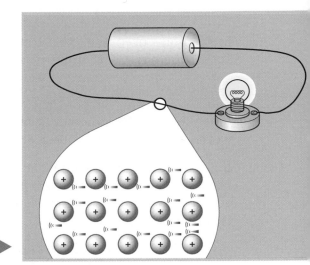

E

Metals are very good at conducting electricity because the outer electrons can move. If a voltage is applied across a piece of metal, all the electrons drift along in the same direction, forming an electric current. The moving electrons can also transfer heat energy, and this is what makes metals so good at conducting heat.

4 **a)** Why are metals good at conducting electricity?
b) Why are metals good at conducting heat?

Metals are strong because the forces holding the ions together are strong. They can be hammered into shape because of the regular arrangement of ions in the metal. If a metal is hit, layers of ions can slide over each other. The ions are still held together by the electrons between them, so the metal bends instead of breaking.

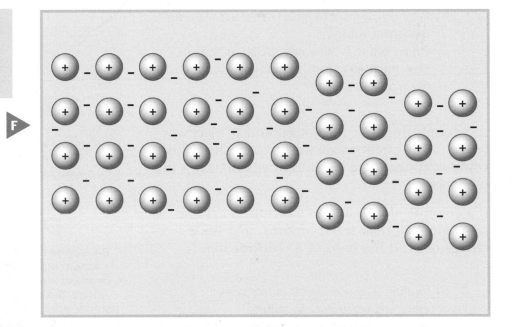

F

5 Why are metals:
a) strong   **b)** malleable?

6 Mercury metal is a liquid at room temperature. It has two electrons in its outer shell.
a) Do you think mercury is a good conductor of heat and electricity? Explain your answer.
b) Do you think solid mercury will be malleable and ductile? Explain your answer.

Summary

Write a paragraph in your own words to answer the topic question at the top of page 144. Include as much information as you can.

Ionic bonding

What happens when a metal reacts with a non-metal?

Metal atoms need to lose electrons to gain full outer shells, and non-metal atoms need to gain electrons.

An atom of sodium has 11 protons in its nucleus, and 11 electrons. One of the electrons is in the outer shell. If the atom could lose that electron, it would then have a full outer shell.

If a sodium atom loses an electron, it still has 11 protons with positive charges, but only 10 electrons with negative charges to balance them. It is now a sodium ion with a charge of +1.

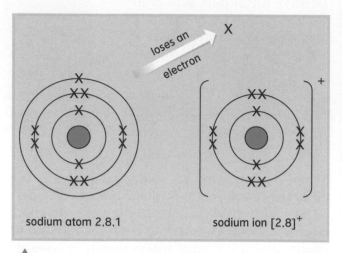

loses an electron X

sodium atom 2,8,1   sodium ion [2,8]⁺

A   **B**

1 a) Explain why metal atoms lose electrons when they form ions.
b) Why do atoms that have lost electrons have a positive charge?
c) Potassium is in the same group as sodium. How many electrons does it need to lose to get a full outer shell?

A chlorine atom has 17 protons and 17 electrons. Seven of the electrons are in the outer shell. If it could gain one more electron, it would have a full outer shell.

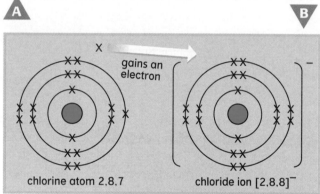

X   gains an electron

chlorine atom 2,8,7   chloride ion [2,8,8]⁻

If a chlorine atom gains an electron, it has one more electron than it has protons, so it has a charge of –1. It has become a **chloride** ion.

2 a) Explain why non-metal atoms gain electrons when they form ions.
b) Why do atoms that have gained electrons have a negative charge?
c) Fluorine is in the same group as chlorine. How many electrons does it need to gain to get a full outer shell?

When sodium and chlorine react together, the sodium atoms lose electrons and the chlorine atoms gain them. The sodium ions and chloride ions have opposite charges, so they are attracted to each other. The forces holding them together are called **ionic bonds**. A **salt** is an ionic compound formed by a reaction between an acid and a base.

C

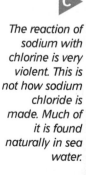

The reaction of sodium with chlorine is very violent. This is not how sodium chloride is made. Much of it is found naturally in sea water.

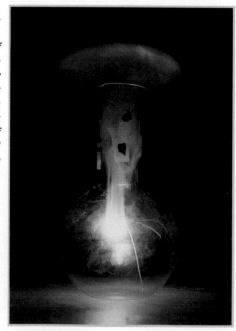

Sodium chloride is a simple example of ionic bonding, because each sodium atom needs to lose one electron, and each chlorine atom needs to gain one. The formula for sodium chloride is NaCl, because there is one chloride ion for every sodium ion.

Some atoms need to lose or gain more than one electron. For example, calcium atoms 2,8,8,2 lose two electrons when they form calcium ions $[2,8,8]^{2+}$. If calcium reacts with chlorine, two chlorine atoms are needed for each calcium atom, because each chlorine can only accept one electron. The overall charge in an ionic compound is zero. The formula for calcium chloride is $CaCl_2$.

The table on page 246 shows the charges on different ions. You can use the charges to work out the formulae of compounds containing different ions. For example, if silver reacts with oxygen, the silver forms Ag^+ ions and the oxygen forms O^{2-} ions. There must be two silver ions for every oxide ion, and the formula for silver oxide is Ag_2O. Some formulae are a bit more difficult to work out, but diagram D shows a quick way of doing it.

Write out the two ions with their charges, and remember the Ag^+ really means Ag^{1+}.

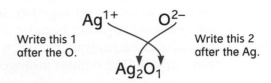

Write this 1 after the O.

Write this 2 after the Ag.

$$Ag_2O_1$$

We don't bother writing the 1s, so silver oxide is Ag_2O.

This works for more complicated examples as well:

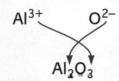

$$Al_2O_3$$

D

3 Explain, in terms of electrons, why the formula for aluminium oxide is Al_2O_3.

4 Work out the formulae for these ionic compounds. (*Hint*: you may need to refer to the table on page 246.)
   a) magnesium chloride
   b) sodium nitrate
   c) ammonium nitrate
   d) ammonium sulphate

5 Magnesium 2,8,2 reacts with chlorine 2,8,8,1 to form magnesium chloride. Draw electronic structure diagrams to show what happens in this reaction.

6 Look at the list of ions on page 246.
   a) In what way is hydrogen acting like a metal when it takes part in ionic bonding?
   b) Why is hydrogen normally regarded as a non-metal?

Some non-metal atoms can form groups which are able to lose or gain electrons to form ions. These are sometimes called **compound ions**. Some examples are the ammonium ion (NH_4^+), the sulphate ion (SO_4^{2-}), and the nitrate ion (NO_3^-). The atoms *within* these ions are held together by a different kind of bonding called covalent bonding – you will find out more about this in topic J14. However, a compound ion behaves just like a non-metal ion when it takes part in reactions with metals. You may need to put brackets around the compound ion when writing it in a formula. For example, silver nitrate is $AgNO_3$, but copper nitrate has to be written as $Cu(NO_3)_2$.

Summary

A storyboard is a set of sketches that shows what will happen when a film is made. Draw a storyboard (including captions and labels) for a short animated film to show what happens when a metal and non-metal react.

Ionic compounds

How can we explain the properties of ionic compounds?

Ionic compounds do not exist as single molecules, but as **giant structures** of billions of ions held together in a regular **ionic lattice**. The ions are held together because the positive and negative charges attract each other. Each ion is attracted to all the other ions around it. The regular arrangement of ions in the lattice means that ionic compounds usually form crystals.

B Iron sulphide crystals.

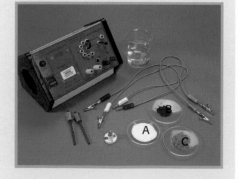

A The structure of iron sulphide.

The forces between the ions are very strong. It takes a lot of energy to make the ions break away from each other, so ionic compounds have very high melting points. Ionic compounds are solids at room temperature.

Ionic compounds cannot conduct electricity when they are solid. There are no electrons to move, and the ions are fixed in place and cannot move around. However, if an ionic solid is melted, the ions break away from each other and are able to move around. Because each ion has an electric charge, a molten ionic compound *can* conduct electricity.

Some ionic compounds dissolve in water. When this happens the positive and negative ions break away from each other and can move around in the water. A solution of an ionic compound can conduct electricity.

? **2** Describe two ways in which you can make an ionic compound conduct electricity, and explain why these methods work.

When an electric current flows through a molten or dissolved ionic compound, the negative ions are attracted to the positive electrode, and the positive ions are attracted to the negative electrode. The ions lose or gain electrons at the electrodes, and turn back into electrically neutral atoms (they have no overall charge).

! Iron sulphide is sometimes called 'Fools Gold' because gold hunters thought it was gold.

? **1** Explain why ionic compounds are solids at room temperature.

P How could you test some different chemicals to find out which ones are ionic compounds?

C

The **cathode** is the electrode connected to the negative terminal of a cell or power supply. Electrons flow out of the cell and down the cathode. Positive ions, called **cations**, are attracted towards the cathode. When they reach the cathode, the positive ions accept electrons and turn back into atoms.

The **anode** is connected to the positive terminal. Electrons flow towards the cell from the anode. Negative ions, called **anions**, are attracted towards the anode, where they give up their extra electrons and turn back into atoms. A gas is often formed at the anode.

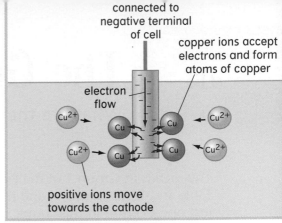

3   Which terminal of a cell is the cathode attached to?

4   Will each of the following ions go to the cathode or the anode during electrolysis?
    a) Cu^{2+} **b)** O^{2-} **c)** Cl^- **d)** H^+

When copper chloride is electrolysed, copper metal forms at the cathode.

We can show what happens at each electrode by writing chemical equations. We use e^- to represent an electron. We usually show what happens at each electrode separately, and so the equations are called **half equations**. We can write the following balanced half equations for the copper chloride example shown in diagrams D and E.

At the cathode: $Cu^{2+} + 2e^- \longrightarrow Cu$

At the anode: $2Cl^- - 2e^- \longrightarrow Cl_2$

When writing half equations it is important to remember the following things:

- The right-hand side must show the product that is actually formed, so in this example we have to show molecules of chlorine (Cl_2), not just atoms of chlorine (Cl).
- We can use a minus sign to show electrons that are given up to the anode. This is the *only* time that we can use minus signs in chemical equations.

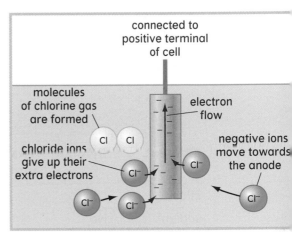

When copper chloride is electrolysed, bubbles of chlorine gas form at the anode.

5   These half equations show what happens when magnesium chloride ($MgCl_2$) is electrolysed.
    $Mg^{2+} + e^- \longrightarrow Mg$ $Cl^- - e^- \longrightarrow Cl_2$
    a) Copy out the equations and balance them.
    b) Which ions are the cations, and which are the anions?

6   Ions in metals also form giant structures. Explain why solid metals conduct electricity, but solid ionic compounds do not.

7   Write balanced half equations to show what happens at each electrode when the following ionic compounds are electrolysed. You will need to work out the correct formula for each compound first.
    a) zinc bromide
    b) aluminium oxide

Summary

Silver bromide is an ionic compound.

A Describe the properties of solid silver bromide, and explain why it has these properties.

B Describe what happens if a solution of silver bromide is electrolysed. Include details of what happens at each electrode, and the half equations for the reaction.

The Group 1 metals

What are the reactions of the Group 1 metals?

The metals in **Group 1** of the Periodic Table are all very reactive, and they all have just one electron in their outer shell.

Three of the Group 1 metals. A

Element	Symbol	Atomic number	Melting point (°C)	Boiling point (°C)	Reactivity
lithium	Li	3	181	1342	least reactive
sodium	Na	11	98	883	
potassium	K	19	63	760	
rubidium	Rb	37	39	686	
caesium	Cs	55	29	669	most reactive

B *The elements in Group 1.*

 1 How do the melting and boiling points of the Group 1 metals change as you go down the Group?

The Group 1 metals all react with non-metals to form ionic compounds. They all form ions with a +1 charge because they all have just one electron in their outer shell.

The Group 1 metals also have very low densities, so they will float on water. They react with water to form a hydroxide and hydrogen gas. Heat from the reaction usually melts the piece of metal into a ball, which moves around on the surface of the water. The heat may also cause the hydrogen gas given off in the reaction to catch fire.

The metals near the bottom of the group are more reactive than the ones near the top. Caesium reacts so fast with water that it explodes.

C *Caesium reacting with water.*

Lithium atoms have just three electrons, arranged in two shells. The single electron in the outer shell is still quite close to the positive charges on the nucleus of the atom, so the forces holding it in place are strong. Caesium atoms have 55 electrons, arranged in six shells. The sixth shell in a caesium atom contains only one electron, and it is this electron that leaves the atom when an ion is formed. This electron is much further away from the nucleus than the outer electron in lithium, so the forces holding it to the atom are not as strong as in lithium. The outer electron can leave the atom more easily; this is why caesium is much more reactive than lithium.

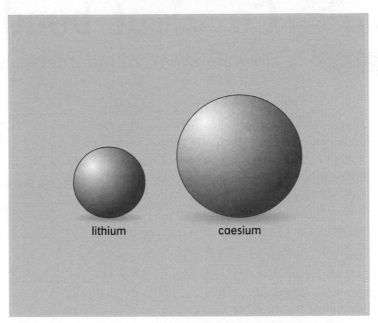

lithium   caesium

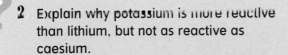 *Caesium atoms are much bigger than lithium atoms, so it is easier for the outer electron to leave the atom.*

The equation for the reaction of lithium with water is:

lithium + water $\longrightarrow$ lithium hydroxide + hydrogen

$$2Li(s) + 2H_2O(l) \longrightarrow 2LiOH(aq) + H_2(g)$$

The equations for the reactions of the other Group 1 metals are similar, since they all form +1 ions.

When metal hydroxides dissolve in water they form an alkaline solution. This is why the Group 1 metals are sometimes called the **alkali metals**.

Summary

You are writing an encyclopaedia entry on 'The alkali metals'. Write a paragraph to summarise the Group 1 metals for the encyclopaedia.

2 Explain why potassium is more reactive than lithium, but not as reactive as caesium.

3 Some universal indicator is added to a tank of water. A piece of sodium is then dropped into the water.
   a) Describe, in as much detail as you can, what you would see if you watched this reaction happening.
   b) Explain why you would see these things.
   c) If you collected the gas given off, how could you test it to check that it was hydrogen?
   d) Write a balanced symbol equation for the reaction of sodium with water.

4 Why do you think the alkali metals are usually stored in bottles of oil rather than being in contact with the air?

5 Look at the positions of beryllium and calcium in the Periodic Table on page 246. Which metal would you expect to be the most reactive? Explain your answer.

6 Why do you think that caesium has a lower melting point than lithium? (*Hint*: you may need to look back at topic J10 on pages 144–145.)

Covalent bonding

How are atoms of non-metals held together?

There are millions of different compounds in your body, and most of the atoms making up these compounds are non-metal atoms. Most non-metal compounds are held together by a different kind of bonding, called **covalent bonding**. In covalent bonding, atoms share electrons.

Chlorine is written as Cl_2. This is because, in chlorine gas, two chlorine **atoms** form one chlorine **molecule**. They share electrons so that both atoms can have a full outer shell of electrons.

When they are gases, most non-metal elements form molecules with two atoms in them. They are called **diatomic gases** ('di' means two). The only non-metals that do not form molecules are the noble gases. They already have full outer electron shells, so they do not need to share electrons.

Atoms can share more than one pair of electrons. Diagram B shows some molecules which share different numbers of electrons.

Two chlorine atoms can have full outer shells if they share electrons. All the electrons are the same as each other – we use dots and crosses to make it easier to see which atoms the electrons were originally from.

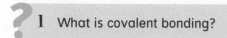

1 What is covalent bonding?

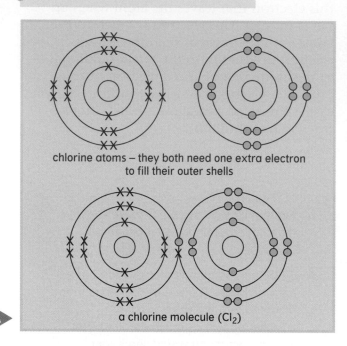

chlorine atoms – they both need one extra electron to fill their outer shells

a chlorine molecule (Cl_2)

 A

2 Look at diagrams A and B. How many *pairs* of electrons do these atoms share?
 a) nitrogen
 b) oxygen
 c) chlorine

3 Why don't the noble gases form diatomic molecules?

B

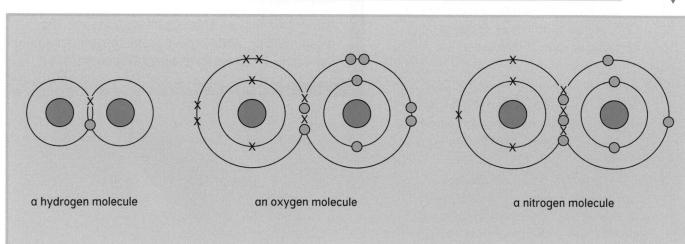

a hydrogen molecule   an oxygen molecule   a nitrogen molecule

Covalent bonds can also form between atoms of different non-metal elements. Picture C shows how hydrogen and carbon share electrons to form covalent bonds. This compound is called methane, and it is a gas.

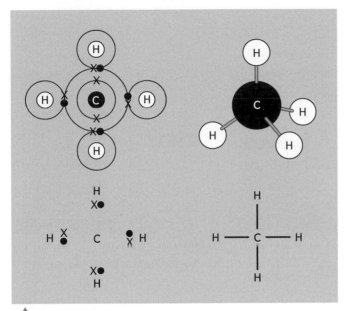

C There are different ways of showing covalent bonds.

Non-metal atoms which form covalent bonds often form molecules. Substances made of molecules are often liquids or gases at room temperature. They have low melting and boiling points. They do not conduct heat or electricity well, even when they are solid or liquid, because there are no charged particles to carry the current.

D *Ammonia and hydrogen chloride are both compounds made from non-metals. They are both gases at room temperature.*

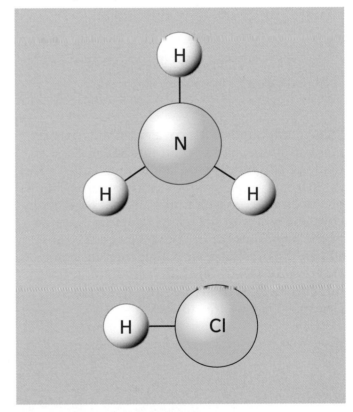

4 Look at picture D. Draw a diagram to show how the electrons are shared between the different atoms in hydrogen chloride.

5 This is part of the equation for the formation of ammonia.
$$N_2 + 3H_2 \rightarrow$$
a) Finish writing the equation, balance it, and add state symbols.
b) Draw a diagram to show how the electrons are shared between the atoms in ammonia.

6 Draw diagrams, similar to the ones in diagram B, to show the electronic structures of these covalent molecules.
a) carbon dioxide
b) ethane (C_2H_4)
c) propene (C_3H_6)

7 Explain how the atoms in calcium carbonate ($CaCO_3$) are held together. (*Hint*: you may need to look back at topic J11.)

Summary

Explain the difference between covalent bonding and ionic bonding, in as much detail as you can. You may need to look back at topic J11.

Covalent giant structures

How do covalent compounds form giant structures?

Some covalently bonded elements or compounds exist as individual molecules. The covalent bonds holding the atoms together are very strong, but there are only weak **intermolecular forces** holding the molecules to each other. This means that most of these substances have low melting and boiling points, and many of them are liquids or gases at room temperature.

Elements or compounds that form molecules do not conduct electricity, because there are no charged particles to carry the current.

A   *All these materials are made from covalently bonded molecules.*

 1   Why is nitrogen a gas at room temperature?

2   Why doesn't oil conduct electricity?

Some compounds with covalent bonds exist as giant structures rather than molecules. Sand is made of **silicon dioxide**, sometimes called **silica** or quartz. A single grain of sand contains billions of silicon and oxygen atoms all held together by covalent bonds in one giant structure. Because of the large number of strong covalent bonds, silicon dioxide has a very high melting point, and the crystals it forms are very hard. It does not conduct electricity because there are no electrons that are free to move.

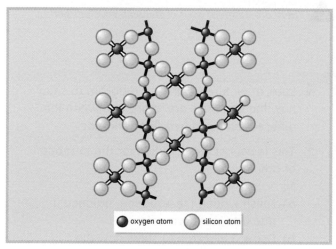

● oxygen atom   ● silicon atom

B   *The structure of silicon dioxide.*

C   *Sand is made from tiny quartz crystals.*

 3   List three properties of silicon dioxide, and explain why it has these properties.

Some elements also form giant covalent structures. Carbon can exist in two covalently bonded forms with very different properties – diamond and graphite.

Each atom in a diamond is joined by four strong covalent bonds to four other atoms in a regular arrangement. This arrangement is so strong that diamond is one of the hardest substances known, and diamonds are used for cutting glass and on drill bits for cutting through rock. Diamond does not conduct electricity, because there are no electrons that can move.

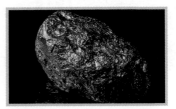

 Diamond.

 A piece of graphite.

4 Write down:
   a) three similarities and
   b) one difference between diamond and silicon dioxide.

Graphite is also made of pure carbon, but the atoms are arranged in rings in flat sheets. Each carbon atom is joined to three others in the same layer with covalent bonds. The strong bonds between the atoms in each layer give graphite a high melting point. There are some electrons that can move along the layers, so graphite can conduct electricity along the layers of atoms.

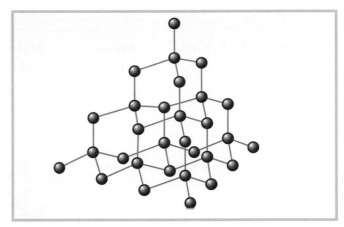

 The structure of diamond.

There are only weak bonds holding the layers together, so the layers can slide over each other easily. The 'lead' in a pencil is actually made of graphite, and layers of graphite are rubbed off the end of the 'lead' when you move the point of a pencil across a piece of paper. Graphite can also be used as a lubricant.

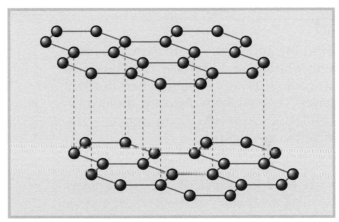

 The structure of graphite.

5 **a)** Write down one similarity in the properties of diamond and graphite.
   b) Write down two differences in their properties.
   c) Explain these differences in terms of the structures of the two materials.

6 Most compounds made of small, covalently bonded molecules are gases at room temperature. Water molecules are small, but water is a liquid at room temperature. Find out why water has such a high melting point compared with other covalent substances of similar molecular size.

Summary

Carbon dioxide consists of small molecules. Carbon dioxide and silicon dioxide are both compounds of a Group 4 element with oxygen. List the properties of carbon dioxide and silicon dioxide, and explain why they are so different.

The halogens

What are the reactions of the elements in Group 7?

The elements in Group 7 of the Periodic Table are called the **halogens**. They all have seven electrons in their outer shell and they are all non-metals.

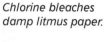

A The elements in Group 7.

Element	Symbol	Atomic number	Molecule of gas	Melting point (°C)	Boiling point (°C)	Reactivity
fluorine	F	9		−220	−188	most reactive
chlorine	Cl	17		−101	−35	
bromine	Br	35		−7	59	
iodine	I	53		114	184	least reactive

Fluorine and chlorine are gases at room temperature, and bromine is a liquid. All the halogens are coloured when they are gases. They all form diatomic molecules (molecules with two atoms joined together covalently).

1 How do the melting and boiling points of the Group 7 elements change as you go down the group?

2 Look at Table A and photograph B. How could you tell the difference between a test tube full of nitrogen and one full of chlorine? There are two ways. (*Hint*: most of the air is made of nitrogen.)

Chlorine bleaches damp litmus paper. **B**

Chlorine gas is poisonous. It was used as a weapon in the first World War (1914–1918). Thousands of soldiers were killed or injured by it.

Fluorine is the most reactive halogen. It has the smallest atoms, so the electrons in the outer shell are nearer to the positive charges in the nucleus in fluorine than they are in iodine. This means it is easier for a fluorine atom to gain an extra electron to fill up its outer shell, so it reacts more easily.

When halogens react with metals they form ionic compounds called **salts**. Halogens all need just one electron to fill their outer shell, and so they all form negative ions with a –1 charge. The ions have a slightly different name to the atoms they were made from:

- a fluorine atom forms a fluoride ion
- a chlorine atom forms a chloride ion.

All halogen atoms form **halide** ions. Fluoride and chloride are examples of halide ions.

3 What are the names of the ions formed when bromine and iodine atoms gain electrons?

The halogens at the top of Group 7 are more reactive than the ones at the bottom. Halogens and metals can react to form halide salts. If a solution of one of these salts is mixed with a solution of a more reactive halogen, a **displacement reaction** happens. The more reactive halogen 'grabs' the metal.

chlorine + potassium bromide $\longrightarrow$ potassium chloride + bromine

$Cl_2(aq)$ + $2KBr(aq)$ $\longrightarrow$ $2KCl(aq)$ + $Br_2(aq)$

Chlorine is more reactive than bromine, so chlorine ends up in the compound.

Bromine is less reactive than chlorine, so it is displaced (pushed out) from the salt.

If you mix iodine solution with potassium bromide solution, nothing happens. This is because the more reactive halogen, bromine, is already part of a salt.

Halide salts have many uses. Sodium fluoride is used in toothpaste. Sodium chloride is used to de-ice roads and silver bromide is used to make photographic paper (see topic J18). Silver iodide can be sprayed onto clouds to make it rain!

Gritting lorries spread sodium chloride onto roads to de-ice them.

4 Copy and complete these word equations. If there is no reaction, write 'no reaction'.
   a) iodine + potassium bromide $\longrightarrow$
   b) chlorine + potassium iodide $\longrightarrow$
   c) bromine + sodium chloride $\longrightarrow$

5 Write balanced symbol equations for the reactions in question 4.

6 Why is the most reactive halogen at the top of the group, when the most reactive alkali metal was at the bottom of Group 1?

Summary

You are writing an encyclopaedia entry on 'The halogens'. Write a paragraph to summarise the halogens for the encyclopaedia.

J17 Using sodium chloride

How do we use sodium chloride?

Sodium chloride is the salt you are probably most familiar with, as you put it on your food. It is also the main substance in sea water that makes it taste 'salty'. It is often called **common salt**. Sodium chloride is also very important because of the other chemicals that can be made from it.

A

A salt mine.

> ! Sodium chloride is an essential chemical in your body. Your body contains about 250 g of salt.

Sodium chloride is obtained from underground deposits or from sea water.

Sodium chloride is an ionic compound, so it conducts electricity when it is dissolved. Sodium chloride is dissolved in water to make **brine**.

Electrolysis is used to split up the chemicals in brine. Chlorine gas is given off at the **anode** (the positive **electrode**). Hydrogen (from the water in the solution) is given off at the **cathode** (the negative electrode). Sodium ions are left in the solution and form sodium hydroxide (the hydroxide comes from the water).

B

Salt being obtained from sea water.

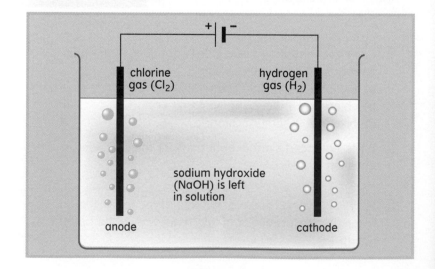

C

chlorine gas (Cl$_2$)

hydrogen gas (H$_2$)

sodium hydroxide (NaOH) is left in solution

anode

cathode

> **?** 1 What is brine?
>
> 2 Name the three products formed when sodium chloride is electrolysed.

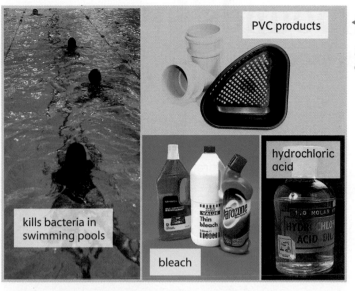

PVC products

hydrochloric acid

kills bacteria in swimming pools

bleach

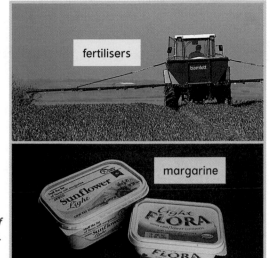

D

Uses of chlorine.

fertilisers

margarine

Uses of hydrogen.

E

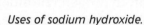

Uses of sodium hydroxide.

F

soap

paper

ceramics

3 Give three uses of chlorine.

4 Give two uses of hydrogen.

5 Give three uses of sodium hydroxide.

6 Hydrogen can also be used as a fuel.
   a) Which element does hydrogen combine with when it is used as a fuel?
   b) Write a balanced symbol equation to show this reaction.

7 Write balanced half equations to show what happens when brine is electrolysed. (*Hint*: the hydrogen gas produced started off as positive hydrogen ions.)

8 Since sodium forms positive ions, you might expect the electrolysis of brine to produce sodium at the cathode. Find out why hydrogen gas is produced instead.

Summary

Copy and complete the concept map below summarising the information on these two pages, or draw one of your own.

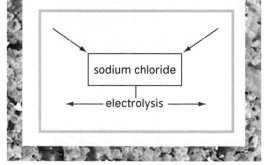

sodium chloride

electrolysis

Halogen compounds

How are halogen compounds useful?

Halogens can form covalent bonds with other non-metals, or ionic bonds with metals. Compounds of the halogens are useful in industry and for photography.

Acids

The halogens react with other non-metals to form molecules with covalent bonds. For instance, chlorine reacts with hydrogen to form hydrogen chloride. Hydrogen chloride is a gas at room temperature.

Hydrogen chloride can be dissolved in water. When it dissolves, it splits up and forms positive hydrogen ions and negative chloride ions. A solution that contains hydrogen ions is an acid. When hydrogen chloride dissolves in water it forms hydrochloric acid.

The other hydrogen halides also form acids when they dissolve in water. Acids are useful for making lots of other chemicals, for cleaning metals before they are rust-proofed, and for making printed circuit boards that are used in computers.

A

Fluorine reacts with sodium to form sodium fluoride. Sodium fluoride can help to stop teeth decaying, particularly in children. It is sometimes added to drinking water. It is also added to many toothpastes.

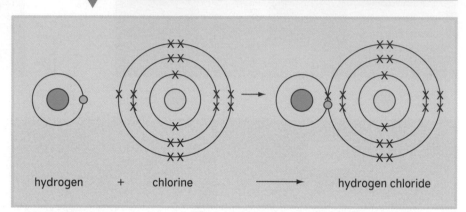

hydrogen + chlorine ⟶ hydrogen chloride

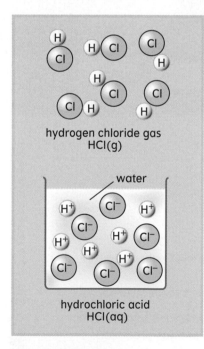

hydrogen chloride gas
HCl(g)

water

hydrochloric acid
HCl(aq)

B

?

1 a) Is hydrogen chloride a molecule or a giant structure?

  b) Write a balanced symbol equation to show what happens when hydrogen and chlorine react to form hydrogen chloride gas.

2 Write a balanced symbol equation to show how hydrobromic acid can be made from hydrogen and bromine. Include the correct state symbols.

C *A printed circuit board.*

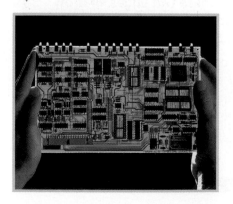

Photography

Silver can react with chlorine, bromine or iodine to form salts, called **silver halides**. The silver and the halide ions are held together with ionic bonds. If light shines on one of the compounds, it breaks apart and silver is formed again. The same thing happens when X-rays shine on them, or the radiation from radioactive substances.

For instance, silver bromide forms silver and bromine when light shines on it:

silver bromide $\longrightarrow$ silver + bromine

$$2AgBr(s) \longrightarrow 2Ag(s) + Br_2(g)$$

This reaction is useful in photography. Tiny particles of silver look black, and any silver bromide that does not react can be removed with other chemicals.

The white parts of the cow reflect more light. The light turns silver bromide to silver, which looks black. This is **a negative**.

D This is what happens when a photograph is taken. Afterwards, the film is treated with other chemicals to stop the rest of the silver bromide changing.

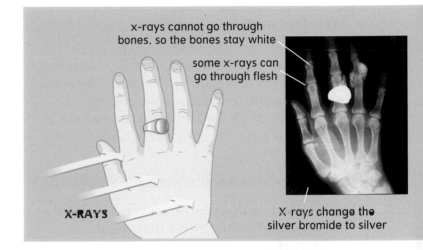

x-rays cannot go through bones, so the bones stay white

some x-rays can go through flesh

X-RAYS

X-rays change the silver bromide to silver

E

P A piece of photographic paper goes dark when light shines on it. How could you investigate what affects the darkness of the paper?

F

? **3** **a)** Which chemical is used on photographic film?

   b) What colour does this turn when light shines on it?

   c) Which chemical causes this colour?

4 If you have an X-ray, your bones show up white on the film. Explain why this happens in as much detail as you can.

5 **a)** Write a word equation to show what happens when silver iodide (AgI) splits up.

   b) Write a balanced symbol equation for the reaction. Put in the state symbols.

6 Why does the amount of blackening on an exposed piece of film depend on both the intensity of the light and the length of time the film is exposed?

! Antoine Becquerel (1852–1908) discovered radioactivity when he left some uranium salt in a drawer with some photographic paper, and discovered that the paper became darkened.

Summary

Produce a magazine or newspaper advert for a company that sells cylinders of halogen gases. The advert should explain briefly the possible uses of the gases.

Structures and bonding

How do we know which type of bonds are in a particular substance?

The type of bonding in a substance depends on the type of atoms in it. Substances with different bonding have different properties.

Metals – metallic bonding

Metal atoms all need to lose one or more electrons to get a full outer shell of electrons. The electrons move around between the metal ions. The positive ions are attracted to the negative electrons and all the ions are held together in a regular structure. This is called metallic bonding.

Substances held together with metallic bonding:

- are good conductors of heat and electricity, because of the electrons that can move

- are strong and malleable, because the layers of ions can move over each other

- usually have high melting and boiling points, because of the strong forces holding the ions together.

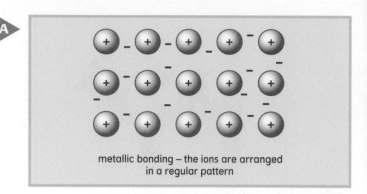

A

metallic bonding – the ions are arranged in a regular pattern

Metals have metallic bonding.

B

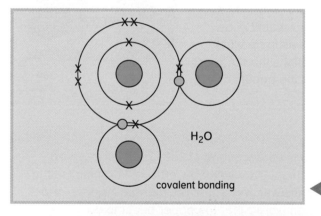

H_2O

covalent bonding

C

D

Water and most of the gases in the air all have covalent bonds.

Non-metals – covalent bonding

The noble gases are non-metals. They are very unreactive because they already have full outer electron shells. All other non-metals need electrons to give them a full outer shell. When different non-metal elements react with each other, they share electrons and form covalent bonds.

Compounds made of non-metals often form molecules. They usually:

- have low melting and boiling points

- are poor conductors of heat and electricity, because none of the electrons are free to move.

Covalently bonded elements or compounds sometimes form giant structures. They usually:

- have high melting and boiling points

- do not conduct heat or electricity well (except for graphite).

Metals and non-metals – ionic bonding

When a metal reacts with a non-metal, the metal atoms lose electrons to form positive ions, and the non-metal atoms gain electrons to form negative ions. The positive and negative ions are attracted to each other, and held together with strong forces. This is ionic bonding.

Substances with ionic bonding:

- form giant structures
- have high melting and boiling points, because of the strong forces between ions
- conduct electricity when they are molten or dissolved, because the electrically charged ions can move around.

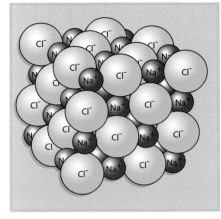

E

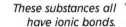

These substances all have ionic bonds. **F**

sodium sulphate copper sulphate

potassium dichromate potassium permanganate

1 Which kind of bonding is formed between:
   a) two non-metal elements
   b) a metal and a non-metal?

2 a) Why are metals good conductors of electricity?
   b) Why do ionic substances conduct electricity when they are melted or dissolved in water?
   c) Why don't most covalent substances conduct electricity?
   d) Graphite is a covalent substance which *does* conduct electricity. Explain why it does so.

3 Why do metals and ionic substances usually have high melting and boiling points?

4 Which kind of bonding produces molecules?

5 You are given a substance and asked to identify the type of bonding holding it together. Describe a series of tests you could carry out, and what the results of each test might tell you.

Summary

Draw a table to summarise the three types of bonding, and the properties of substances with those types of bonding. You could start your table like this:

	Metallic	**Ionic**	**Covalent**	
			(molecules)	**(giant structures)**
forms between	metal atoms	metals and non-metals		
atoms gain full outer shells by	losing electrons			
melting points				

Further questions

1 This diagram represents an atom.

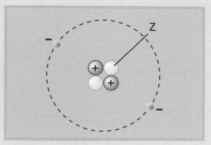

a) What is represented by Z? (1)

b) Copy and complete this table to show the relative masses and charges of the particles in atoms.

	Mass	Charge
proton	1	
neutron		
electron	negligible	−1

(3)

2 This symbol represents an atom of chlorine.

$$\begin{matrix} 35 \\ \textbf{Cl} \\ 17 \end{matrix}$$

a) How many protons does a chlorine atom have? (1)

b) How many electrons does it have? (1)

c) How many neutrons does it have? (1)

d) A different isotope of chlorine has a mass number of 37. How many protons does this isotope have? (1)

e) How many neutrons does this isotope have? (1)

3 A magnesium atom has 12 electrons.

a) Draw a diagram to show the electronic structure of a magnesium atom. (3)

b) Will the atom gain or lose electrons when it forms an ion? (1)

c) Choose the correct way of writing the electronic structure of a magnesium ion from the list.

$[2,8,1]^+$ $[2,8]^{2+}$ $[2,8,1]^-$ $[2,8,8]$ $[2,8]^{2-}$ (1)

4 Hydrogen and oxygen react together to form water. A hydrogen atom has one electron, and an oxygen atom has eight electrons.

a) Hydrogen forms molecules with the formula H_2. What kind of bonding holds the two hydrogen atoms together? (1)

b) Draw a diagram to show the electronic structure of a hydrogen molecule. (1)

c) Copy and complete this equation to show the reaction. Balance the equation and add state symbols.

$$H_2 + O_2 \longrightarrow$$

(3)

5 These diagrams show the electronic structures of calcium and fluorine atoms.

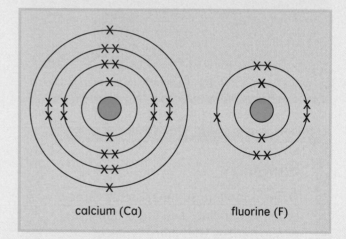

calcium (Ca)   fluorine (F)

a) Which of these two elements is a non-metal? (1)

b) What will be the charge on a calcium ion? (1)

c) How many electrons does fluorine need to gain to get a full outer shell? (1)

d) Write down the formula for calcium fluoride. (1)

e) Will solid calcium fluoride conduct electricity? (1)

f) Write balanced half equations to show what would happen at the electrodes if molten calcium fluoride is electrolysed. (3)

g) Which is the cation in these half equations? (1)

6 This diagram shows part of the Periodic Table.

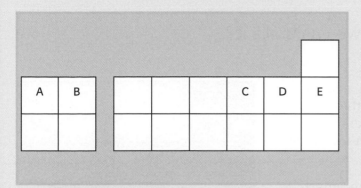

a) Write down the letters of two elements that you would expect to be metals. (2)

b) Which element will have a full outer shell of electrons? (1)

c) Which two elements will form molecules when they are gases? (2)

d) Which element will have the highest mass number? (1)

7 Helium, neon and argon are called noble gases. They are in Group 0 of the Periodic Table.

a) Which of these diagrams shows a noble gas? (1)

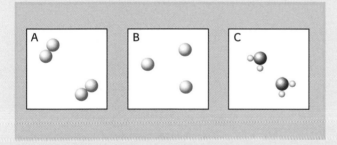

b) Give one use for helium. (1)

c) Name one other noble gas and give a use for it. (1)

8 Nitrogen molecules consist of two nitrogen atoms covalently bonded together. Pure carbon can exist as diamond or graphite. In both forms the carbon atoms are held together by covalent bonds.

a) List the physical properties of these three substances (i.e. their melting points, and whether or not they conduct heat or electricity). (6)

b) Explain the differences in their properties in terms of their structures. (6)

9 Sodium chloride is a compound of a metal and a non-metal.

a) Which element in sodium chloride is a metal? (1)

b) What kind of bonding holds sodium chloride together? (1)

c) Name two places that large quantities of sodium chloride can be found. (2)

d) What is brine? (1)

e) Electrolysis can be used to split up brine into chlorine, hydrogen and sodium hydroxide solution. Give one use for each of these products. (3)

f) How could you test a gas to see if it was chlorine? (1)

10 Three of the elements in Group 7 of the Periodic Table are fluorine, chlorine and bromine. Fluorine and chlorine are gases at room temperature.

a) Which diagram represents chlorine gas?

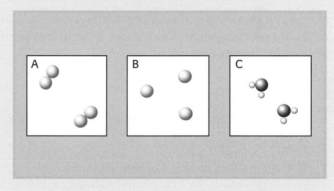

b) Which of these three Group 7 elements is the most reactive? (2)

c) Explain why this element is the most reactive. (2)

d) Copy and complete these word equations to show what will happen. If there is no reaction, write 'no reaction'.

i) sodium fluoride solution + chlorine $\longrightarrow$

ii) sodium bromide solution + chlorine $\longrightarrow$ (2)

11 What sort of bonding would you expect to find in each of the following?

a) sodium bromide   b) hydrogen chloride gas

c) carbon dioxide   d) water

e) iron   f) chlorine gas (6)

Speed

What is speed and how can we calculate it?

Even when we are standing still on the Earth we are actually travelling at extremely high speeds. This is because the Earth is constantly spinning on its axis and travelling around the Sun. Even the Sun isn't standing still; it is travelling at an incredibly high speed around our galaxy.

Speed tells us how far something travels in a certain length of time. The faster something is going, the higher its speed, and the further it will travel in a certain time.

! The fastest land mammal (the cheetah) and the fastest fish (the sailfish) have the same highest recorded speed of 110 km/h.

? 1 At top speed, how far would a sailfish travel in an hour?

A

Speed can be measured in many different units. The most common units are **metres per second** (m/s), **kilometres per hour** (km/h) and **miles per hour** (mph).

E **Calculating speed**

The speed of an object can be worked out if you know:

● the distance it covered

● the time it took to cover that distance.

speed	=	**distance**	÷	**time**
(metres per second, m/s)		**(metres, m)**		**(seconds, s)**

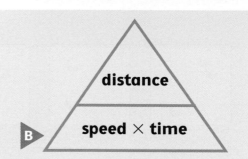

B distance / speed × time

Worked examples

A An athlete runs 100 metres in 10 seconds. What is the speed of the athlete?

speed = distance ÷ time
    = 100 m ÷ 10 s
    = 10 m/s

B A car travels 200 kilometres in 4 hours. What is the speed of the car?

speed = distance ÷ time
    = 200 km ÷ 4 h
    = 50 km/h

Note: the units for speed depend on the units you have used for distance and time.

? 2 Write down three different units for speed.

P How can you make an elastic band car? How can you make it go faster?

Velocity

Scientists often talk about **velocity** instead of speed. Velocity and speed both tell you how fast something is moving. If you only know the speed of an object you can't guess where it will be an hour later because you don't know which direction it is travelling in. Velocity tells us the speed and *direction* of an object's movement. Look at picture C.

- The speed of rabbit A is 2 metres per second.
- The velocity of rabbit B is 2 metres per second going north.

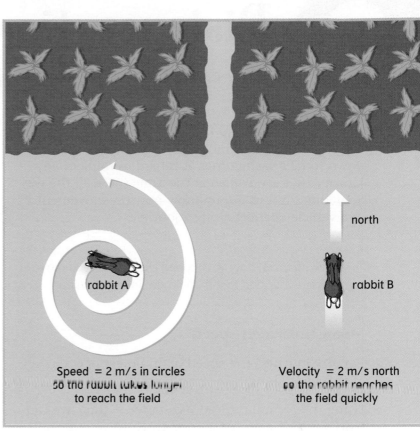

Speed = 2 m/s in circles so the rabbit takes longer to reach the field

Velocity = 2 m/s north so the rabbit reaches the field quickly

3 What does velocity tell you about the movement of an object that speed does not?

4 Copy and complete the table below:

Speed (m/s)	Distance (m)	Time (s)
	100	5
	45	9
	40	20
	20	2
	6	3

5 Two trains are travelling at 100 km/h. One train is travelling north and the other south. Write a sentence comparing the speeds and velocities of these two trains.

6 Work out how far the following people will travel:
   a) A man walking at 2 miles per hour for 3 hours.
   b) A student running at 5 metres per second for 10 seconds.
   c) A baby crawling at 0.1 metres per second for half a minute.

7 Work out how fast a car travelling at 108 km/h is going in metres per second.

8 The Olympic Games were held in the UK in 1948. Here are some of the results:
Melvin Patton ran 200 metres in 21.1 seconds.
Dorothy Manly had a mean (average) speed of 8.2 m/s in the 100 metres.
Curtis Stone completed 5 kilometres in 14 minutes and 39.4 seconds.
Henry Eriksson ran the 1500 metres in 3 minutes and 49.8 seconds.
   a) Which athlete ran the fastest?
   b) If all the athletes ran at a constant speed, only one would have had a constant velocity. Which one? Explain your answer.
   c) Find out how fast the winner of the woman's 100 m sprint was at the last Olympics.

Summary

When a new module is joined to the International Space Station, it approaches at about 0.1 m/s. It is important that it meets the docking port on the space station exactly. Design a fact sheet for visitors to a space museum to explain how velocity is calculated and why scientists at ground control need to know the velocity of a new module rather than just its speed.

Distance–time graphs

How can we show an object's journey on a graph?

At the start of a Grand Prix race the cars are stationary. They speed up at an incredible rate but have to slow down to take each corner. It is hard to think of any journey that is travelled at the same speed all the way. Sometimes it is useful to know how the movement of a vehicle changes along a journey.

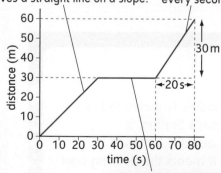

A

 1 Write down how your speed changes as you move from your bed to the bathroom in the morning.

Mean (average) speed

For any journey, the speed of an object may change as it travels along.

Using the formula: speed = distance ÷ time, we can work out the speed of an object. However, this tells us the **mean** (average) speed of the object over the whole journey. The object may have started slowly and then got faster, but the formula can only show us the mean speed. To show how the movement changes during a journey we can use a **distance–time graph**.

 2 Why is the mean speed often different from the actual speed of an object at a certain point on a journey?

Distance–time graphs

Distance–time graphs show how far an object has moved at different times. Time is plotted on the *x*-axis and distance is plotted on the *y*-axis.

The speed can be calculated by finding the gradient (steepness) of the line. This is done by dividing the change on the *y*-axis by the change on the *x*-axis.

Worked example

Look at the right-hand part of the line in graph B.

Change in distance	= 60 – 30 = 30 m
Change in time	= 80 – 60 = 20 s
Gradient	= 30 m ÷ 20 s
Speed	= 1.5 m/s

B

If an object is travelling at a steady speed then its distance from the start will be increasing steadily. This gives a straight line on a slope.

The steeper the slope, the faster the speed, as the distance is increasing by a larger amount in every second.

30 m

20 s

If an object is stationary (standing still) at any point then its distance from the start will not change with time. This gives a straight, horizontal line.

 3 On a distance–time graph, what type of line shows an object that is stationary?

If an object is getting faster, the slope must get steeper so the line curves upwards. If the object is slowing down the line must get less steep.

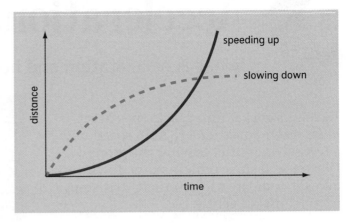

4 On a distance–time graph, what happens to the line on the graph if an object speeds up?

P How could you draw a distance–time graph for a car on a track?

5 Draw a sketch of a distance–time graph for the following journeys:

a) A girl runs at a steady speed to a bus stop, where she suddenly stops. She gets on a bus. The bus travels at a steady speed that is faster than the girl's running speed.

b) A driver parks the car on a hill but forgets to leave the hand-brake on. The car starts to move and speeds up until it reaches a steady speed. Unfortunately there is a river at the bottom of the hill which the car rolls into. The car slows down and falls at a slower, steady speed in the water until it hits the bottom where it stops.

6 a) Describe the following journey travelled by a snail, using the distance–time graph E:

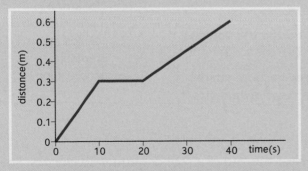

b) For how long was the snail stationary?

c) What was the mean speed of the snail over the whole journey?

d) Find the actual speed of the snail during each 10 seconds of its journey by calculating the gradient for each 10 second time interval.

e) Convert your answers to part d) into cm/s.

Cheetahs can only run at 110 km/h for short distances. The fastest mammals over very long distances are sled dogs. Teams of these can cover 1000 km in less than 10 days.

D *The Iditarod race covers 1000 km.*

Summary

Write a short story about a race and then draw a labelled distance–time graph for it.

Acceleration

What is acceleration and how can we calculate it?

To send a rocket into space, the rocket must reach an extremely high speed only a few seconds after leaving the ground. During a crash, a vehicle slows down very quickly compared to a vehicle that stops when it brakes gently.

These things involve an object changing velocity, but it is not just the new velocity that is important, it is how *quickly* the object *changes* velocity.

A

? **1** Put the following objects in order, starting with the object that can change velocity most quickly.

> lorry   fighter plane   bicycle   steam roller

! In 1975, the fastest recorded bowler, Jeffrey Robert, accelerated a cricket ball to just over 160 km/h.

The **acceleration** of an object tells us how quickly its velocity is changing. The more the velocity of an object changes in a certain time, the greater the acceleration. Acceleration is measured in **metres per second squared (m/s²)**.

E Calculating acceleration

The acceleration of an object can be worked out if you know:

- the change in velocity of the object
- the time it took to change velocity.

$$\text{acceleration} = \text{change in velocity} \div \text{time taken to change the velocity}$$
$$\text{(m/s}^2) \qquad\qquad \text{(m/s)} \qquad\qquad\qquad \text{(s)}$$

Note: The units of acceleration are metres per second **squared** because metres per second are divided by seconds, and m/s² is easier to write than m/s/s.

? **2** A Mini car can go from 0 km/h to 100 km/h in 10 seconds, whereas a Ferrari can go from 0 km/h to 100 km/h in 5 seconds. Which car has the greatest acceleration?

Worked examples

A At take-off, a plane accelerates from rest to 40 m/s in 10 seconds. What is the acceleration of the plane?

Change in velocity	=	final velocity − velocity at start
	=	40 − 0
	=	40 m/s.
Acceleration	=	change in velocity ÷ time taken
	=	40 m/s ÷ 10 s
	=	4 m/s².

B Near the end of a race, a sprinter accelerates. She was running at 7 m/s but accelerates to 9 m/s in 4 seconds. What is the acceleration of the sprinter?

Change in velocity	=	final velocity − velocity at start
	=	9 − 7
	=	2 m/s.
Acceleration	=	change in velocity ÷ time taken
	=	2 m/s ÷ 4 s
	=	0.5 m/s².

? 3 What is the unit for acceleration?

acceleration of 2 m/s²

Deceleration

When we talk about acceleration we usually think of things speeding up. However, there are just as many situations where objects are slowing down. This is called **deceleration**. To calculate deceleration we can use exactly the same formula as for acceleration. The only difference is that the answer will be a negative number if the object is slowing down.

C acceleration of −5 m/s²

? 4 Copy and complete table D.

D

Velocity at start (m/s)		Final velocity (m/s)	Change in velocity (m/s) = final velocity – velocity at start	Time taken (s)	Acceleration (m/s²)
a)	0	10		5	
b)	5	4		0.5	
c)	3	9		2	
d)	12	5		7	
e)	4	8		1	

5 In the table above which of the answers show an object which is decelerating?

6 Which has the greatest deceleration, a runner going from 10 m/s to 2 m/s in 5 s or a runner going from 10 m/s to 5 m/s in 2 s?

7 A car is driving north at 20 m/s and does a U-turn so that it ends up driving south at 20 m/s. If the U-turn takes 5 seconds to complete, what is the acceleration? (*Hint*: the car has changed direction, so it has changed velocity.)

8 A car is going round a roundabout at a steady speed of 20 miles per hour. Explain why it is accelerating, even though its speed is not changing.

Summary

Write a few sentences to answer the topic question at the top of page 170. Include in your answer all the words in bold on these two pages.

Velocity- time graphs

How can we show the change in velocity of an object on a graph?

The distance an object travels can be represented on a distance–time graph. You can also show how the velocity of an object changes, using a **velocity–time graph**. This can tell us more information about the movement of the object, including its acceleration.

Velocity–time graphs

Velocity–time graphs show how the velocity of an object has changed at different times. Time is plotted on the *x*-axis and velocity is plotted on the *y*-axis.

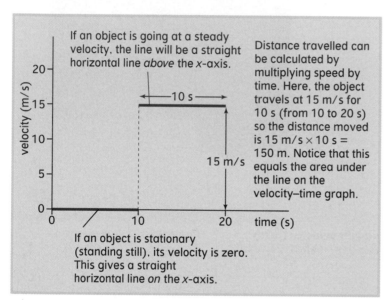

If an object is going at a steady velocity, the line will be a straight horizontal line *above* the *x*-axis.

Distance travelled can be calculated by multiplying speed by time. Here, the object travels at 15 m/s for 10 s (from 10 to 20 s) so the distance moved is 15 m/s × 10 s = 150 m. Notice that this equals the area under the line on the velocity–time graph.

If an object is stationary (standing still), its velocity is zero. This gives a straight horizontal line *on* the *x*-axis.

 A

Mount St. Helens erupted in 1980, causing rocks to travel at velocities up to 400 km/h (250 mph).

B

 1 On a velocity–time graph, what type of line shows an object that is:
  a) stationary
  b) travelling at a steady velocity
  c) accelerating?

 C

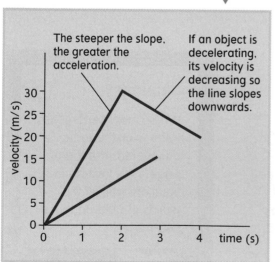

The steeper the slope, the greater the acceleration.

If an object is decelerating, its velocity is decreasing so the line slopes downwards.

The gradient of the line on a velocity–time graph gives the acceleration. This is because this gradient is worked out by dividing a change in velocity by the time for that change.

Worked example

Look at the lower line on graph C.

Change in velocity	= 15 m/s – 0 m/s = 15 m/s
Change in time	= 3 s – 0 s = 3 s
Gradient	= 15 m/s ÷ 3 s
Acceleration	= 5 m/s^2

It is easy to confuse distance–time graphs with velocity–time graphs. Always check the axes on the graph to see which sort it is before answering a question.

2 a) Explain what the gradient of a velocity–time graph shows.
b) Explain what the gradient of a distance–time graph shows.

3 How can you find the distance travelled by an object from its velocity–time graph?

4 Draw a velocity–time graph for the following journey:

A boy taking part in a 100 m race accelerates steadily for the first 4 seconds, reaching a velocity of 8 m/s. He runs at this steady velocity for 6 seconds before finally accelerating to 10 m/s during the remaining 3 seconds of the race.

Here is a journey with both graphs drawn to point out the differences:

A child starts an egg and spoon race, accelerating steadily (A) until reaching a steady velocity (B). He then drops the egg and suddenly stops to pick it up (C). He accelerates again (D) and reaches a steady velocity that is slower than the last time (E), until he reaches the end of the race where he gently decelerates (F) before stopping (G).

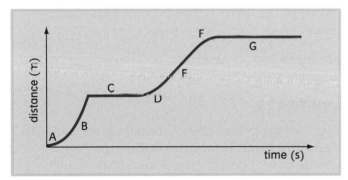

 A distance–time graph.

5 For the egg and spoon race velocity–time graph, F, calculate:
a) the acceleration for each of the line sections, A to G
b) the total distance the child ran.

6 Draw a velocity–time graph for a parachutist, from the moment she jumps from the plane until she lands safely on the ground.

P How can you find the speed of an object using ticker tape?

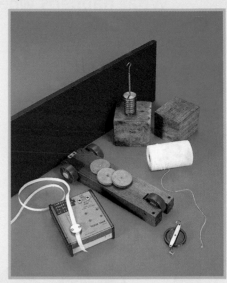

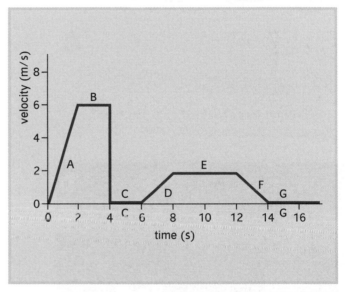

A velocity–time graph.

Summary

Write a list of bullet-points summarising the key features of a velocity–time graph, including the things that can be calculated from one. Draw an example and describe the journey that it shows.

Balanced forces

What happens when forces are balanced?

A

1 What is a force?

2 What three things can a force do?

The world could not exist without forces. The forces in our skeletons and muscles hold our bodies up so that we are not floppy lumps on the floor. The forces in the Universe keep the planets in their positions around the Sun and hold the stars together.

 The strongest muscle in the human body is called the masseter. It produces the force needed to raise the lower jaw for biting and chewing.

What is a force?

A force is a push or a pull. This means a force can:

- change the velocity of an object
- change the shape of an object
- change the direction that an object is moving in.

When we talk about forces, we say that a force **acts** on an object. This means the force is either pushing or pulling the object. There are very few situations where there is only one force acting on an object. We need to be able to work out what happens to objects when there is more than one force acting.

Forces are measured in **newtons**, **N**. This unit is named after a scientist called Sir Isaac Newton.

Balanced forces

If the forces acting on an object are **balanced** they will cancel each other out. Forces can only cancel out if they are acting in opposite directions, so the forces must be parallel to each other.

In a tug of war competition the teams are pulling in opposite directions. If both teams pull with exactly the same force, then the force to the left cancels out the force to the right so there is no movement in either direction. The forces are balanced.

B

For forces to balance they must be the same size but act in opposite directions.

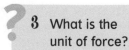
3 What is the unit of force?

If forces are balanced it is as if there is no force at all. The movement of the object will not change because there is no remaining force to change the movement.

Equal and opposite forces

When an object is resting on a surface, the **weight** of the object is pushing down on that surface. Something has to stop the object sinking down into the surface. There is another force pushing up on the object that cancels out the object's weight. This force comes from the surface.

Whenever an object rests on a surface, the weight pushing down on the surface is cancelled out by an equal force pushing up on the object.

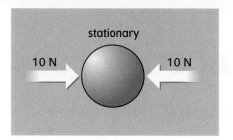
stationary

10 N → ← 10 N

 C If an object is stationary and the forces acting on it are balanced then the object will remain stationary.

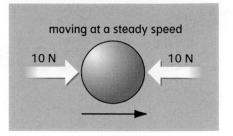
moving at a steady speed

10 N → ← 10 N

 D If an object is moving and the forces acting on it are balanced then it will carry on moving at the same speed. There is no force to speed it up or slow it down.

E
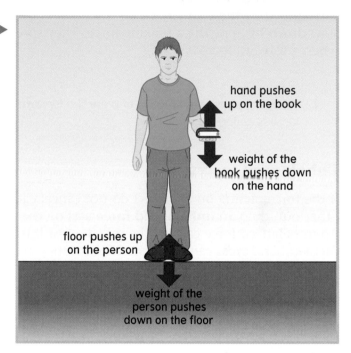

hand pushes up on the book

weight of the book pushes down on the hand

floor pushes up on the person

weight of the person pushes down on the floor

P How could you investigate whether still water can push?

F
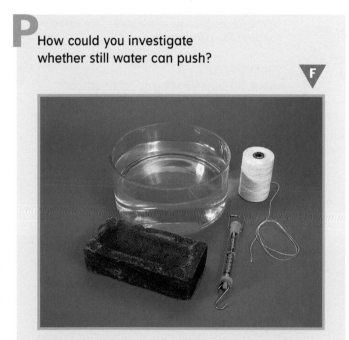

? 4 a) If forces are balanced, what two things can you say about them?
b) A force of 20 N acts downwards on a stationary object. What force must act upwards on the object for it to remain stationary?

5 Explain how a book can rest on a table, without falling through the table.

Summary

For each of the following situations, draw a picture showing the forces that are balanced. Explain what happens in each case because the forces are balanced.

- a tug of war where neither team is winning
- your teacher sitting still on a chair
- a car driving at constant velocity
- a submarine stationary at a constant depth

Unbalanced forces

How will an unbalanced force change the way an object moves?

If balanced forces act on an object then its movement will not change. We need to be able to work out what happens when **unbalanced** forces act on an object. You will already have a good idea about this as you are surrounded by these situations all the time. Vehicles slow down by applying a braking force. They speed up when a forward force is acting.

 1 What happens to the motion of a car if a forward force is acting on it?

Unbalanced forces

If the forces acting on an object do not cancel each other out, then an **unbalanced force** acts on the object. An unbalanced force can also be called a **resultant force**. (Remember: Forces can only cancel out if they are parallel to each other.)

The unbalanced force will be in the direction of the biggest force.

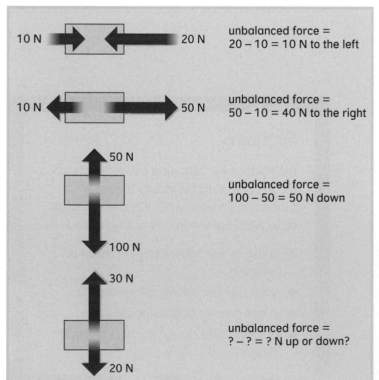

10 N   20 N   unbalanced force = 20 − 10 = 10 N to the left

10 N   50 N   unbalanced force = 50 − 10 = 40 N to the right

50 N   100 N   unbalanced force = 100 − 50 = 50 N down

30 N   20 N   unbalanced force = ? − ? = ? N up or down?

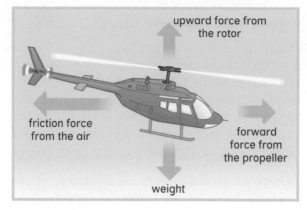

A When all the forces are balanced, the speed and direction of the helicopter stays the same. If the forces become unbalanced, the speed or direction will change.

! About 50 000 years ago, a rock from space hit the Earth with enough force to destroy a whole city. It landed in an isolated region of Arizona, USA. **B**

2 The answer to the last part in diagram C has been left out. Draw the box and forces and complete the answer to give the unbalanced force on the box.

3 True or false?

'Forces that are at right angles to each other cannot cancel each other out.'

Changing movement

When an unbalanced force acts on an object, it will change the way the object moves. There are four things to remember that tell us how the movement will change:

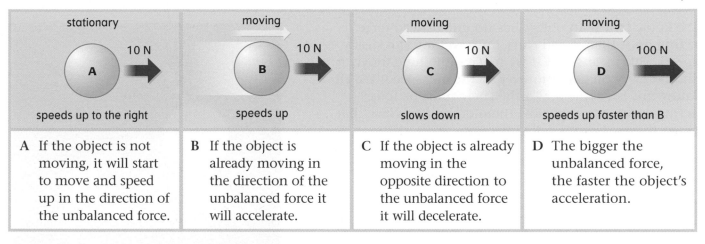

stationary	moving	moving	moving
A — 10 N	B — 10 N	C ← 10 N	D — 100 N
speeds up to the right	speeds up	slows down	speeds up faster than B

A If the object is not moving, it will start to move and speed up in the direction of the unbalanced force.	B If the object is already moving in the direction of the unbalanced force it will accelerate.	C If the object is already moving in the opposite direction to the unbalanced force it will decelerate.	D The bigger the unbalanced force, the faster the object's acceleration.

D

4 Draw a diagram showing the friction force and forward force on a car that is speeding up. Remember, the size of the force arrows can show which of the forces is the largest.

5 a) Work out the resultant force in each of the situations in diagram F.

b) Describe how the motion of the objects will change using the following words:

accelerate   decelerate   stay still

F

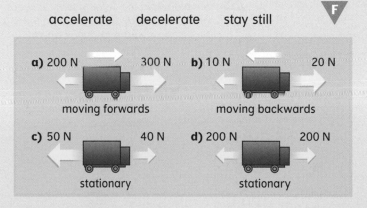

a) 200 N → 300 N
moving forwards

b) 10 N ← 20 N
moving backwards

c) 50 N ← 40 N →
stationary

d) 200 N ← 200 N →
stationary

6 The forces in table G all act on a submarine at different times. Write down what happens to the submarine at each time.

G

	Up force	Down force	Forward force	Backward force
a)	1000 N	3000 N	2000 N	1500 N
b)	5000 N	3000 N	0 N	0 N
c)	3000 N	3000 N	0 N	500 N
d)	3000 N	3000 N	1000 N	1000 N

P How could you power a rocket with water?

E

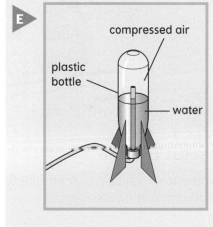

compressed air

plastic bottle

water

Summary

Write a list of bullet points to answer the topic question at the top of page 176. Include all the words in bold on these two pages.

177

Friction

What is friction and how does it affect how an object moves?

We know that if an object has no unbalanced force acting on it then it will carry on travelling at a steady speed. This means that if we make something move, it should carry on going forever at a steady speed! We all know this isn't true on Earth. There must be forces acting on objects that slow them down. The force that slows things down is called **friction**.

> **1 a)** What part of a car provides the forward force that can speed the car up?
> **b)** What force tries to slow a car down?

Friction is a force. It is caused by surfaces sliding over each other. Friction always tries to *slow things down*. Friction always acts in the opposite direction to any movement.

sledge movement

friction of the snow on the runners

 This is Voyager 2 which was sent to fly past the planets in the Solar System. It keeps going at a steady speed because there is no friction in space to slow it down.

Useful friction

Sometimes friction can be helpful. Here are some examples:

 Friction stops the ladder falling down.

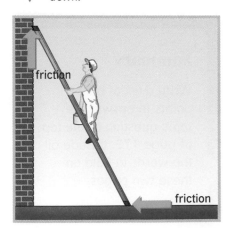

friction

friction

D Friction between the brake pad and the wheel stops the wheel turning.

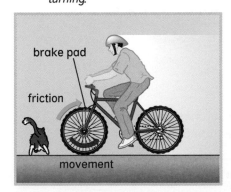

brake pad

friction

movement

E Friction between the bottle and the fingers stops the bottle slipping.

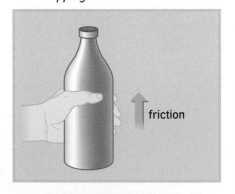

friction

> **2** Use the word 'friction' in your answers to these questions.
> **a)** Why do trainers have rubber on the soles?
> **b)** Why do toothbrushes often have rubber strips on their handles?

P How could you find out what combination of surfaces produces the most friction?

Bicycles and cars have tyres made of rubber to help them grip the road. Water on the road reduces friction. There are grooves in the tyres called 'tread' to help push water out of the way when it is wet. Racing cars use tyres with deep, wide grooves in wet weather. If there is not enough friction, the wheels on a vehicle will go round without the vehicle moving forward. This is what happens when a car tries to travel on ice.

? **3** Why is it hard to walk on ice?

Unwanted friction

Friction is not always useful. In a car engine, friction can make parts of the metal wear away. Oil is used to reduce friction; it acts as a **lubricant**. Friction also makes surfaces heat up. Try rubbing your hands together quickly. Can you feel the heat energy? If there is not enough oil in a car engine to lubricate the parts, the engine can get too hot. This will damage parts of the engine.

! Teflon is used to coat non-stick frying pans. However, it is used on many other surfaces to reduce friction, including saws, zips and even bullets.

? **4** Look at each of the following pictures. For each picture:
a) write down whether the friction is useful or unwanted
b) explain your answer
c) suggest what might reduce the friction. **G**

walking

car engine

removing a lid

5 What are the units for friction?

6 Explain why:
a) mountain bike tyres are made from rubber
b) the tyres have grooves in them.

7 Give four examples of friction on moving objects, and explain the energy transfer that the friction causes in each case.

Summary

Write a paragraph in your own words which explains:

● what friction is
● what its effects are
● how to reduce friction.

Your paragraph should contain some examples of useful and unwanted friction.

Braking and stopping

What affects the time it takes for a vehicle to slow down?

It is not long before you can start learning to drive. Driving has obviously got a lot to do with moving, but more importantly you need to be able to stop. This is not as easy as it sounds. It is hard to work out how much space you need to stop a car, because it depends on how fast you are travelling, your **reaction time**, the type of car you have and the type of road you are driving on.

A

1 **a)** Is it harder or easier to stop a vehicle on an icy road than a normal dry road?
   b) Use your knowledge of friction to explain your answer to part a).

! When travelling at 30 mph you are travelling the length of an articulated lorry every second.

Stopping distance

The distance it takes for a car to slow down and stop is divided into two parts:

- **Thinking distance** – the distance the car travels while the driver thinks about braking.
- **Braking distance** – the distance the car travels after the brakes have been pressed.

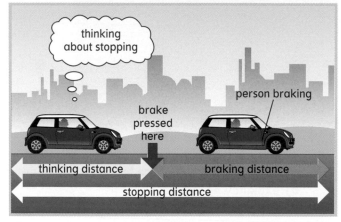

B

E The total stopping distance of a vehicle is the thinking distance and the braking distance added together:

stopping distance = thinking distance + braking distance

Thinking distance

When a driver sees a red light, it takes time for the brain to send a message to the foot to press the brake. This is the driver's **reaction time**. While this is happening the vehicle is still moving forward at its original speed.

- The faster the vehicle is moving, the further it will travel during the reaction time.
- The longer it takes the driver to react, the further the vehicle will travel during the reaction time.

P Can you find your reaction time? C

2 What is the thinking distance?

A driver's reaction time will be increased if the driver is tired, has taken drugs or drunk alcohol. This is why the police are trying so hard to stop people driving under the influence of drugs or alcohol. The longer a person's reaction time is, the longer it will take for a vehicle to stop in an emergency.

Poor visibility, due to fog or heavy rain, makes it harder for drivers to see when they need to stop.

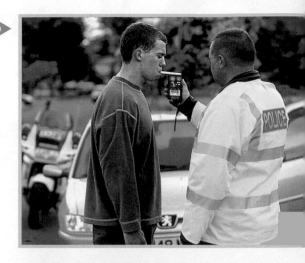
D

3 a) What three main things will increase a driver's reaction time?
 b) What effect will an increased reaction time have on the thinking distance?
 c) What effect will it have on the braking distance?
 d) What effect will it have on the overall stopping distance?

Braking distance

Once a driver has pressed the brakes, the vehicle begins to slow down.

- The faster the vehicle is moving, the longer it will take to slow down, for a certain **braking force**.

- If a bigger braking force is used to stop the vehicle, the time for the vehicle to stop will decrease.

If the road is wet or icy, this will increase the braking distance. If too big a braking force is used, the tyres may slide on the road because there is not enough friction. Vehicles must also be well maintained. If the brake pads on a vehicle are worn down it will take longer for a vehicle to slow down when the brakes are applied.

E The brake pads of a Formula 1 car glow, due to the amount of force used.

4 Copy and complete this table of stopping distances. F

Speed (m/s)	Conditions	Reaction time (s)	Thinking distance (m)	Braking distance (m)	Overall stopping distance (m)
10	normal	1	10	8	
	drunk driver		15		23
	wet road		10	10	

5 a) On a wet road, a driver travelling at 10 m/s suddenly sees a cat run into the road in front. Draw a velocity–time graph to show what happens when the driver brakes evenly to a complete stop. (*Hint*: you will need to use the information from question 4, remembering that the distance is the area under a velocity–time graph.)

 b) Work out the deceleration of the car once the driver starts to brake.

Summary

A Explain the meaning of each of the headings in table F.

B Explain how and why the following will change the stopping distance:

- wet road
- drunk driver
- tired driver
- fog.

Moving through fluids

How can liquids and gases affect how an object moves?

When two solid surfaces move over each other, friction tries to stop the movement. Sometimes an object isn't moving on a solid surface, but it still experiences a friction force that slows it down. For instance, if you are swimming and you stop propelling yourself forward, the water slows you down until you stop moving. When you throw a ball it doesn't keep going forever, the air slows it down.

A *When a plane is flying, the air it moves through pushes against the front surfaces of the plane.*

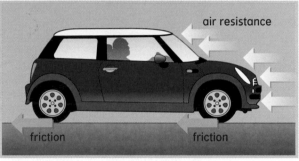

B

 1 What tries to slow a plane down when it is flying?

Air resistance and drag

Liquids and gases are called **fluids**. The type of friction that objects feel when they are moving through a fluid is called **drag**. If the object is moving in the air, then this friction force is sometimes called **air resistance**. Drag is caused by the particles in a fluid hitting the front surface of the object. This makes a force that pushes in the opposite direction to the movement of the object.

 2 What causes air resistance?

3 What two forces try to slow a car down when it is travelling along a road?

 When a shuttle re-enters the Earth's atmosphere, the friction caused by the atmosphere raises the surface temperature of the shuttle to over 950 °C.

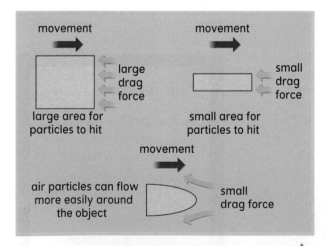

C

 4 Write down three examples of streamlining that people have used in order to reduce drag. Remember, it's not just used in vehicles; think about what athletes do to reduce drag.

The bigger the front **surface area** of an object, the more particles can hit the object. This means the drag force or air resistance will be bigger. Some objects are specially designed to reduce drag by making the area of the front surface smaller. The shape of the front surface also changes the amount of drag. Some shapes make it easier for the liquid or gas to flow over them. This is called **streamlining**. Streamlining reduces drag.

D The faster this skysurfer falls, the bigger the force pushing on the board.

P How could you investigate the force needed to move an object at different speeds?

E

Speed and drag

When you cycle down a hill and get faster you might have noticed that the force of the wind pushing against you gets stronger. This is the case for all moving objects. The faster they travel, the bigger the force pushing against them from the liquid or gas they are travelling through.

> The higher the speed of an object, the bigger the drag or air resistance.

Imagine a submarine under water. If it travels at a low speed, water can move slowly out of the way so there is only a small amount of drag. If the submarine speeds up, the water has to be pushed out of the way faster, so the force on the front of the submarine is larger.

A new type of one-man submarine. Notice the shapes of the front surfaces. F

5 a) What pushes against the front of a lorry as it travels along a motorway?
b) Will this push get larger or smaller if the lorry slows down?

6 Put the pictures in box F in order, starting with the one with the least amount of drag: G

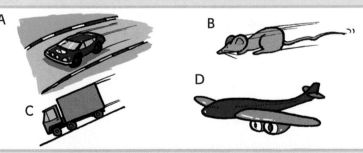

A
B
C
D

7 What happens to the air resistance on an aeroplane as it slows down?

8 a) A woman is running at a steady speed. The air resistance acting on her is 20 N and the friction force acting on her (between her shoes and the ground) is 2 N. What force must her legs be providing to push her forward?
b) How and why would her leg force be different if her steady speed was faster?

Summary

Explain what each of these words/phrases means and give two examples of each one.

- fluid
- drag
- streamlining
- drag changing with speed

K10 Unbalanced forces and acceleration

What affects the acceleration of an object?

When car designers are working on the new cars of the future, they are constantly trying to improve the performance of the car; making it accelerate better and use as little fuel as possible. So how do designers do this?

- Streamlining the body of the car reduces air resistance, which makes the car use less fuel and accelerate more easily.
- Reducing the **mass** of the car also helps.

 1 What helps to reduce the air resistance of a vehicle?

Acceleration and force

We know that an unbalanced force will make an object speed up (accelerate) or slow down (decelerate). The size of the acceleration depends on the size of the unbalanced force.

For an object of a certain mass, the bigger the force the bigger the acceleration or deceleration.

Acceleration and mass

It would be unfair to race a car against a lorry, even if they both had the same engines inside. This is because a car has much less mass to accelerate than a lorry. Motor bikes have even less mass to accelerate.

The size of the acceleration or deceleration of an object depends on the mass of the object.

The bigger the mass of an object, the bigger the force that is needed to produce the same acceleration.

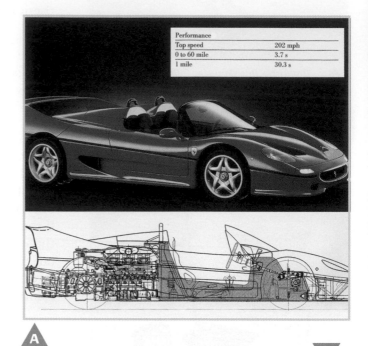

Performance	
Top speed	202 mph
0 to 60 mile	3.7 s
1 mile	30.3 s

A

B

forward force = 2500 N
acceleration = 5 m/s²

forward force = 500 N
acceleration = 1 m/s²

Newton's Second Law

We can work out the force accelerating an object if we know:

- its mass
- the acceleration.

force = mass × acceleration
(N)   (kg)   (m/s²)

Worked example

If a bungee jumper with a mass of 80 kg accelerates upwards from the bottom of his fall at 5 m/s², what overall force is acting on him?

force = mass × acceleration
    = 80 kg × 5 m/s²
    = 400 N

We can rearrange the equation to work out the mass or acceleration.

Worked example

A motorcycle is pushed by a force from its engine of 1000 N. It has a mass of 200 kg. What is it acceleration?

$$\text{force} = \text{mass} \times \text{acceleration}$$

$$\text{so} \quad \frac{\text{force}}{\text{mass}} = \text{acceleration}$$

$$\text{or} \quad \text{acceleration} = \frac{\text{force}}{\text{mass}}$$

$$= \frac{1000 \text{ N}}{200 \text{ kg}}$$

$$= 5 \text{ m/s}^2$$

4 Calculate the masses of the cars in picture B.

5 For each of the following, calculate the missing quantity, showing your working and giving the correct units:
   a) mass = 50 kg, acceleration = 10 m/s², force = ?
   b) force = 10 000 N, acceleration = 125 m/s², mass = ?
   c) mass = 75 kg, force = 15 N, acceleration = ?

2 a) Cyclist A is able to produce twice the forward force of cyclist B. Which cyclist will have the greatest acceleration if they have the same mass?
   b) Both cycles have exactly the same brakes, which the cyclists press with the same force. What can you say about the deceleration of the cyclists if they have the same mass?

3 A 3000 N force is acting on each of the objects in the list.
   A A car of mass 2000 kg
   B A mouse of mass 0.05 kg
   C A person of mass 60 kg
   D A plane of mass 50 000 kg
   a) Put the objects in order, starting with the one with the most acceleration.
   b) Calculate the acceleration in each case.

One newton is the force needed to give a mass of one kilogram an acceleration of one metre per second squared.

P How can you investigate what happens to the acceleration of a trolley when you increase its mass?

C

Summary

Imagine you are writing a brochure for the car shown in picture A. Design an introductory page which explains what affects the acceleration of a car. Include how scientists would calculate the car's acceleration, and what your company's design team have done to get the best possible acceleration in your car.

Gravity, mass and weight

What is weight and how can we calculate it?

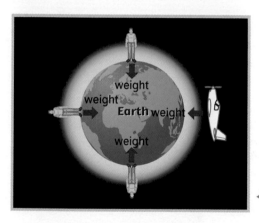

A Astronauts wear special boots which add extra mass and make them heavier.

B

When astronauts got to the Moon, they found that walking across the surface of the Moon was very different from walking on the Earth. This is because they had less **weight** on the Moon. There was less force pulling them down towards the ground.

 1 How can astronauts make themselves heavier so they can walk more easily on the moon?

Gravity and weight

Any object that is falling towards the ground, will speed up as it falls. The object accelerates. This is always true and it happens because of **gravity**. The force of gravity is called weight.

All objects attract each other by gravity. You will be attracting this book and this book will be attracting you, but the force is so small that you can't detect it. The Earth is so huge that the attractive force between the Earth and you is noticeable and keeps you on the ground. The weight of any object always points to the centre of the Earth.

2 True or false?
  a) The force of gravity is called weight.
  b) Objects always fall at a steady speed.

The gravitational field strength around a black hole is so strong that even light is pulled in towards it. This means we cannot see black holes as no light comes from them. We can sometimes tell they are there as gases from nearby stars are pulled into the black hole with such a large acceleration that the gases emit X-rays.

3 On the planet Pluto there is less gravity than there is on the Earth.
  a) Would your weight be more or less on Pluto than it is on the Earth?
  b) Would your acceleration be more or less on Pluto than on the Earth if you fell?

The strength of gravity is called the **gravitational field strength**. Gravity or gravitational field strength is measured in **newtons per kilogram (N/kg)**.

Each planet has a different gravitational field strength.

- The bigger the gravitational field strength, the faster an object will accelerate when it falls towards the surface of the planet.
- The bigger the gravitational field strength, the bigger the weight of a certain object.

The gravitational field strength on the Earth is 10 N/kg. This means that each kilogram of mass has a weight of 10 newtons.

Mass

We know that if gravity changes, the weight of an object also changes. However, the object itself does not change. The **mass** is the amount of **matter** in an object and this only changes if something is cut off or added to the object. So, if you go to the Moon you may weigh less but you won't have changed mass and so you will look exactly the same. Mass is measured in kilograms (kg).

losing mass and weight

only losing weight

C

Calculating weight

The weight of an object can be worked out if you know:

- the mass of the object
- the gravitational field strength.

weight = mass × gravitational field strength
(N)   (kg)   (N/kg)

Weight is a force, so it is measured in newtons (N).

Worked example

A girl of mass 65 kg goes to the Moon where the gravitational field strength is 1.6 N/kg. What will her weight be on the Moon?

weight = mass   ×   gravitational field strength
       = 65   ×   1.6
       = 104 N

8 If your mass were 80 kg, calculate how much you would weigh on Earth, the Moon and Jupiter. (The gravitational field strength on Jupiter is 25 N/kg.)

9 Explain the effects of the following on mass, weight and acceleration caused by gravity.
   a) The effects on a hot air balloon of throwing two 10 kg sandbags out of the basket.
   b) The effects on a submarine of firing a torpedo.

4 Write down whether each of these events will change the mass *and* the weight of something or *only* the weight.

   a) Moving an object from Earth to the Moon.
   b) Cutting your hair.
   c) Feeding a cat.
   d) Going to Mars.

5 Copy and complete the following table:

Weight (N)	Mass (kg)	Gravity (N/kg)
	50	10
	100	10
	20	5
	2	3
	60	4

6 What units is mass measured in?

7 An astronaut has a mass of 70 kg. He travels from the Earth to the Moon, where the gravitational field strength is 1.6 N/kg.
   a) What is the astronaut's weight on the Moon?
   b) What is the change in the astronaut's weight as he travels from the Earth to the Moon?
   c) What could cause his mass to change on the trip?

Summary

Draw a cartoon strip about two astronauts who go on a trip to the Moon. Your story should explain everything on these two pages, including the differences between gravity, mass and weight, and some calculations of weight on Earth and the Moon.

Terminal velocity

What is terminal velocity?

If an object falls, the gravitational pull of the Earth makes the object accelerate. The faster the object travels in the air the bigger the air resistance trying to slow it down. So can an object carry on getting faster forever as it falls?

The answer is no since forces become balanced, and the object will travel at a steady speed.

Air resistance and terminal velocity

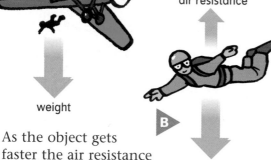

A When an object falls, it accelerates as its weight pulls it down.

air resistance

B

weight

weight

As the object gets faster the air resistance gets bigger.

Eventually the object goes so fast that its air resistance is as big as the weight. The forces are balanced so the object stops accelerating and falls at a steady speed. This is called its **terminal velocity**.

? 3 What happens to the air resistance of a parachutist when the parachute is opened?

4 When an object is travelling at its terminal velocity, what can you say about the forces acting on it?

? 1 What is the name of the force that:
  a) pulls objects towards the Earth
  b) tries to slow things down as they travel through the air?

2 What will happen to the speed of a falling object if the weight pulling down on the object is equal to the air resistance pushing up on the object?

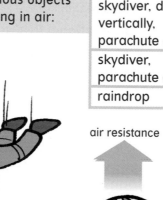

air resistance

C

weight

! This table shows approximate terminal velocities for various objects falling in air:

Object	Terminal velocity
skydiver, lying flat, parachute closed	56 m/s
skydiver, diving vertically, parachute closed	143 m/s
skydiver, parachute open	3 m/s
raindrop	76 m/s

The object can increase its air resistance by increasing its surface area or by being less streamlined. Now the upward force is bigger than the downward weight. This will make the object slow down.

All fluids (i.e. all liquids and gases) have the same sort of frictional effects, so falling through oil or water, for example, will also lead to a terminal velocity.

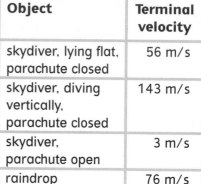

air resistance

D

weight

air resistance

E weight

As the object slows down, the air resistance decreases until it reaches the same size as the weight. The forces are now balanced again so the object falls at a new steady speed. It has a new terminal velocity.

How could you find out the best shape for a parachute?

The engine in a vehicle produces a forward force that pushes the vehicle forward. This is called the **driving force**. Every vehicle has a maximum driving force that its engine can produce.

Vehicles have a maximum velocity, when the maximum driving force is cancelled out by friction and air resistance. When the forces are balanced the vehicle cannot accelerate any more and will travel at a steady speed.

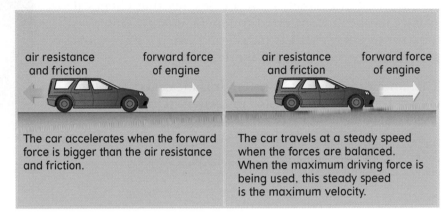

air resistance and friction | forward force of engine

The car accelerates when the forward force is bigger than the air resistance and friction.

air resistance and friction | forward force of engine

The car travels at a steady speed when the forces are balanced. When the maximum driving force is being used, this steady speed is the maximum velocity.

5 If you jump out of a very high aeroplane you won't accelerate all the way down to the ground. Why not?

6 A bird is flying back to its nest holding a grape. Whilst hovering over a lake, the bird loses its grip on the grape which then falls.
   a) Explain what will happen to the speed of the grape as it falls through the air.
   b) What will happen to the speed of the grape when it hits the water?

7 a) Explain why a fisherman who has caught an old boot can only reel it in at a certain maximum speed.
   b) If he had caught a live fish, suggest a reason why the maximum speed to reel it in would be less than for the boot. Give a reason why the maximum speed could be more than for the boot.

8 An Australian parachutist called Rodd Millner is planning to skydive from the very upper limit of the atmosphere. Explain why, even if he maintains the same body shape, his terminal velocity will change as he falls lower and lower in the atmosphere. Consider only the time *before* he opens his parachute.

Summary

Using your own words, and diagrams to help if you wish, explain what terminal velocity is, and how it would be reached by a stone released at the surface of a deep lake.

Work and energy transfer

How can we calculate the amount of work done?

When a force moves something we say that **work** is done. This involves changing one form of **energy** into another. For instance, when an engine moves a car forward, **chemical energy** stored in the fuel is changed into **kinetic (movement) energy**. We say that chemical energy has been transferred to kinetic energy. The amount of energy that is transferred when a force moves something is known as the **work done**.

The amount of energy transferred is measured in **joules** (J). So, the work done is also measured in joules.

 1 Explain why the unit for work done is 'joules'.

A *These people have to do work to push the car.*

E **Calculating the work done**

The work done can be found if you know:

- the force applied
- the distance over which the force is applied.

work done = force applied × distance moved in the direction of the force
   (J)   (N)   (m)

Worked examples

A A car pushes itself forward with a force of 1000 N. If it moves 200 m, what is the work done by the car?

Work done = force applied × distance moved in the direction of the force

= 1000 N × 200 m

= 200 000 J.

B A crane lifts a load off the ground to a height of 20 m. If the weight of the load is 500 N, what is the work done by the crane?

Work done = force applied × distance moved in the direction of the force

= 500 N × 20 m

= 10 000 J.

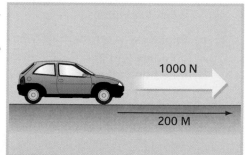

B *The force and the distance must be in the same direction.*

1000 N
200 M

C the crane pulls up with a force of 500 N

20 m
500 N

P How would you work out how much work you have done today? **D**

Elastic potential energy

Work is done whenever a force is applied over a distance. This means that if a force changes the shape of an object, work must be done.

When you stretch a spring or elastic band, you use a force over a distance. Work is being done, so energy is being transferred. The energy that you use to do the work is changed into stored energy in the spring or elastic band. This stored energy is called **elastic potential energy**. **E**

elastic band

Newton meter

stretched elastic band

6 a) The crate that the man in picture G is pushing has a mass of 20 kg. What is its weight?
  b) How much work would the man have to do to lift it vertically 1 m onto the back of the truck?

2 m

G

  c) If the man pushes it up the plank, the force he works against is 125 N. How much work does this require?
  d) In both cases, the crate gains the same amount of potential energy. Why does pushing it up the plank need more work?
  e) Why might the man still prefer to use the plank, even though he wastes energy with that method?

2 If something is lifted it gains gravitational potential energy. 100 J of chemical energy is changed into gravitational potential energy when a gardener picks up a large plant. How much work does the gardener do?

3 Copy and complete the table below:

Work done = (J)	Force applied × (N)	Distance moved in the direction of the force (m)
	23	2
	4	50
	35	4
	14	10
	10	24

4 Draw three situations where work is being done. Show on your diagrams the force and direction of the distance moved. Here is an example:

F

5 Which requires more work to be done, lifting a weight of 10 N a height of 0.5 m or pushing the same weight a distance of 2 m against a friction force of 5 N?

Summary

Define and explain the scientific use of the word 'work'. Include an explanation of how to calculate it, with a worked example of your own.

Kinetic energy

What is kinetic energy and how can we calculate it?

Life would be very boring if we couldn't move around. In fact all of our daily activities need movement energy, even thinking. **Kinetic energy** is the scientific name for movement energy.

Kinetic energy and mass

If a bicycle and a lorry are driving towards you at the same speed, it is more worrying if you are standing in front of the lorry. The lorry has got more kinetic energy than the bicycle, which makes it do more damage if it hits an object. Two objects travelling at the same speed can have different amounts of kinetic energy, because they have different amounts of mass.

> *The bigger the mass of an object, the greater its kinetic energy at a certain speed.*

? **1** **a)** If a hippo and a rat are both running at 1 m/s, which has the most kinetic energy?
b) Explain your answer.

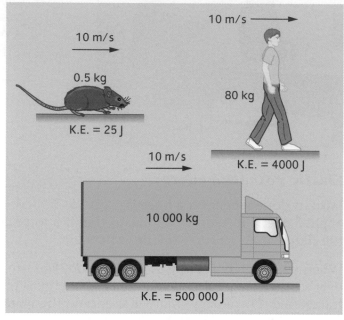

A *Things travelling at the same speed have different amounts of kinetic energy (K.E.) because they have different masses.*

! The wind speed in a tornado funnel can exceed 200 mph.

Kinetic energy and speed

Although the mass of an object affects its kinetic energy, the speed of the object is even more important. The faster a vehicle is travelling, the harder it is to stop as it has more kinetic energy to change into other forms of energy. In fact, if you double the speed of an object it will have *four* times more kinetic energy.

> *The greater the speed of an object, the greater its kinetic energy.*

? **2** Why is a car travelling at 10 m/s harder to stop than a car travelling at 5 m/s?

The faster the wind speed, the greater the damage it causes as it has much more energy. **B**

E Calculating kinetic energy

The kinetic energy of an object can be found if you know:

- the mass of the object
- the speed of the object.

$$\text{kinetic energy} = \tfrac{1}{2} \times \text{mass} \times \text{speed}^2$$
$$\text{(J)} \qquad\qquad \text{(kg)} \quad \text{(m/s)}$$

As kinetic energy is a type of energy it is measured in joules (J).

 3 Look at the equation. What must you remember to do to the speed of an object when you are working out its kinetic energy?

Worked examples

A A car has a mass of 1000 kg and is travelling at 40 m/s. How much kinetic energy does it have?

$$\begin{aligned}
\text{kinetic energy} &= \tfrac{1}{2} \times \text{mass} \times \text{speed}^2 \\
&= 0.5 \times 1000 \times (40)^2 \\
&= 800\,000 \text{ J.}
\end{aligned}$$

B A ball with a mass of 300 g is thrown with a speed of 5 m/s. How much kinetic energy was given to the ball?

$$\begin{aligned}
\text{kinetic energy} &= \tfrac{1}{2} \times \text{mass} \times \text{speed}^2 \\
&= 0.5 \times 0.3 \times (5)^2 \\
&= 3.75 \text{ J.}
\end{aligned}$$

(Remember there are 1000 g in 1 kg!)

Kinetic energy and friction

The more kinetic energy an object has, the more energy it has to transfer to stop it moving. Most vehicles use friction to slow them down. The kinetic energy is transferred to heat energy as the wheels do work against the friction in the brakes.

 4 Copy and complete the table below:

Mass (kg)	Speed (m/s)	Speed²	Kinetic energy (J)
10	5		
20	5		
10	10		
10	20		

5 An ice skater travelling at 2 m/s accelerates to twice this speed. What does his kinetic energy become?

6 Table F on page 181 gives car stopping distances at various speeds. Over the braking distance, the brakes do work transferring the kinetic energy of the car to heat.
   a) If the car has a mass of 1000 kg, calculate its kinetic energy at 10 m/s.
   b) By re-arranging the equation for work done, calculate the braking force under normal conditions.
   c) By how much is the braking force reduced in wet conditions?

P How could you find out how much kinetic energy you have when you run?

C

Summary

Using your own words and examples, answer the topic question at the top of page 192.

The Solar System

What is in the Solar System?

Planets move around the Sun very quickly and since they are so large, they have enormous kinetic energies.

Hundreds of years ago, people believed that the Earth was the centre of the Universe, and everything else went around the Earth. It wasn't until the middle of the 1500s that a scientist called Nicolaus Copernicus showed that the planets actually travel around the Sun.

Planet	Mass	Kinetic energy
Earth	6×10^{24} kg	2.65×10^{33} J
Jupiter	2×10^{27} kg	1.62×10^{35} J
Pluto	1.2×10^{22} kg	1.34×10^{29} J

A The kinetic energies of the planets due to their movement around the Sun.

The Solar System

1 What is at the centre of our Solar System?

B

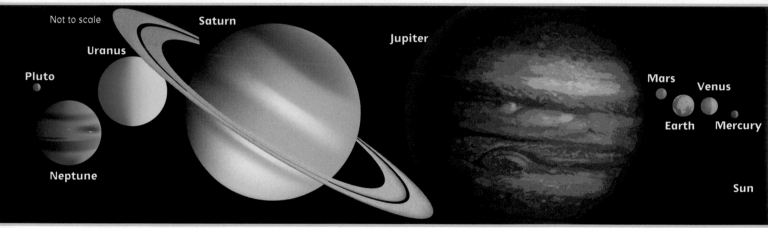

Not to scale

Pluto • Neptune • Uranus • Saturn • Jupiter • Mars • Venus • Earth • Mercury • Sun

In our **Solar System** there is one star which we call the Sun. Nine planets **orbit** (move around) the Sun at different distances from it. The orbits are not circular; they are ellipses (ovals) with the Sun close to the centre. The further away the planet is from the Sun, the longer it will take to complete one orbit.

Stars versus planets

In our Solar System there is only one star. However, from Earth we are able to see billions of other stars that are outside the Solar System. There are a few important differences between planets and stars.

We can see other planets from the Earth because they reflect the light from the Sun. In fact, they look just like stars. Planets are constantly moving around the Sun whereas the stars stay in fixed patterns in the sky. These fixed patterns are called **constellations**. We can tell which of the bright lights in the sky are planets because they will move across the fixed patterns of stars.

Planets:	**Stars:**
• orbit the Sun or another star • do not give out light • reflect light from the Sun or other stars	• stay in a fixed pattern in the sky • give out their own light

C

D

The stars remain in a fixed pattern. Planets move slowly across the pattern of stars.

2 Write down the two main differences between planets and stars.

When we look at other planets from the Earth, the position of the planets in the constellations depends on where the planet and the Earth are in their orbits around the Sun.

The movement of the Earth

The Earth orbits (goes around) the Sun every $364\frac{1}{4}$ days. This gives us the length of our year. At the same time, the Earth spins on a **tilted axis**. It takes 24 hours for the Earth to spin around once. This gives us the length of our day. The side of the Earth that is facing the Sun is in daylight while the other side is in darkness.

Comets

A comet is a lump of rock and ice. Comets also orbit the Sun, but their orbits are even less circular than the planets, with the Sun near to one end of the orbit. It is when the comet travels close to the Sun that the ice melts and a tail of dust and water vapour can be seen reflecting the Sun's light.

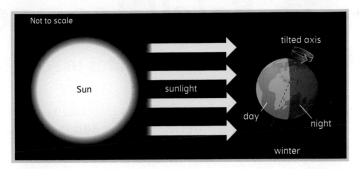

E

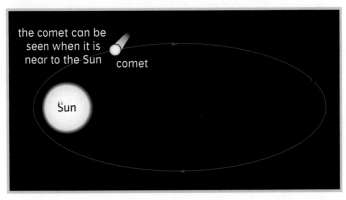

F

3　Why can we see comets when they are near to the Sun?

4　The diagram shows a recently discovered solar system. What are the things labelled a–d?

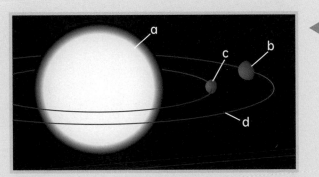

G

5　Explain why we have day and night on Earth.

6　Explain why the days are longer in the summer than in the winter.

7　From the information given in table A on page 194, calculate the speed of movement of the Earth, Jupiter and Pluto.

As it takes $365\frac{1}{4}$ days for the Earth to orbit the Sun, every four years there is an extra day in February. This is called a leap year.

Summary

Draw a fully labelled diagram of the inner part of our Solar System, out as far as Mars. Note on it all movements of the Earth. Include the orbit of a comet which travels close to the Sun (inside Mercury's orbit) and then travels out as far as Mars before returning again. Mark on its orbit the parts where the comet might be visible from Earth.

195

Satellites and orbits

What are satellites used for? What affects the size of an orbit?

A satellite is an object that orbits another larger object. Planets are **natural satellites** of the Sun, and moons are natural satellites of the planets.

A

Orbit size

For an object to stay in a particular orbit it must be travelling at the correct speed. If the speed of the object changes, then the size of the orbit will have to change. In fact, the faster the object is travelling the smaller the orbit can be.

It is the combination of the speed of an object and its gravitational attraction to a larger object that keeps it in orbit.

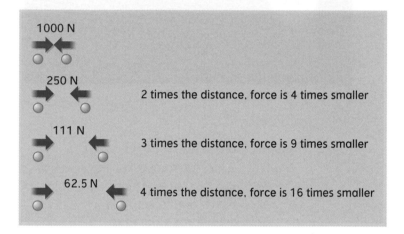

1000 N

250 N — 2 times the distance, force is 4 times smaller

111 N — 3 times the distance, force is 9 times smaller

62.5 N — 4 times the distance, force is 16 times smaller

B

Millions of homes now have **satellite dishes**. These dishes pick up television signals that have been sent from all over the world. The signals are **emitted** (given out) in one part of the world and sent into space where they are received by a **satellite**. The satellite then sends the signal back to satellite dishes on a different part of the Earth.

There are two main types of man-made satellites which orbit the Earth. Each type has a different orbit and different uses.

Geostationary orbit satellites

A **geostationary orbit** is one where the satellite stays above a fixed point on the Earth and follows that point around as the Earth rotates. This means that the satellite takes 24 hours to complete one whole orbit around the Earth.

Gravity and distance

The closer any objects are to each other, the stronger the force of gravity is between them. As objects move closer together they attract each other more. The increase in force is not in **proportion** with the decrease in the distance. This means that the force does not double when the distance is halved. In fact, if the distance between two planets is halved, the gravitational force between them will be *four* times larger, not twice as large.

P How could you find out what happens to the size of an orbit if the force causing it changes size?

C

 The Pegasus is the smallest rocket to launch a satellite into space. It is only 15 m long.

?

1 How long does it take for a satellite on a geostationary orbit to complete one orbit? Choose the correct answer from the list.

   24 hours   24 days   12 hours

2 Explain how a satellite on a geostationary orbit can always be above the same point on the Earth.

Geostationary satellites are usually placed in an orbit very high above the equator. There is only a limited amount of space to put them in, so only around 400 geostationary satellites can be in orbit at any one time. If there are more than this their signals can start to affect each other.

Geostationary orbit satellites are used for communications, including satellite television and telephones.

Polar orbit satellites

Satellites in a **polar orbit** move around the Earth, going over the poles during each orbit. Polar orbits are usually much closer to the Earth than geostationary orbits, and the satellite can orbit the Earth more than once a day. As these satellites move around in their orbits, the Earth is spinning around beneath them and this allows the satellites to scan the entire Earth each day.

For a satellite to stay in a particular orbit it must be travelling at the correct speed. The smaller the orbit of the satellite, the faster it must be travelling. As satellites in polar orbits are closer to the Earth than geostationary orbits they must travel more quickly.

Polar orbit satellites are used for **monitoring** the weather conditions on Earth and also for spying.

Satellites are above the Earth's atmosphere. This means that they can see into space far more clearly than we can from Earth. Scientists trying to find out about the Universe often use satellites to observe space without the **atmosphere** being in the way.

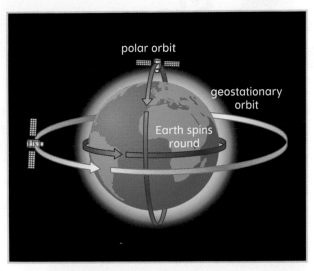

 A satellite on a polar orbit can scan the whole of the Earth as it spins. A satellite in a geostationary orbit stays above one point on the Earth.

 3 Write down two differences between a polar orbit and a geostationary orbit.

4 Write down one use of a polar orbit satellite.

 There is room for about only 400 geostationary satellites or they would interfere with each other's signals.

 5 Why can a satellite see into space more easily than a telescope on Earth?

6 What is the name of the natural satellite that orbits the Earth?

7 Describe how the Olympic games being held in one country can be seen on televisions on the other side of the world.

8 What force keeps satellites in orbit?

9 What would happen to the Earth's orbit around the Sun if the Earth slowed down?

10 Explain the limitations of spy satellites:
   a) if they are in a polar orbit
   b) if they are in a geostationary orbit.

Summary

Write a paragraph summarising the similarities and differences between polar and geostationary orbits and what satellites in those orbits are used for. Include factors that could affect the sizes of the orbits

Stars

How are stars formed?

A The Orion constellation.

Stars are made from dust and gas in space. The gravitational attraction between any particles pulls them together. As the number of particles builds up, the gravitational attraction pulling in more particles of gas gets stronger, until a star exists.

Planets form in a similar way, but don't reach such a large size. The mass of the planet can be attracted to the larger mass of a nearby star and this causes the planet to orbit the star.

? 1 What type of force makes a star form?

There are millions of stars in every galaxy. Scientists have spent centuries recording the positions of the stars in the night sky, putting them into groups called **constellations**.

Nuclear-powered stars

Stars are so enormous that the force of gravity pulling the gas into them is very strong. This holds the star together tightly, but also causes the temperature to get extremely hot. The high temperature makes the star try to **expand** (get bigger).

Squashing gas particles closer together raises the temperature, and when the atoms in a star are forced together **nuclear fusion** reactions can happen. These reactions cause the nuclei of lighter elements (mainly hydrogen and helium) to join together, forming heavier elements. A lot of energy is given out. This raises the star's temperature even more and the star gives out radiation. We can see stars because of this radiation.

The Universe is mainly hydrogen (78%) and partly helium (21%), with a very small amount of all the other elements (1%). The heavier elements are thought to be made in stars through nuclear fusion reactions. These heavier elements are found on Earth, which suggests that our Solar System was formed from the remains of earlier stars which exploded.

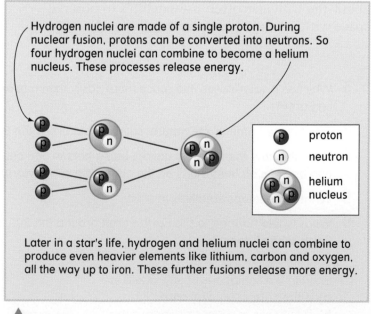

Hydrogen nuclei are made of a single proton. During nuclear fusion, protons can be converted into neutrons. So four hydrogen nuclei can combine to become a helium nucleus. These processes release energy.

p	proton
n	neutron
p n n p	helium nucleus

Later in a star's life, hydrogen and helium nuclei can combine to produce even heavier elements like lithium, carbon and oxygen, all the way up to iron. These further fusions release more energy.

B Nuclear fusion.

The life of a star

So, there is a gravitational force pulling the star inwards and another force caused by the heat pushing the star outwards. Provided that these forces are balanced, the star is **stable** and stays a similar size. Our Sun is in this stage of its life and can stay like this for billions of years.

As a star loses energy it expands until it forms a **red giant**. After more energy is lost, the star collapses as the gravitational force becomes the larger force and pulls the star in on itself. The type of star that forms next depends on the mass of the red giant.

If the red giant is not too massive it becomes a **white dwarf**. The matter in a white dwarf is pulled together so hard that it can be millions of times denser than materials we have here on Earth.

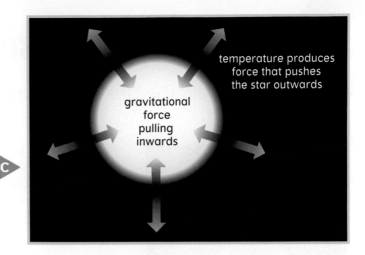

C temperature produces force that pushes the star outwards

gravitational force pulling inwards

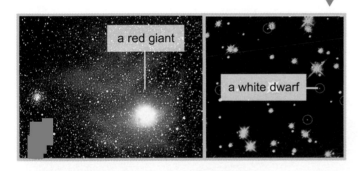

a red giant

a white dwarf

D

If the red giant is massive enough, it can **contract** (get smaller) so quickly that it causes a huge explosion. All the dust and gas in the star gets thrown into space. This is called a **supernova**. Any matter that is left behind forms a small, dense **neutron star**.

If enough matter is left behind, this may be so dense, and its gravitational field so strong that nothing can escape from it, not even light or other forms of electromagnetic radiation. It is then called a **black hole**.

A supernova. E

neutron star

? **2** Explain why our Sun is in the stable stage of its life. Write about forces in your answer.

! The Crab Nebula is a star that exploded into a supernova. This produced the brightest star in the sky, visible even during the day for 3 weeks during 1054.

? **3** When will a red giant form a neutron star instead of a white dwarf?

4 What is a supernova?

5 What is a black hole?

6 Describe the simplest nuclear fusion reaction in stars.

7 a) Why might somebody say 'We are all made from stardust'?

b) What evidence would they have to back up this suggestion?

Summary

Draw a flowchart showing the development of a star including all the possible types of star it could become. Include on your connecting arrows the conditions needed and the processes which occur.

The Universe

How did the Universe begin?

 A galaxy.

Our Sun and the planets orbiting the Sun are called the **Solar System**. The Sun is just one star in a group of stars called a **galaxy**. Our galaxy is called the **Milky Way**. There are at least a billion different galaxies in the Universe. The distances between the planets in the Solar System are enormous, but the distances between stars in a galaxy are even larger. Larger still are the distances between the galaxies.

1 Put the following in order, starting with the largest:

Earth   Moon   Milky Way   Sun   Universe   Solar System

2 What is the scientific name for a group of stars?

The Universe

Many scientists believe that the Universe began with an enormous explosion, called the Big Bang. All the energy and matter that existed was flung outwards into space. The explosion was so massive that scientists believe that the Universe is still getting larger as all the matter continues to move outwards. Over millions of years the stars and planets were formed from this matter and energy.

The evidence

The main evidence that stars and galaxies are moving apart comes from the **red-shift** of starlight. Stars give out a huge range of colours of light, including many that our eyes cannot see, like ultraviolet light. Usually stars emit all wavelengths (colours) – a **spectrum** – but each star's spectrum will have some gaps where colours are not present. Those missing colours are caused by certain elements being present. The gaps are like a fingerprint for the chemicals in the star and we can check the fingerprint against chemicals in lab experiments on Earth. This can tell us what a star is made from.

The big bang.

When we look at light from other galaxies we see the fingerprint *pattern* we would expect but the wavelengths (colours) are wrong. The whole pattern has been shifted towards the red end of the spectrum. This red-shift is caused by the galaxy moving away from us. It is observed for virtually all galaxies, meaning that they are moving away from our own galaxy.

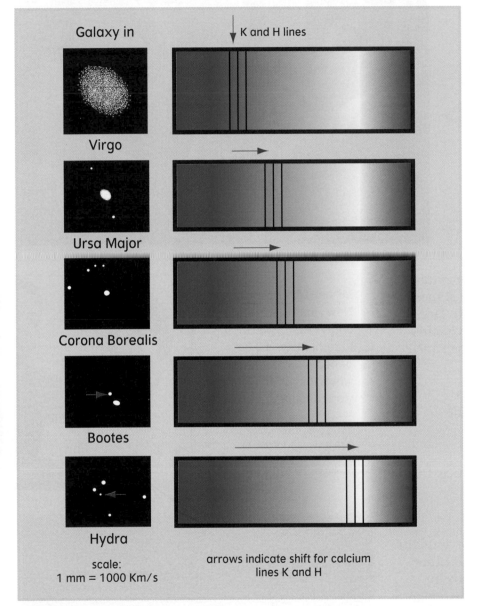

 Images and spectra of five different galaxies.

The Big Bang

It turns out that the red-shift is bigger for more distant galaxies, which means they are moving away from us faster than nearby galaxies. Long ago all the galaxies would be closer together. So, scientists suggest that if we went back far enough in time (billions of years) all the galaxies would be in the same place, about to start moving apart. Scientists call this time the Big Bang.

?

3 What is 'red-shift' in astronomy?

4 How do scientists believe the Universe began?

5 Why do scientists believe all the matter in the Universe was originally in one place?

!

Scientific estimates for the age of the Universe range from 10 to 20 billion years old. This means the diameter of the Universe could be between 190 000 billion billion kilometres and 380 000 billion billion kilometres. The best estimates are roughly in the middle of these ranges.

? **6** Look at the spectra of light for the galaxies in picture C.
   a) Which is the most distant galaxy?
   b) Which is the fastest moving galaxy, and what tells us its speed?

Summary

Write a paragraph summarising the ideas and evidence that scientists have about the origin of the Universe.

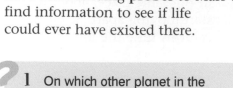 **Life in the Universe**

Is there life beyond the Earth?

Films like E.T., Star Wars and Men in Black are based on the idea that there are other life forms living on planets in space. Scientists are trying to find evidence for life on other planets and have been sending **probes** to Mars to find information to see if life could ever have existed there.

A

> **? 1** On which other planet in the Solar System are we trying to find evidence of extra-terrestrial life at the moment?

Finding proof that there is or has been extra-terrestrial life of some kind does not just mean we actually have to see creatures face to face. There are many ways that we can prove other forms of life have existed outside of the Earth.

> **? 2 a)** Do you think we can prove that dinosaurs ever existed on Earth?
> **b)** What evidence do we have?

There are three main ways we can look for evidence of other life forms:

Finding fossils

By sending robots to the Moon and eventually to other planets, samples of rocks and other materials can be brought back to Earth for scientists to investigate. Robots can also take pictures of the planets that can be sent back to Earth. This has been done for Mars and Europa (a natural satellite that orbits Jupiter).

> **? 3** What two things can robots bring back to Earth for scientists to investigate?

! Mr and Mrs Hill from New Hampshire underwent hypnosis to remember a 3 hour period of time, during which they believed they were abducted by aliens.

Barney and Betty Hill, allegedly abducted by aliens in Virginia, USA in 1961.

B

A robot exploring Mars. **C**

Receiving signals from space

Radio telescopes can pick up radio signals from outer space. This is called the search for extra-terrestrial intelligence (SETI). Scientists have to try to sort out what could be meaningful signals, sent from other life forms, from the general background **noise** that is picked up. They monitor a narrow band of wavelengths to do this. They have been trying to detect signals for over 40 years, but have not found anything yet. This may be because other life forms don't have the same technology that we do.

4 Why do you think we have not yet received radio signals from extra-terrestrial life in outer-space?

Finding chemical changes caused by organisms

Living organisms change their environment. If these changes can be detected it can provide evidence that they exist. An example of this on Earth is the amount of oxygen in the air. If there was no life on Earth the amount of oxygen would be much lower.

The type of life that exists on Earth depends mainly on carbon and water to survive. Scientists get excited if they find these substances on other planets as it makes it more likely that life may have existed there.

D A radio telescope.

5 What two main things do living creatures on Earth need to survive?

6 Why do you think it is easier to send a robot to Mars to look for evidence than it is to send a human? Use the words 'temperature', 'atmosphere' and 'oxygen' in your answer.

7 Scientists at the SETI project have picked up radio signals. Why have they not claimed that there is extra-terrestrial life?

8 How could scientists decide which planets are best to send probes to?

E

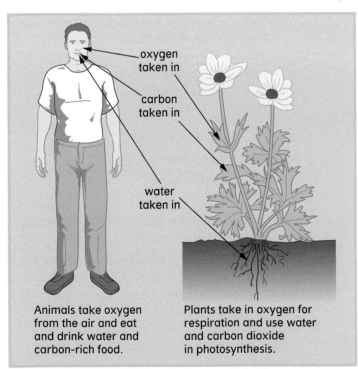

oxygen taken in

carbon taken in

water taken in

Animals take oxygen from the air and eat and drink water and carbon-rich food.

Plants take in oxygen for respiration and use water and carbon dioxide in photosynthesis.

Summary

Write a script for a short radio news item which explains to listeners the ways in which scientists are searching for life beyond the Earth.

1 A woman walks to work each morning. The graph shows her journey.

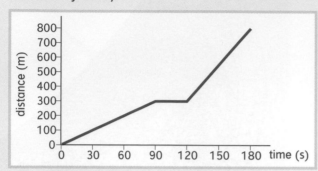

a) Between what times was the woman:

i) standing still?

ii) moving the fastest? (2)

b) Calculate the woman's mean (average) speed for the whole journey. Show your working. (2)

c) Calculate the woman's fastest speed. Show your working. (2)

2 The submarine in the diagram is travelling at a steady speed.

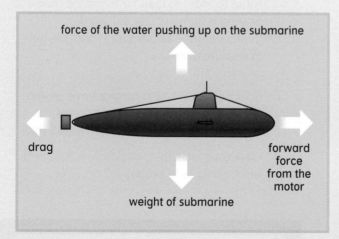

force of the water pushing up on the submarine

drag

forward force from the motor

weight of submarine

a) Explain why the forward force of the motor is not making the submarine accelerate. (1)

b) The forward force increases.

i) What happens to the movement of the submarine?

ii) Explain your answer. (2)

3 A car accelerates from 0 m/s to 30 m/s in 5 seconds. It then travels at a constant velocity for 10 seconds, before it slows down and stops in a further 5 seconds.

a) Calculate the acceleration of the car. Show your working. (2)

b) Draw a velocity-time graph of the journey. (3)

c) What is the deceleration of the car at the end of the journey? (2)

d) Work out how far the car travelled. (2)

4 The diagram shows the forces acting on a car.

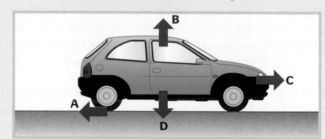

a) Choose the correct forces from the list to label the forces A to D. (4)

> friction   upward force of the ground
> driving force of the motor   weight

b) Copy and complete the following table, stating whether the car will speed up, slow down or stay the same speed. (3)

Force A is bigger than force C	
Force A is smaller than force C	
Force A is equal to force C	

5 **a)** A motorcyclist and her bike have a total mass of 250 kg. What is their combined weight? (1)

b) If the bike can reach a speed of 40 m/s from rest in 5 seconds, what is its acceleration? (2)

c) What overall forward force would be needed to give this acceleration? (2)

d) Why would the engine's force need to vary to keep this constant acceleration for the whole 5 seconds? (3)

6 a) Copy and complete the table, placing the conditions into the correct columns.

Increase thinking distance	Increase braking distance

Conditions:

driver who is drunk

ice on the road

worn brake pads

driver who is tired

rain (5)

b) Describe how an airbag can protect a driver or passenger during a crash. Use the following words in your answer: force, decelerate. (2)

7 A student has to lift a pile of books onto a table. Calculate the amount of work done lifting the books. Show your working. (2)

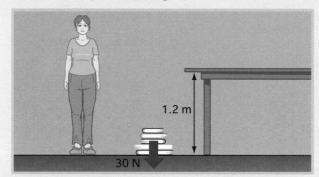

1.2 m

30 N

8 a) Choose the correct satellite orbit, polar or geostationary, to fit each of the sentences.

i) Can observe the whole of the Earth in one day.

ii) Takes 24 hours to make one complete orbit.

iii) Used for communications and satellite television.

iv) Used to monitor the weather. (4)

b) How are scientists trying to gather evidence for extra-terrestrial life? (3)

9 a) Why is nuclear fusion important for stars? (1)

b) Define the term 'galaxy'. (1)

c) Why do scientists believe the Universe is expanding? (3)

10

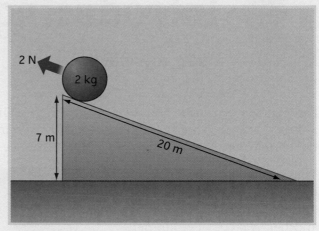

2 N

2 kg

7 m

20 m

a) Calculate the work done against friction as the ball rolls down the slope.

b) The ball is travelling at 10 m/s at the bottom of the slope. Use the equation to find the amount of kinetic energy the ball has.

kinetic energy $= \frac{1}{2} \times$ mass $\times$ speed^2 (4)

11 a) Copy and complete the sentences:

The Earth _____ the Sun in _____ days. The Earth spins on its axis once every 24 _____. (3)

b) i) At night, how can we see the stars in the sky?

ii) At night, how can we see the Moon and other planets in the sky? (2)

c) Stars and planets look similar in the night sky. Explain how we can tell which of the bright lights are stars and which are planets. (1)

12 a) Copy and complete the table:

Object mass (kg)	Planet gravitational field strength (N/kg)	Weight of the object on the planet (N)
2	10	
5	10	
10	1.6	
0.2	8	
6	16	

(5)

b) i) Explain why the weights of astronauts change when they go to the Moon.

ii) An astronaut has a mass of 80 kg on the Earth. What is the mass of the astronaut on the Moon? (2)

Introducing waves

What are waves?

Earthquakes can cause a lot of damage, often killing people and animals, and destroying buildings. Earthquakes are shock waves travelling through the Earth and along its surface.

These waves are called **seismic waves** and carry a lot of **kinetic energy** from one place to another. A piece of equipment called a **seismograph** is used to detect seismic waves. Scientists can learn about the structure of the Earth by studying how the seismic waves pass through it.

One full swing of a wave from the top to the bottom and back again is called an **oscillation**. The time taken for one complete oscillation is called the **period**.

B *As the Earth's surface moves, the seismograph records the size of the shake and the time it arrives.*

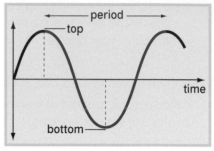

C *One oscillation (shown in red).*

1 How could an earthquake in Germany be detected in Spain?

2 An earthquake occurs in San Francisco and is detected by a seismograph. Look at diagram D.
  a) How long did the shock wave take to reach the seismograph?
  b) How many oscillations took place during the first second of the shock wave?
  c) What is the period of this shock wave?

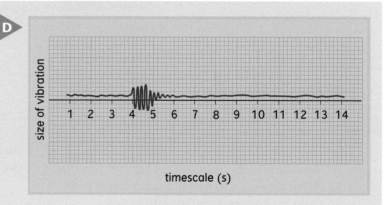

D

size of vibration

1 2 3 4 5 6 7 8 9 10 11 12 13 14

timescale (s)

There are two main types of seismic waves: **transverse** waves and **longitudinal** waves. You can study both types of waves using a spring. Both types of waves have features in common:

- part of the spring is disturbed when the wave passes through
- regular patterns can be seen
- energy moves from one end of the spring to the other.

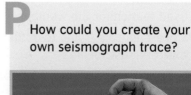

P How could you create your own seismograph trace?

E

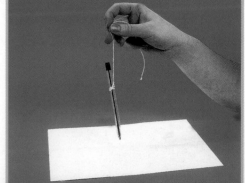

! In 1976, an earthquake in Tangshan, China killed 242 000 people.

Transverse waves

When the end of a spring is moved up and down, all parts of the spring move up and down repeatedly as energy passes from one end to the other. The spring is disturbed *at right angles* to the direction that the wave travels. This type of wave is called a transverse wave.

Longitudinal waves

If the end of the spring is pushed forwards and backwards, sections of the spring are squashed or stretched as the energy passes from one end to the other. The spring is disturbed *in the same direction* that the wave travels. This type of wave is called a longitudinal wave.

Regions where the spring is squashed together are called **compressions** and those where the spring is stretched out are called **rarefactions**. Longitudinal waves are sometimes called compression waves.

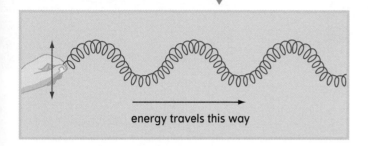

F

energy travels this way

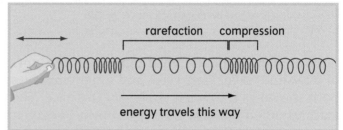

G

rarefaction   compression

energy travels this way

3 Waves can be seen on the surface of bath water. Look at diagram H.

H

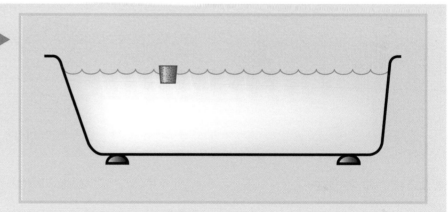

  a) Are the surface water waves transverse or longitudinal?

  b) Describe the motion of the cork floating on the surface.

4 Longitudinal waves are sometimes called compression waves. Why is this?

5 Copy the table. Use ticks to compare transverse and longitudinal waves.

Feature	Transverse waves	Longitudinal waves
these waves transfer energy		
regular disturbances can be seen		
disturbances move from side to side		
disturbances move forward and back		

6 Why do seagulls sitting on the sea bob up and down as the waves pass, but not move in towards the beach with the waves?

7 **a)** How do waves transfer energy along a spring without any mass travelling from one end to the other?

  b) What variables could be changed when sending waves along a spring?

Summary

Draw a diagram of a transverse wave and a longitudinal wave. Write notes to explain the differences between them.

Speed of waves

How fast do waves travel?

Often seismographs will show two vibrations caused by the same earthquake. The earthquake creates two different types of wave which travel at different speeds.

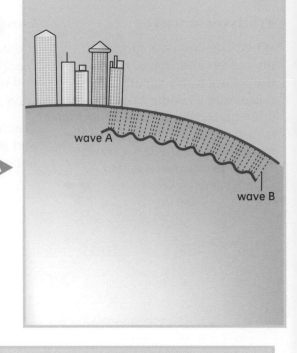

A

wave A

wave B

? 1 Diagram A shows seismic waves passing through the Earth. Which wave is longitudinal, A or B?

Look at diagram B. The **seismograph trace** shows the shape of a seismic wave. Transverse and longitudinal waves are both shown as transverse waves on the trace. The main features of a transverse wave are shown in diagram C.

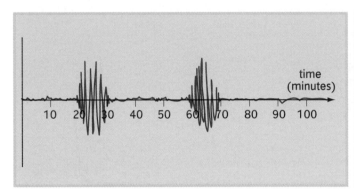

time (minutes)

10 20 30 40 50 60 70 80 90 100

B A seismograph trace.

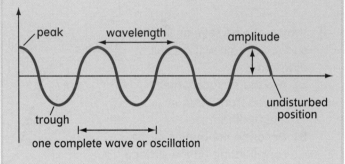

peak   wavelength   amplitude

trough

undisturbed position

one complete wave or oscillation

C A transverse wave.

The number of complete waves (oscillations) detected by the seismograph every second is the **frequency**. Frequency is measured in **hertz** (Hz). If three waves pass the seismograph in 1 second, then the frequency is 3 hertz.

The length of one complete wave is called the **wavelength**. Wavelength is measured from any point on one wave to exactly the same point on the next wave. Wavelength is measured in metres.

The height of a peak measured from the undisturbed position is the **amplitude**. The stronger the earthquake, the bigger the amplitude of the seismic waves.

? 2 Jake is studying a seismograph trace. Eight waves pass each second.
  a) What is the frequency of the wave?
  b) How many complete waves (oscillations) will pass in 4 seconds?
  c) What is the period of one oscillation?

? 3 Copy diagram D. Add these labels: amplitude, wavelength.

D

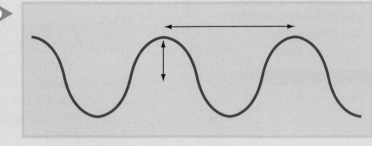

E

You can work out the speed of a wave if you know:

- how many waves pass each second (the **frequency**)
- how long each wave is (the **wavelength**).

wave speed = frequency × wavelength
(m/s)   (Hz)   (m)

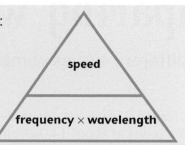

speed

frequency × wavelength

4 A wave's frequency is 100 Hertz and its wavelength is 12 m. What is its speed?

Worked example

The frequency of a sound wave is 165 hertz. Its wavelength is 2 metres. What is its speed?

Frequency   = 165 Hz
Wavelength   = 2 m
Speed   = frequency × wavelength
             = 165 × 2
             = 330 m/s.

Earthquakes at sea cause very fast waves, which slow down when they reach land. Their amplitude increases as they slow down. The amplitude can be up to 75 m, so these waves can be very destructive.

E

5 Look at diagram G. Both waves travel at the same speed.

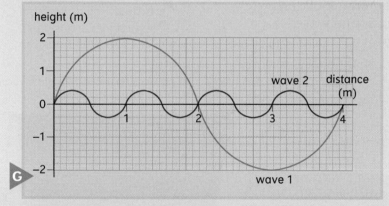

G

a) Use the diagram to find the amplitude of each wave.
b) Write down the wavelength of each wave.
c) Wave 1 has a frequency of 2.1 Hz. What is the frequency of wave 2?
d) Calculate the speed of each wave.

P

How could you measure the speed of seismic waves in water?

F

6 The table below gives information about four different waves. Copy and complete the table.

	Frequency (Hz)	Wavelength (m)	Speed (m/s)
Wave 1	300	1.1	
Wave 2	100		330
Wave 3	100		1500
Wave 4	5×10^{14}	600×10^{-9}	

Summary

A Explain the meaning of each word written in bold on these two pages.

B Copy the wave speed equation. Show how it can be rearranged to make frequency or wavelength the subject of the equation.

Comparing waves

How do different waves compare?

Longitudinal seismic waves (called P waves) travel at about 2000 m/s near the surface of the Earth. They travel at about 14 000 m/s deep inside the Earth. This is because the inside of the Earth is more **dense** than the surface. If scientists can work out the speed of a longitudinal seismic wave, they can work out what sort of rock it travelled through.

Speeds of P waves in different sorts of rock.

granite - 5900 m/s

basalt - 6400 m/s

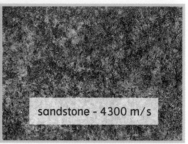

sandstone - 4300 m/s

1 a) Which rock is the most dense? Explain your answer.

b) Calculate the difference between the speeds of P waves in basalt and sandstone.

2 In which material will sound waves travel fastest – oil or wood? Explain your answer.

Sound also travels as a longitudinal wave. Sound waves travel faster in solids (6000 m/s in steel), slower in liquids (1500 m/s in water) and slowest in gases (340 m/s in air). Sound waves do not travel at all in empty space (a **vacuum**).

Seismic P waves are produced by parts of the Earth vibrating. Sound waves are also produced from vibrating objects. If you feel your throat when you speak, you can feel your 'voice box' vibrating.

 Sound does not travel through a vacuum. Astronauts must talk using radio links.

Light also travels as waves but light waves are transverse waves. Light waves are produced by glowing objects such as the Sun, a light bulb or a flame. These waves travel fastest in a vacuum, but more slowly through **transparent** materials such as glass, Perspex and water. Light will not travel through **opaque** materials (things which are not see-through).

3 Write down four differences between light waves and sound waves.

4 In what ways are sound waves and seismic P waves similar?

	Light	**Sound**
cause of the energy	glowing object	vibrating object
travels quickest through:	empty space (vacuum)	solids
speed in air	300 000 000 m/s	340 m/s
type of wave	transverse	longitudinal

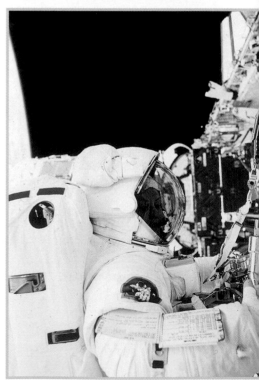

5 Copy and complete the table:

	Transverse wave	Longitudinal wave
a sketch of the wave	amplitude, wavelength	compression, rarefaction
example of each type of wave		
Will the wave travel through:		
● air		
● a vacuum		
● glass		
● wood		
● water		

! When things go faster than sound they are said to break the sound barrier. In certain weather conditions, you can see where the shock waves are produced as the sound barrier is broken. **E**

P How could you investigate what affects the sound that a vibrating object makes? **F**

Summary

Copy table C and add an extra column to include information about seismic P waves.

6 After an earthquake, people trapped under fallen buildings call for help but often can't be heard. People are advised to tap on metal pipes instead. Why?

7 Use ideas about particles and longitudinal waves to explain why sound does not travel through a vacuum.

8 If the Sun is 149 600 000 000 m from us and its light takes 500 s to reach us, how fast does light travel?

Reflection and refraction

What are reflection and refraction and how are they useful?

Reflection

Waves travel in straight lines. A straight arrow showing the direction that the wave travels in is called a **ray**. We can often see rays of light.

You can see the Moon at night because rays of sunlight **reflect** off it.

Many diagrams showing reflected light rays use an imaginary line called the **normal** drawn at right angles to the surface. All angles are measured using the normal.

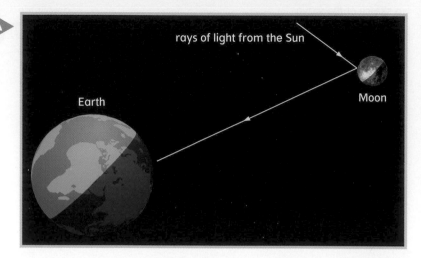

rays of light from the Sun

Earth

Moon

 B *A ray of light being reflected.*

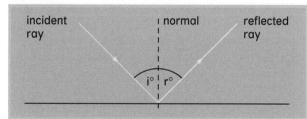

incident ray

normal

reflected ray

$i°$ $r°$

1 A ray of light hits a plane mirror at an angle of 52° to the normal. What will the angle of reflection be?

2 Copy and complete diagram C. Show how the ray reflects from the mirror, so that Georgia can see her feet in the mirror.

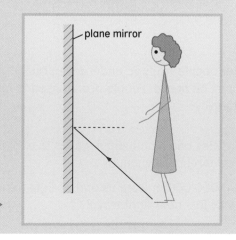

plane mirror

C

 Reflected light from lasers is used to read the bar codes on items bought in shops.

The **angle of incidence** is called angle **i°** and the **angle of reflection** is called angle **r°**. The law of reflection states that:

> *the angle of incidence = the angle of reflection*
> or $i° = r°$

Different types of waves can be reflected:

- Sound waves reflecting off hard surfaces are heard as **echoes**.
- Light reflects from objects into our eyes, allowing us to see things.
- Waves travelling along ropes and springs can be reflected.
- Water waves reflect off river banks and harbour walls.
- Transverse seismic waves (called S waves) reflect inside the Earth when they reach the liquid core.

Refraction of light

Rays of light travelling into glass or water slow down and change direction. This is called **refraction**. The substance through which the light is travelling is called the **medium**. Sound waves also refract when they cross the boundary between two different substances.

Mirages are caused when light is refracted as it travels between a layer of hot air rising from hot ground, and a layer of cooler air above. **D**

Seeing refraction

You can use a block of glass and a ray box to see refraction. **E**

Waves travelling along the normal do not change direction. **F**

Waves arriving at any other angle do change direction. **G**

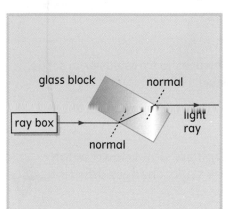

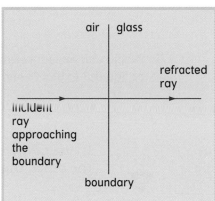

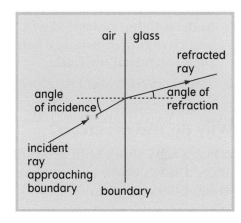

? 3 Copy diagrams H and I. Draw in the missing light rays.

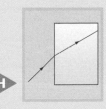 **H**

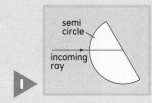 **I**

P How could you find out if light refracts more in different materials? **J**

Summary

A Write down the meanings of these words: medium, reflection, refraction, incident ray, reflected ray, refracted ray, normal.

B Copy diagram B and write out the law of reflection.

? 4 Copy diagram K. **K**

a) Add lines to show a ray of light travelling from the fish to the surface of the water and refracting into the boy's eye.

b) Show on your drawing where the fish would appear to be for the boy. (*Hint*: it's a straight line.)

c) Describe where the boy would appear to be for the fish.

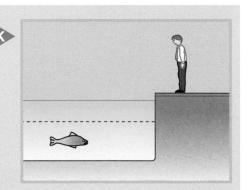

Waves and the Earth

What can seismic waves tell us about the Earth's structure?

All waves change speed when they enter different media. When waves enter the medium at an angle to the normal, they are refracted.

- Light travels at 300 000 000 m/s in a vacuum and at about 200 000 000 m/s in glass.
- Surface water waves travel fastest in deep water, slowing down and changing direction when they reach shallow water.
- Sound waves travel fastest in solids and slowest in gases.

 1 Why do water waves slow down as they approach a beach?

2 Copy and complete this table.

Type of wave	The waves travel fastest in:	The waves travel slowest in:
light waves		
sound waves	solids	
	deep water	

3 Would you expect seismic P waves to travel faster in solids or liquids? Explain your answer.

Why do waves refract?

When a tank slows both caterpillars at once, it slows down and continues in a straight line.

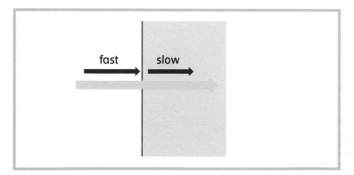

If one of the caterpillars slows down before the other, then the tanks changes direction.

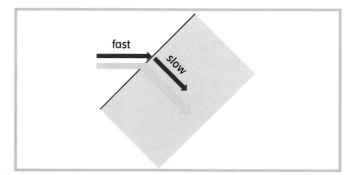

If both sides of a light ray are slowed by the same amount it continues in a straight line.

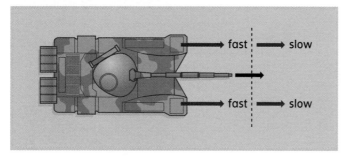

If one side slows down before the other then the ray of light turns (refracts).

 4 Explain why waves approaching a beach at an angle tend to turn in towards the beach.

Seismic wave refraction

The study of seismic waves from earthquakes has revealed that the Earth is made up of many layers. As the shock waves pass from one layer to another they are refracted and slight changes in direction occur. Gradual changes in the density of the rock cause gradual changes in the direction of the waves and they follow a curved path.

More abrupt changes in direction occur as the seismic waves pass between the mantle and the outer core or as they pass between the outer core and the inner core.

The two main types of seismic waves are **S waves** and **P waves**.

S waves are transverse waves and travel through the solid mantle. An S wave shadow is observed on the opposite side of the Earth to the earthquake and this implies that part of the core is liquid because transverse S waves cannot pass through it.

P waves are longitudinal waves like sound waves. They can travel through the liquid outer core and the inner core, and are refracted as they pass from one layer to another.

 E *S waves travel through the mantle but not the core.*

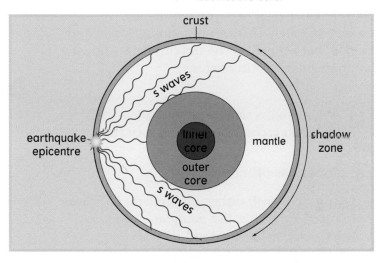

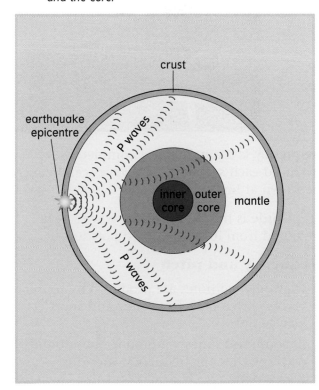

F *P waves travel through both the mantle and the core.*

?

5 Look at diagram E. How can S waves from earthquakes be used to measure the size of the Earth's outer core?

6 a) What will happen to the speed of P waves as they travel from one side of the Earth to the other?
b) Why do seismic waves get refracted as they pass from one layer to another?

Summary

Draw a diagram of the Earth showing both P waves and S waves travelling away from an earthquake. Explain why the waves follow the paths you have shown. Label the S wave shadow zone and explain why S waves do not reach this region.

Sound and ultrasound

How can we see sound waves?

We detect sound waves using our ears. However, electrical systems can be used to produce high frequency oscillations, making sound waves that are too high pitched for us to hear. These waves are called **ultrasound**. Hospitals use ultrasound to examine (scan) unborn babies. The high frequency of ultrasound means that it will partially reflect when it meets the boundary between two different media. The ultrasound waves pass safely through the mother's skin and muscle, but **reflect** off the unborn baby, showing its bones, heart and other organs.

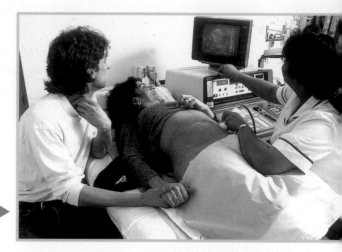

A

 1 What are the similarities and differences between sound waves and ultrasound?

Ultrasound has other uses:

- **Quality control**: ultrasound reflects off cracks in metal structures like aeroplane wings so these defects can be found.
- **Cleaning**: Delicate mechanisms can be placed in liquids and ultrasound waves passed through the liquid. This dislodges the dirt and cleans the mechanism without the need for it to be taken apart.

Picture B shows an **oscilloscope** being used by a sound engineer. The screen displays a sound wave. Sound waves are longitudinal but to make measurements easier the oscilloscope displays the wave as a transverse wave. This is called a **trace**. There are squares on the screen to let the engineer work out the frequency and amplitude of the waves.

! Whales communicate underwater using ultrasound. Their messages can travel many kilometres through the water.

2 Write down three uses of ultrasound waves.

B

3 Copy diagram C. Draw another wave with:
   a) twice the amplitude but the same wavelength
   b) the same amplitude but half the wavelength.

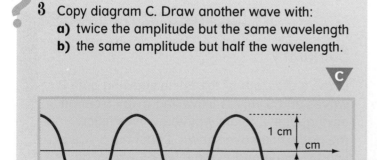

C

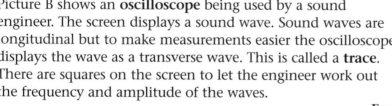

1 cm
cm
1 cm

Frequency is the number of complete waves produced each second. More waves can be seen on screen at high frequency.

Amplitude is the height of the wave's peak measured from its undisturbed position.

Frequency and pitch

- High-pitched notes are produced by sound waves with a high frequency and short wavelength.
- Low-pitched notes are produced by sound waves with a low frequency and long wavelength.

Sound waves range from low rumbles (below 20 Hz) to very high-pitched sounds, above 20 000 Hz. We cannot hear sounds higher than 20 000 Hz.

Amplitude and loudness

- Loud notes are produced by sound waves that have large amplitudes.
- Quiet notes are produced by sound waves that have small amplitudes.

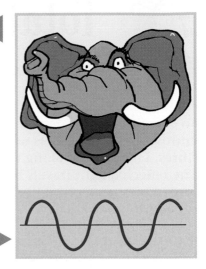

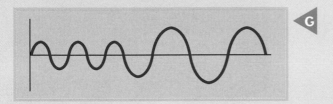

4 Look at diagram G. Copy and label the drawing, showing where the sound is

a) quiet   **b)** loud
c) high pitched   **d)** low pitched.

5 Counter-tenors are men who can sing very high but they have normal speaking voices. Diagram H shows the trace of a counter-tenor speaking. Copy the trace and draw another one to show his trace when singing loudly at a concert.

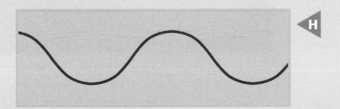

P How can you compare the pitch of different notes using an oscilloscope?

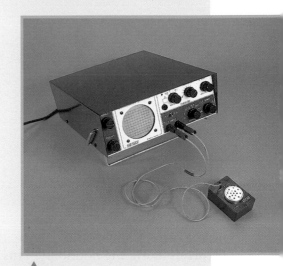

6 Diagram I shows pulses of ultrasound being used to detect a crack in a piece of metal. Ultrasound partially reflects from the surface created by the crack.

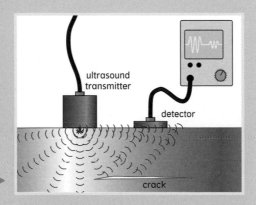

ultrasound transmitter

detector

crack

Explain how the trace on the oscilloscope could be used to calculate how far down the crack is.

Summary

Write five short paragraphs to explain the meaning of the following words: amplitude, frequency, loudness, pitch, ultrasound.

Total internal reflection

What is total internal reflection?

To examine the inside of a patient, doctors often use **endoscopes**. These tools use bundles of **optical fibres**. Light travels along the fibres into the patient. The reflected light travels back along other fibres to form a picture. Optical fibres use **total internal reflection** to do this.

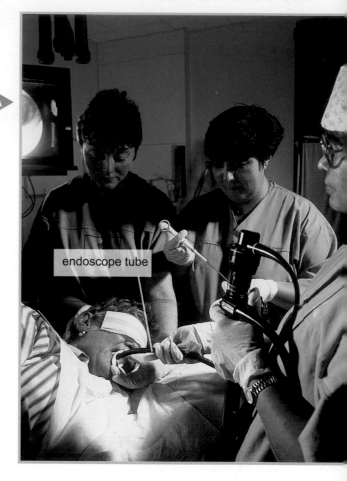

A

endoscope tube

 1 a) Why are endoscopes used in hospitals?
 b) Write down one other use for an endoscope.

Light normally changes direction when it travels from glass, Perspex or water into the air, because of refraction.

B

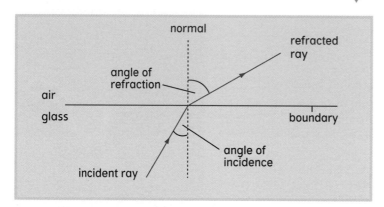

At a certain angle of incidence, the refracted light travels along the boundary. This angle is called the **critical angle**.

C

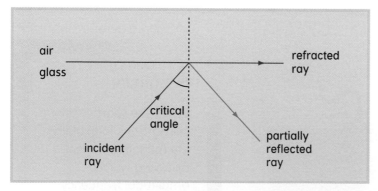

Above this angle, all the light reflects back from the inside surface and none passes through. The surface acts like a mirror. This is total internal reflection.

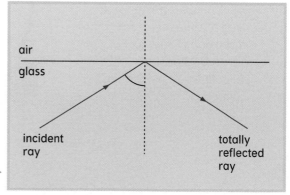

D

 2 Look at diagram C. What is the angle of refraction when the angle between the incident ray and the normal is equal to the critical angle?

P How could you find the critical angle for glass?

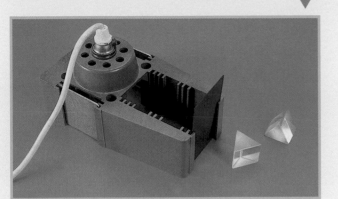

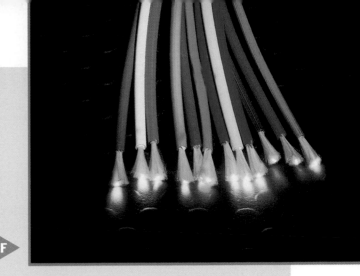

F

The thinnest optical fibres are a billionth of a metre wide and up to 10 km long.

Cat's eyes in the road reflect light from a driver's headlights back into the driver's eyes, lighting up the centre of the road. A prism in a cat's eye uses total internal reflection.

G

Diagram H shows how *repeated* total internal reflection occurs in optical fibres in endoscopes.

H

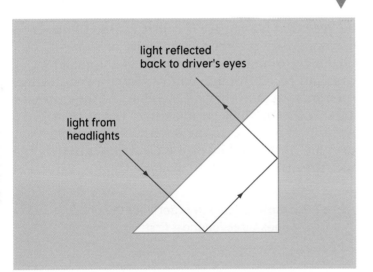

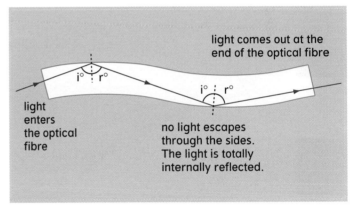

?

3 Why are two bundles of optical fibres needed in an endoscope?

4 Bubbles of gas in lemonade sometimes look shiny. Explain why this happens.

5 Cat's eyes are made using prisms rather than mirrors. What are the advantages of prisms compared to mirrors?

6 Write a sentence explaining how an endoscope can be used to examine the inside of a footballer's damaged knee.

7 Draw a diagram of a periscope using two prisms to reflect the light.

Summary

A Draw a diagram to show a ray of light passing through an optical fibre.

B Use the terms 'critical angle' and 'total internal reflection' to explain why light does not escape through the sides of the optical fibre.

Dispersion

What is dispersion?

Sunlight is made up of different colours of light. These colours can be separated as the light rays shine through raindrops. The spread of colours is called the **visible spectrum**. You can also see a spectrum when white light shines through a prism. This separation of colours is called **dispersion**.

We see a spectrum because different colours of light travel at different speeds through a raindrop or prism. Each colour changes direction (refracts) by a different amount as it moves from air into water or glass, and back out again. Diagram B shows how dispersion occurs.

1 a) What is the weather like when we see rainbows?

b) If you are looking at a rainbow, is the Sun behind you or in front of you?

The light that we can see is called **visible light**. Light waves are members of a family of waves called **electromagnetic waves**. All electromagnetic waves can travel through empty space (**a vacuum**). When in a vacuum they all travel at the same speed (300 000 000 m/s). Electromagnetic waves form a spectrum of waves carrying energy. Visible light waves are in the middle of the **electromagnetic spectrum**. This is shown in diagram C.

2 a) Put these colours in order with the one that changes direction most first:

red　　　　blue　　　　yellow

b) Which of the colours in a) has the longest wavelength?

c) Which one has the highest frequency?

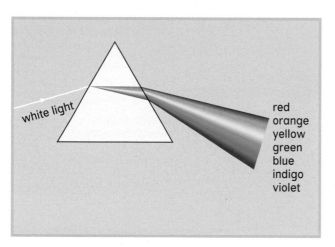

white light

red
orange
yellow
green
blue
indigo
violet

B This is how a prism disperses white light into a spectrum. Red light changes direction least. Violet (purple) light changes direction most.

C The electromagnetic spectrum.

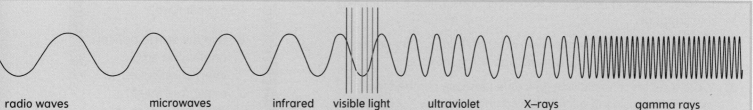

| radio waves | microwaves | infrared | visible light (visible spectrum) | ultraviolet | X–rays | gamma rays |
| 1000 m | 1 m | 1 mm | 0.001 mm | 0.000 001 mm | | 0.000 000 001 mm |

wavelength

3 Use diagram C to write down the names of the waves with the longest and the shortest wavelengths.

! Sometimes, because of repeated total internal reflection in the rain drops, you get a double rainbow. Notice the order of colours in each one.

D

! Because of dispersion, all the colours of the visible spectrum can be seen on bubbles and thin films of oil.

E

P How could you create a rainbow?

F

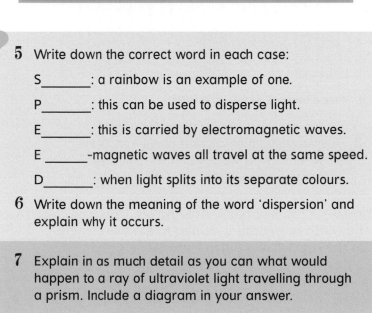

4 What is the speed of:
a) a light wave?
b) a radio wave?

Summary

A Starting with gamma rays, make a list of the electromagnetic spectrum in order of decreasing frequency. Add notes to indicate how wavelength and frequency change as you go down your list.

B State two things that all electromagnetic waves have in common.

5 Write down the correct word in each case:

S_____ : a rainbow is an example of one.

P_____ : this can be used to disperse light.

E_____ : this is carried by electromagnetic waves.

E_____-magnetic waves all travel at the same speed.

D_____ : when light splits into its separate colours.

6 Write down the meaning of the word 'dispersion' and explain why it occurs.

7 Explain in as much detail as you can what would happen to a ray of ultraviolet light travelling through a prism. Include a diagram in your answer.

Diffraction

What is diffraction and how is it useful?

When waves enter a harbour, they often spread into parts of the harbour that are not in front of the entrance. When waves spread through a gap or around objects it is called **diffraction**.

 1 What effect allows the water waves to spread into the harbour?

When a wave is diffracted, its wavelength does not change. However, the size of its wavelength affects how much it is diffracted. Diagrams B and C show different water waves diffracting through a gap.

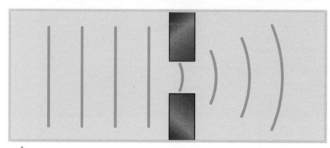

B *These waves are strongly diffracted.*

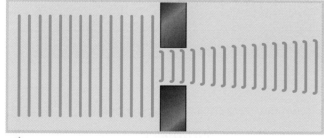

C *These waves are weakly diffracted.*

 2 The wavelength of voices is about 1 m. Is the wave strongly or weakly diffracted through a doorway, 1 m wide?

Normally a hill will block radio waves. However, if the width of the hill is similar to the wavelength then the radio waves diffract strongly around the hill, improving radio reception. Radio waves used for TV do not diffract as much around hills because their wavelength is shorter than the waves used to transmit radio broadcasts.

A

If the wavelength is similar to the size of the gap, then the wave curves as it passes through the gap, and spreads out a lot on the far side. It is strongly diffracted.

If the wavelength is much smaller than the size of the gap, the wave does not curve or spread out much. It is weakly diffracted.

The same rule applies to all waves spreading around objects.

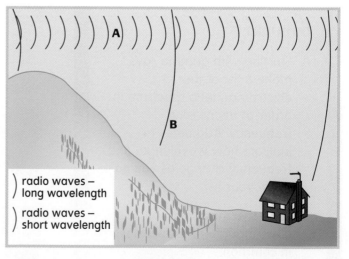

radio waves – long wavelength

radio waves – short wavelength

D *Long radio waves are received more clearly than short radio waves because they diffract strongly around the hill.*

3 Look at diagram D.
  a) Explain why the house might receive some radio stations well but have poor reception for other radio stations.
  b) Television signals have a shorter wavelength than radio signals. Why might the owner of the house need to change the direction of the television aerial?

P How would you find out whether high- or low-pitched notes are diffracted the most through a gap?

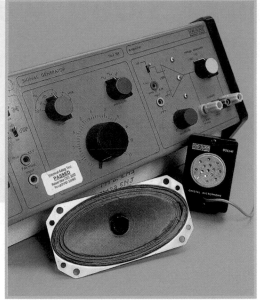

E

4 If members of a class are chatting outside a room, what effect allows their voices to spread through the doorway and fill the room?

5 Which one of these waves cannot be diffracted? Choose the correct answer.

  A water waves **B** sound waves **C** waves on a spring

6 Look at diagram B.
  a) Has diffraction caused a change in wavelength?
  b) Do you think diffraction will change the amplitude of the waves? Give reasons for your answer.

7 What makes a wave diffract more strongly? Choose the correct answer.

  A a longer wavelength **B** greater amplitude
  C moving between different materials

8 Diagram F shows sound waves passing a building. **F**

  a) What effect makes the waves curve after passing the building?
  b) Would the waves curve more or less if the building was much wider?
  c) You cannot see sound waves. How could you tell that diffraction had happened?

Sounds can sometimes still be heard even though there is a building blocking their direct path. This is because sound waves are also diffracted. Longer wavelengths are diffracted more, so low-pitched sound waves can diffract easily around the corners of buildings.

Water waves entering a harbour can be seen to diffract. Electromagnetic waves and sound can also be diffracted, providing evidence that they travel as waves.

Summary

A Draw waves going through a wide gap and through a narrow gap. Draw all the waves with equal wavelength.

B Write a paragraph for a TV and radio listings magazine to explain why houses in valleys may get good radio reception but poor TV reception.

223

Long wavelength electromagnetic waves

How do long wavelength electromagnetic waves behave?

TV and radio programmes are transmitted using electromagnetic waves called radio waves. Other electromagnetic waves are used for different purposes depending on their wavelengths:

- heating and cooking (3 cm)
- transmitting (sending) pictures and sounds round the world (1–2000 m)
- talking to astronauts in space (1 m)
- communicating underwater with submarines (100 km)
- tracking ships, and aeroplanes (1 cm).

The wavelengths of the different electromagnetic waves gives each type of wave its properties and uses. Electromagnetic waves are also called **electromagnetic radiation**.

?

1 What affects a wave's properties and uses?

2 What three things can happen to electromagnetic waves?

P Which wavelengths are used more often for local and national radio broadcasts?

Each type of radiation can be **absorbed** (taken in), **transmitted** (allowed through) or **reflected** by different substances. If radiation is absorbed by something it often heats up.

Sometimes the radiation that is absorbed creates an electric current in something. This current vibrates at the same frequency as the absorbed wave. This is how radio waves are turned into signals that you can hear in a radio.

Radio waves

- Typical wavelength: 200 m.
- Properties: They are reflected by an electrically charged layer in the Earth's upper atmosphere. This allows the waves to reach distant places despite the Earth's curved surface.
- Uses: They are used to transmit radio and TV broadcasts.

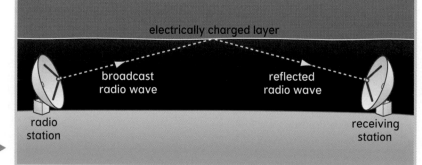

electrically charged layer

broadcast radio wave

reflected radio wave

radio station

receiving station

B

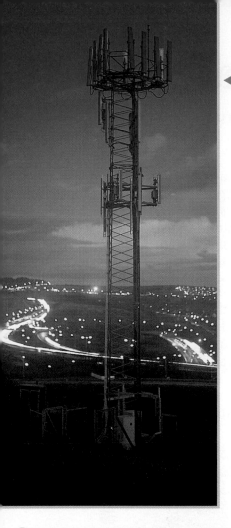

Microwaves

- Typical wavelength: 2.8 cm.
- Properties: They are absorbed by water molecules in food, passing on their energy so the food heats up. Microwaves are transmitted (pass through) the Earth's atmosphere easily.
- Uses: They are used to cook food using microwave ovens, for sending information to satellites and communicating within mobile phone networks.

Infrared radiation

- Typical wavelength: 0.5 mm.
- Properties: All hot objects give out infrared radiation. You can feel it as heat. Infrared radiation passes through the Earth's atmosphere and can be sent as a narrow beam.
- Uses: Infrared radiation is used in grills, toasters and electric fires. It is also sent as narrow beams from remote controls to operate electrical equipment. Infra-red radiation is also used to send information through optical fibre telephone cables.

! It was first discovered that microwaves could cook things when pigeons near new microwave transmitters in World War Two were dying because they were cooked! Different wavelength microwaves are used in microwave ovens and mobile phones!

?

3 a) Why can microwaves be used to communicate with satellites?

b) Why are microwaves not used for communicating with submarines?

4 What type of radiation do each of these use?
a) a video remote control
b) a TV station
c) mobile phones.

5 A radio station in Moscow sends broadcasts to Siberia.
a) What type of electromagnetic wave is used?
b) Explain how the atmosphere helps the broadcast travel a long distance. Draw a diagram as part of your answer.
c) If a different station sends out microwaves, why don't they reach Siberia?

6 When cooking with microwaves:
a) why does moist food cook quicker than dry food
b) why is it not advisable to wrap food in aluminium foil? (There are two reasons.)

Summary

A State two uses of each of the three types of long wavelength electromagnetic waves.

A Explain why different wavelengths are used in different situations.

Analogue and digital signals

How are analogue and digital signals different?

In the past, smoke signals and yodelling allowed people to send messages across valleys in mountainous areas. Now we can talk on the phone to people on the other side of the world.

Speech and music can be changed into electrical signals, and sent along electrical cables. These signals can also be sent using radio waves, microwaves and infrared waves. Speech and music can also be changed into light or infrared waves, which are sent along optical fibres.

Analogue signals

A

When we speak, the frequency and amplitude of the sound waves we make change continuously. Like sound waves, electromagnetic signals also change continuously. They are examples of **analogue signals**. Analogue signals are signals that can change frequency and amplitude continuously.

B

Digital signals

Morse code was used on ships to send messages as a series of long or short beeps. The signal was either on or off. Sound waves and electromagnetic signals can be changed into a series of beeps (**pulses**). Signals like this are called **digital signals**.

The light reflecting off this bar code is converted into a digital signal.
C

? 1 Complete the table to show if the signals coming from each item vary continuously or are on/off. The first one has been done for you:

	Can it vary continuously?	Is it only on or off?
the light from a lamp controlled by a dimmer switch	yes	no
the light from a torch		
the temperature of a drink		
the sound of a door bell		

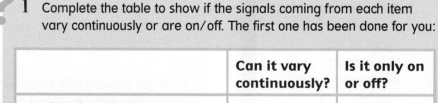

P Find out how Morse code can be used to send signals.

Less distortion, better quality

Digital signals are used more and more for television, radio and telephone. More information can be sent as digital signals through optical fibres compared with electrical analogue signals sent through cables of the same thickness. Information sent along cables becomes distorted (altered) because different frequencies weaken by different amounts and random noise is picked up. With analogue signals the distortions are amplified by the receiver but digital signals that are distorted can be restored by the receiver.

? 3 State two advantages of transmitting digital television signals through optical fibres compared to transmitting analogue signals using high-frequency radio waves.

Diagram E shows how an analogue signal can be distorted after transmission. The strength of the signal can be increased but this does not remove the distortion.

Look at diagram F. A digital signal is a sequence of pulses that can still be recognised even if they have been severely distorted during transmission. Electronic systems can restore the signal to its original condition.

? 4 What are the similarities between the signals produced by a bar code and those produced by Morse code? (*Hint*: you can find a bar code on the cover of this book.)

5 A digital camera contains millions of light detectors. When a photo is taken, light shines on these detectors and a picture is built up using information about the colour of light shining on each detector. Explain what a small part of a picture from a digital camera would look like if you looked very closely at it.

6 Explain why television signals become weakened and distorted as they travel from the transmitter to a television aerial.

? 2 Which of the examples in diagram D are analogue signals?

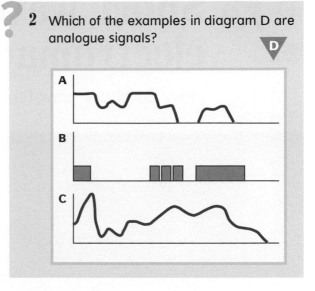

! Digital recordings do not suffer from the hisses or crackles that can be heard on analogue recordings.

E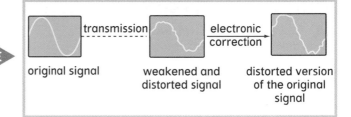

original signal — transmission — weakened and distorted signal — electronic correction — distorted version of the original signal

F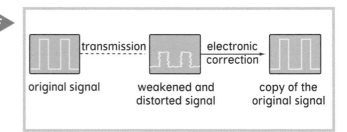

original signal — transmission — weakened and distorted signal — electronic correction — copy of the original signal

Summary

Design a newspaper advertisement for a company selling digital radio receivers. The advertisement should explain why digital radio produces better quality sound than analogue radio. Include diagrams in your advert.

Short wavelength electromagnetic waves

How do short wavelength electromagnetic waves behave?

A *This bank note has a fluorescent marker that shows up under ultraviolet light.*

Some waves have wavelengths much shorter than visible light.

Banks and shops check bank notes using **ultraviolet** radiation. Ultraviolet radiation cannot be seen. However, if it shines on bank notes, ultraviolet radiation changes to purple light so the bank notes glow purple. This effect is called **fluorescence**. It does not happen with fake bank notes.

? 1 Why are fluorescent dyes used on tickets for big sporting occasions?

P Find out how fake objects can be detected and personal belongings marked invisibly. **C**

Ultraviolet radiation

- Typical wavelength: 0.001 mm.
- Properties: Ultraviolet radiation is reflected as visible, purple light by special materials called **fluorescent materials**.
- Uses: Ultraviolet radiation is used to detect fraud. It is also used in fluorescent lights and sunbeds. Valuable equipment can be marked with ink that is only visible under ultraviolet radiation.

B *A special coating in a fluorescent light absorbs the ultraviolet radiation given out inside the light. The coating then gives out visible light.*

! Aeroplanes that fly very high are exposed to strong ultraviolet rays from the Sun. The atmosphere gives people on the ground some protection from these rays.

X-radiation

- Typical wavelength: 0.000 001 mm.
- Properties: X-rays are absorbed by materials like bones and metals, but they pass through skin and cloth easily.
- Uses: X-rays are used to detect cracks in metals and breaks in bones by producing shadow pictures.

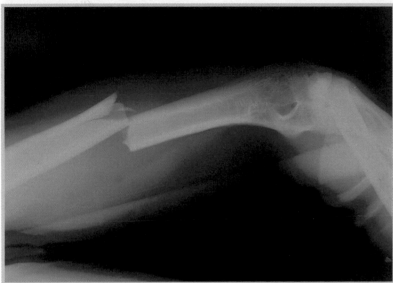

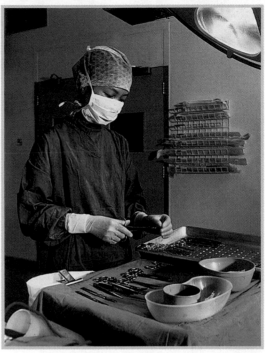

Gamma radiation

- Typical wavelength: 0.000 000 001 mm.
- Properties: Gamma rays can kill living cells. They have a high frequency and so gamma rays carry a lot of energy.
- Uses: Gamma radiation can be used to treat cancer by killing cancer cells. It can keep food fresh and **sterilise** surgical equipment by killing harmful bacteria.

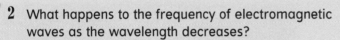

2 What happens to the frequency of electromagnetic waves as the wavelength decreases?

3 Choose the correct type of radiation in each case.
   a) It is used to treat cancer.
   b) It is used to look for cracks in metal aeroplane parts.
   c) It is used in sunbeds.

Summary

Write summary notes on the similarities and differences between the three different types of short wavelength electromagnetic waves.

4 a) Why is luggage passed through an X-ray machine at airports?
   b) Why are people not asked to walk through these X-ray machines?

5 Invisible ink, which fluoresces (glows purple) when ultraviolet light shines on it, helps the police to trace stolen goods. Explain why it is a better choice than normal ink for marking items of property.

6 Use the information in the text to calculate the frequency of typical X-rays. (*Hint*: the speed of electromagnetic waves in air is 300 000 000 m/s.)

Radiation and living cells

How does radiation affect living cells?

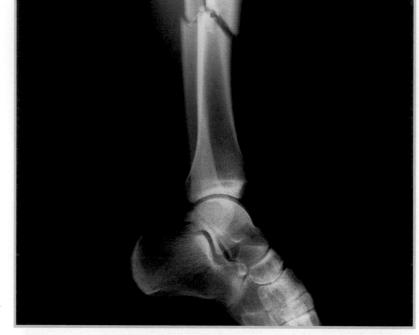

When a patient is treated for cancer, gamma radiation can be used to kill the cancer cells. In low doses, gamma rays cause cancer but high doses directed at cancer cells will kill them. They also kill bacteria which cause infections. Gamma rays are also used to **sterilise** (disinfect) the equipment used in operations. Some food we buy is treated with gamma rays to preserve it by killing the bacteria in it.

 1 List three uses of gamma rays.

The bones show up because X-rays cannot pass through them. **A**

Other types of electromagnetic waves (radiation) can also affect living cells:

B The colour of your skin can protect you from skin cancer.

- **X-rays** usually pass through the soft parts of the body but some cells absorb the rays. High doses kill cells but lower doses can cause cancer.

- **Ultraviolet radiation** (UV) in high doses kills cells. UV from the Sun can cause skin cancer. This is more common in fair-skinned people because light skin does not absorb UV as well as dark skin and so more UV reaches deeper tissue where the cancer forms. Dark skin absorbs UV better so dark-skinned people have less risk of skin cancer.

 In Australia, skin cancer is a real danger. The slogan 'Slip Slap Slop' is used to advertise this danger. This stands for: slip on a top, slap on a hat, slop on sun protection cream.

- **Infrared radiation** (IR) is absorbed by the skin and felt as heat.

C

- **Microwaves** are absorbed by the water in cells. The water heats up and can damage or kill the cells.

Too much of these types of electromagnetic radiation is dangerous. The longer you are exposed to the radiation, the more dangerous it is. Gamma rays are more harmful than X-rays, which are more harmful than UV. You can reduce the risks by reducing the time of exposure and wearing protective clothing.

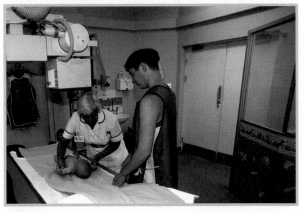

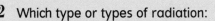
E *The father wears a lead apron to protect him from X-rays. The nurse will stand behind the shield on the right when the X-ray is taken.*

 How could you find out what sources of (safe) radiation there are in the room? **F**

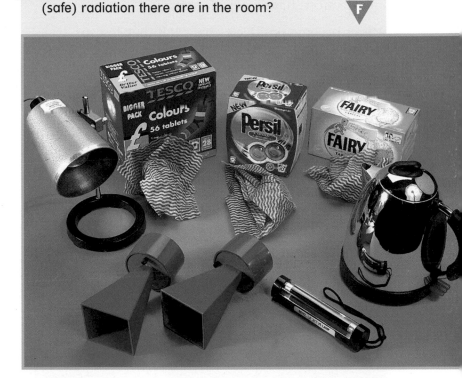

?

2 Which type or types of radiation:
  a) can cause cancer
  b) comes from the Sun
  c) is absorbed by water in cells?

3 How can people who operate X-ray machines reduce the risk of getting cancer?

4 How can you protect yourself from skin cancer?

5 Why do microwave ovens have a switch that automatically switches them off when you open the door?

6 When cancer is treated, several gamma ray sources are carefully angled so the cancer cells receive a large dose but other cells get smaller doses. The rest of the body is shielded using lead sheets.
  a) Why is it important that only the cancer cells get a high dose?
  b) How are other parts of the body protected?
  c) Why do the nurses leave the room when patients are being treated?

7 It is possible to measure the water content of different soil samples using microwaves. How do you think this is done?

Summary

Design a health information leaflet highlighting the dangers of electromagnetic radiation and how people can protect themselves.

Ionisation

What is ionisation?

Gamma rays are dangerous because they can alter atoms. An **atom** contains a central **nucleus** containing **protons** and **neutrons**. Around this are **electrons**.

Atoms normally have an equal number of positive and negative charges, so their overall charge is **neutral**. Protons have a positive charge, neutrons have no charge and electrons have a negative charge.

Atoms become positively charged if they lose an electron, and negatively charged if they gain an electron. Atoms which have become charged are called **ions**.

Gamma rays can knock electrons off atoms and turn them into ions. The atoms have been **ionised**. Gamma rays are an example of **ionising radiation**.

There are three main types of ionising radiation, **alpha** (α), **beta** (β) and **gamma** (γ). They are emitted from the nuclei of atoms undergoing nuclear decay. X-rays and ultraviolet radiation are other examples of ionising radiation.

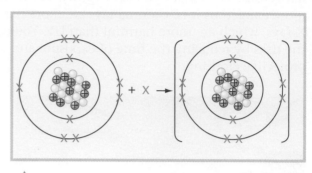

A *An ion is an atom that has gained an electron . . .*

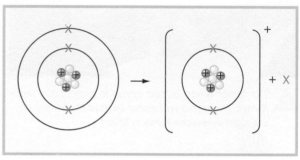

B *. . . or lost an electron.*

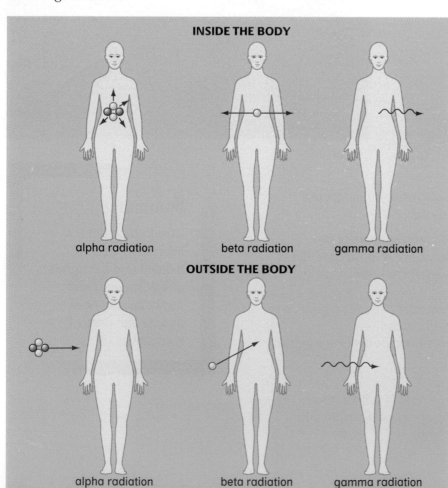

INSIDE THE BODY

alpha radiation   beta radiation   gamma radiation

OUTSIDE THE BODY

alpha radiation   beta radiation   gamma radiation

? **1** Explain what is meant by the term 'ionising radiation'.

If atoms in the molecules of living cells are ionised, the cells are damaged. This upsets the processes in these cells, causing cancer and other illnesses. Damage to cells happens only if the cells absorb the radiation. The radiation is less dangerous if it cannot reach the cells or if it passes straight through them without being absorbed.

C *Alpha radiation cannot pass in or out of the body through skin. Beta and gamma radiation can enter and escape from the body through skin.*

Alpha (α) radiation

The skin absorbs this type of ionising radiation. Alpha radiation cannot pass through into the cells inside the body and so it is the least dangerous type outside the body.

However, if something containing alpha radiation gets inside you, it is strongly absorbed by cells inside the body, causing damage. This means that alpha radiation is the most dangerous type inside the body.

Beta (β) and gamma (γ) radiation

Both of these types pass easily through skin and are absorbed by cells inside the body, causing damage. Beta and gamma radiation are most dangerous outside the body. However, if something giving out these types of radiation gets inside you, the radiation is more likely to escape from the body and not be absorbed by living cells. This means that beta and gamma radiation are less dangerous inside the body than alpha radiation.

The amount of damage caused depends on:

- the type of radiation
- whether the radiation is inside or outside the body
- the amount of radiation you are exposed to (large doses over a long time are most damaging).

Radioactive metals give out ionising radiation but can be safely used in certain batteries. These batteries are used in heart pacemakers, saving millions of lives each year.

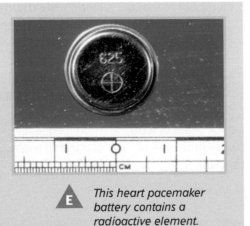

E This heart pacemaker battery contains a radioactive element.

D The hazard symbol for radiation.

2 Why is beta radiation less dangerous inside the body than alpha radiation?

3 Complete the sentences:
   a) When atoms become charged they have been _____.
   b) Alpha radiation is not harmful _____ the body.
   c) Atoms and molecules are normally _____.

4 Copy and label diagram F to show how different types of radiation pass through the body.

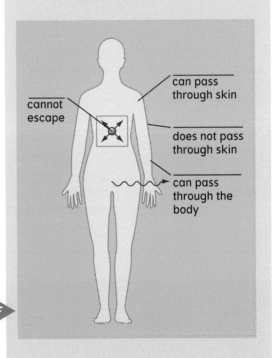

_____ can pass through skin

_____ cannot escape

_____ does not pass through skin

_____ can pass through the body

F

Summary

Write paragraphs to explain the meaning of each of the words written in bold on these two pages.

5 X-rays are used to provide shadow pictures of bones inside the human body. Explain the disadvantages of using gamma radiation in place of X-rays.

Ionising radiation
How do the different types of radiation behave?

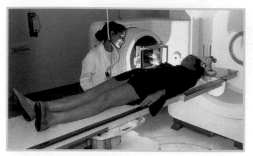

A Gamma radiation is used in hospitals to kill cancer cells.

Radioactive substances emit (give out) ionising radiation from the nuclei of their atoms all the time. Different radioactive substances give out different types of ionising radiation – alpha, beta or gamma.

Radioactive materials come in different strengths. Some substances are very radioactive. They need to be carefully stored, for example inside lead containers.

The three main types of ionising radiation are described in table B.

B

Name of radiation	Symbol	Passes through:	Is absorbed by:	Nature
alpha	α	very short distances in air	a few cm of air, a thin sheet of paper, skin	Positively charged particle. Contains two protons and two neutrons (helium nucleus).
beta	β	air and paper	a thin sheet of metal	Negatively charged electron with high energy. Emitted from the nucleus when a neutron becomes a proton.
gamma	γ	most things except thick lead and concrete	a thick sheet of lead, a very thick wall of concrete	High frequency electromagnetic wave.

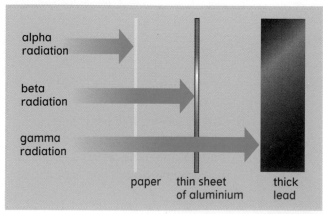

C Different types of radiation are absorbed by different amounts in different materials.

? **1** Use table B to answer these questions:
 a) How can concrete protect people from gamma radiation?
 b) Could this page absorb beta radiation?
 c) Could alpha radiation be safely stored in a strong, cardboard box?

2 Why is an alpha particle sometimes described as a helium nucleus?

Radioactive nuclear fuel is transported in steel flasks. Each flask has a mass of 50 tonnes. **D**

Other materials contain very small amounts of radioactivity. They are found in the air, the ground, building materials and food. **Cosmic radiation**, produced by the nuclear reactions in stars, reaches us from space. The radiation surrounding us from all these sources is called **background radiation**. Background radiation cannot be altered; it is always around us. However strange it seems, background radiation is a part of normal life.

? 3 Write down three sources of background radiation.

E A Geiger counter is used to measure the amount of radiation given off by something.

F Examples of items that give out background radiation.

? 4 Copy and complete these sentences:
B_____ radiation surrounds us all the time.
Radioactive substances e_____ ionising radiation.
T_____ sheets of lead are needed to absorb gamma rays.
A_____ radiation is easily absorbed by skin.

5 Write a sentence explaining to a pupil in year 7 what is meant by background radiation.

6 What type of radiation do each of these sentences refer to?
   a) It is used to kill cells in order to save lives.
   b) It can't travel far without being absorbed.
   c) It travels through air but can't pass though thin metal.

7 Alpha and beta radiation can be deflected by a magnetic field.
   a) Why is gamma radiation not deflected by a magnetic field?
   b) If alpha radiation was deflected upwards by a magnetic field, which way would beta radiation be deflected? Explain your answer.

! 200 million gamma waves pass through your body every hour from the soil and buildings.

Summary

Copy diagram C and add labels to describe the other differences between the three types of ionising radiation.

235

Isotopes

What are isotopes?

Many **elements** contain atoms of different types. The different types of atom are called **isotopes**. Some isotopes are radioactive.

One type of water ('heavy water') has more mass than normal water because it contains an isotope of hydrogen called deuterium. Molecules of water always contain atoms of two elements: hydrogen and oxygen.

Each different element has a different number of protons in the nucleus of its atoms, and different numbers of electrons circling the nucleus. This gives each element its particular chemical properties.

All the atoms of the same element have the same number of protons in the nucleus and the same number of electrons circling around it.

Different isotopes of an element have a different number of neutrons, but the same number of protons and electrons, in their atoms.

Diagram A compares the two isotopes of hydrogen. It also shows an oxygen atom.

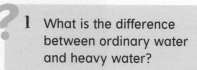

1 What is the difference between ordinary water and heavy water?

A

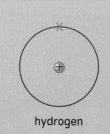

hydrogen

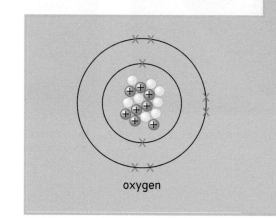

oxygen

deuterium

2 What is it that makes hydrogen and oxygen different elements?

3 What gives an element its chemical properties?

4 a) What is it that makes deuterium the same element as hydrogen?

  b) How is deuterium different from hydrogen?

5 Using the same headings as table B, draw a table to compare hydrogen, deuterium and oxygen.

Neutrons and protons are known as **nucleons**. The **mass** (or **nucleon**) **number** of an element is the total number of neutrons and protons in the nucleus. Hydrogen has one proton and no neutrons. Its mass number is 1. Deuterium has one neutron and one proton. Its mass number is 2.

 B

Element	Protons	Neutrons	Electrons	Mass number
carbon-12	6	6	6	12
carbon-14	6	8	6	14
lithium-6	3	3	3	6
lithium-7	3	4	3	7
uranium-235	92	143	92	235
uranium-238	92	146	92	238

6 What is the mass number of:
   a) helium, which has two neutrons and two protons
   b) carbon, which has six neutrons and six protons?

Some isotopes are radioactive (e.g carbon-14). These are called **radioactive isotopes** (or **radioisotopes** or **radionuclides**). These have atoms with unstable nuclei. As the nucleus splits up (disintegrates), it forms a different element by changing the number of protons it has and emitting (giving out) radiation.

Nuclear fission

Nuclear fission is the process by which a uranium-235 atom breaks up when it is hit by relatively slow-moving neutrons. As the nucleus of the atom splits it releases energy and more neutrons. The neutrons emitted hit and break up other uranium atoms, which then emit even more neutrons. A **chain reaction** is set up releasing more and more energy.

The quantity of energy released during a single nuclear fission is very large compared to the energy released when a chemical bond is made between two atoms in the process of combustion. Nuclear power stations therefore require a much smaller mass of fuel than fossil fuel power stations. The new atoms formed during nuclear fission are also radioactive.

7 Using the same headings as table B, draw a table to compare carbon-12, carbon-13, carbon-14, oxygen-16, oxygen-17 and oxygen-18.

8 A radioisotope of hydrogen is tritium. Which of these can it not do?
   A emit radiation
   B receive broadcasts
   C behave like ordinary hydrogen in some ways.

9 Uranium-235 and uranium-238 are isotopes of uranium. The nucleus of a uranium-235 atom contains 92 protons.
   a) How many protons will the nucleus of uranium-238 contain?
   b) How many more neutrons does uranium-238 have than uranium-235?
   c) How many neutrons does a uranium-238 nucleus contain?
   d) How many electrons will orbit the nucleus in an atom of uranium-235?

The isotope of uranium (uranium-235) used in power stations forms only 1% of the uranium on Earth.

D *A nuclear fission chain reaction.*

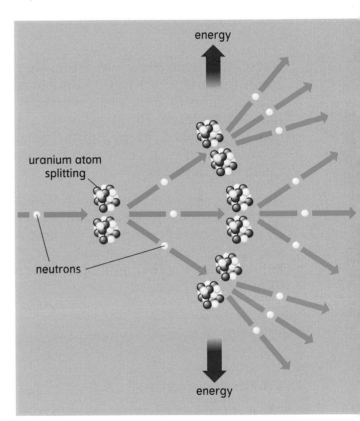

uranium atom splitting

neutrons

energy

energy

Summary

A Draw two diagrams showing the atomic structure of carbon-12 and carbon-14. Use your diagrams to help explain the meaning of the word **isotope**.

B Explain why a chain reaction occurs during nuclear fission.

Half-lives

What happens to a radioactive material over time?

Before a leak can be mended in an underground pipe, you need to know where it is. A radioactive **tracer** is injected at one end of the pipe and a detector is used to discover where the radiation collects. From this, workers can tell where the problem is. The radiation is safe to use because the radioactivity dies away after a short time.

 1 Why is the radioactive substance used to find leaks safe to use?

Radioactive materials are **unstable**. They have atoms with nuclei whch constantly break up forming different atoms. This is called **radioactive decay**. The atoms of the original material are called **parent atoms**. The number of parent atoms that break apart in a second is called the **count-rate**.

Over time, the count-rate falls. The time taken for the count-rate to fall to half its value from when you started counting is the **half-life** of the material. Different materials have different half-lives ranging from millionths of a second to millions of years.

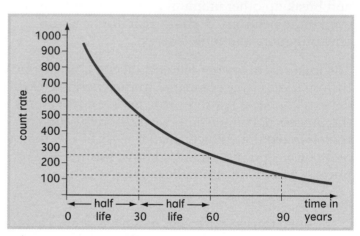

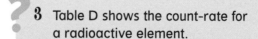
B Every 30 years, the count rate in caesium halves.

 2 What happens to the count-rate over time?

Worked example

What is the half life of this element?

Time (minutes)	Count-rate
0	100
2	70
4	50
6	40

C

- The original count-rate is 100.
- Half of the original count-rate is 50.
- The count-rate is 50 after 4 minutes.
- So the half-life is 4 minutes.

3 Table D shows the count-rate for a radioactive element.

D

Time (minutes)	Count-rate
0	60
10	45
20	37
30	30
40	23

a) What is the original count-rate?
b) What is half of the original count-rate?
c) After how many minutes is the count-rate 30?
d) What is the half-life for this element?

You can calculate how many parent atoms are left in a sample. During one half-life, the number of parent atoms left in the material will halve.

Worked example

The half-life of radon gas is 4 days. There are 1000 atoms of radon to begin with. How many parent atoms will be left after 8 days?

- After 4 days there will be half the number of parent atoms (500 atoms).
- After another 4 days, there are half of 500 atoms (250).
- So after 8 days there will be 250 parent atoms left.

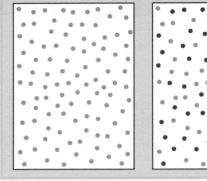

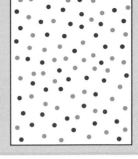

 In one half-life, half the parent atoms decay. You can never tell which atom will decay next.

4 Look at table F.

F

Material	Half-life	Original count-rate	Number of parent atoms
X	10 minutes	100	1 000
Y	3 days	80	20 000
Z	7 years	200	500

Which material, X, Y, or Z:
a) has the longest half-life
b) has a count-rate of 50 after 10 minutes
c) has 10 000 parent atoms after 3 days?

5 Carbon-14 has a half-life of 5600 years. There are 2000 atoms initially.
a) How long will it take for 1000 carbon atoms to decay?
b) If the sample is 11 200 years old, how many parent atoms remain?
c) Radium-226 has a half-life of 1600 years. There are 2000 atoms originally. How many radium atoms remain after 3200 years?
d) Explain which sample you expect to be the least radioactive after 3200 years.

6 Radioactive isotopes are sometimes injected into the body during medical examinations. A detector is then used to measure how much of the isotope builds up in a particular part of the body.
a) Why would a radioactive isotope with a half-life of 18 years not be suitable for this purpose?
b) What problems would the medical staff have if they used a radioactive isotope with a half-life of 5 seconds?

! Uranium-235 is used in nuclear power stations. Its half-life is 700 million years.

P You can make a model of radioactive decay using cubes like these. You drop them, remove some and drop them again. How would you decide which cubes to remove?

G

Summary

Sketch a graph to show the count rate against time for an isotope with a half-life of 10 minutes. Use your graph to help explain the meaning of the term 'half-life'.

Using radioactive isotopes

How can we use radioactive isotopes?

Many people use aluminium foil when cooking. When the foil is made, its thickness can be closely controlled using radiation. When a beam of beta radiation is directed at the foil, the foil absorbs more or less beta radiation, depending on its thickness – thicker foil absorbs more radiation; thinner foil lets more radiation pass through.

A detector on the other side senses how much radiation passes through, warning workers if the thickness changes by too much.

Other things can be checked in the same way:

- the thickness of sheets of paper
- the quality of welded metal joints
- the level of powders in packets.

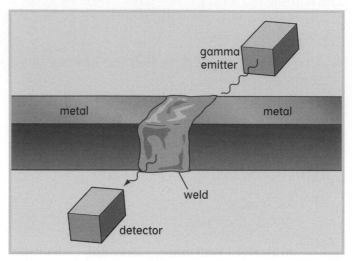

 A Faults in the weld affect the radiation. This change is picked up by a detector.

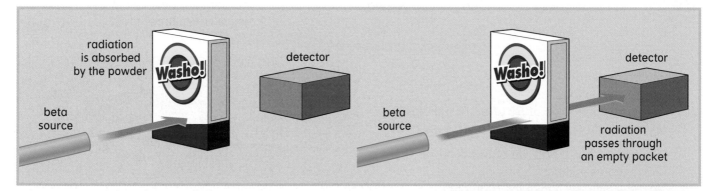

B

 1 Why would alpha radiation and gamma radiation not be suitable for checking the level of powders in packets?

Carbon dating

All living things contain a certain amount of radioactive carbon atoms (carbon-14). When these radioisotopes decay, they become nitrogen atoms that are no longer radioactive. Over time, the material becomes less radioactive. The half-life of carbon-14 is 5600 years. The count-rate will halve in 5600 years and fall to a quarter of its original value in 11 200 years. The original count rate can be estimated by comparing the dead organism to something similar that is alive today. By measuring the count rate for the dead organism it is possible to discover how old it is.

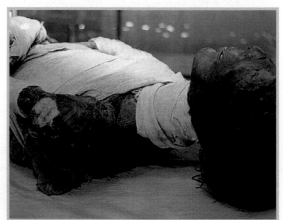

Measuring the amount of C-14 in Egyptian mummies can accurately date them as thousands of years old. This photo is of Tuthmosis IV and he is over 3400 years old. **C**

Dating rocks

Rocks can be dated using a similar technique to carbon dating. Igneous rocks contain a uranium isotope that decays via a series of relatively short-lived radioisotopes to produce stable isotopes of lead. The relative proportions of uranium and lead within a sample of igneous rock vary depending on how old the rock is and can be used to date the rock sample. Some igneous rocks can also be dated using argon gas trapped inside the rock. This argon gas has been produced because the rock originally contained the radioisotope potassium-40 that then decays to argon. Therefore the older the rock is, the more trapped argon gas it will contain.

Other radioactive materials behave in the same way, so, for example, rocks from the Moon can be dated too.

People who work with radiation need to know how much radiation they have been exposed to. To help monitor this, the person wears a **radiation badge** containing photographic film. After a period of time, the film is developed.

- A darker developed film means more radiation exposure.
- A lighter developed film means less radiation exposure.

Living things can also be dated using radiation. This is Methuselah, the worlds oldest living thing. It's a bristle cone pine tree **D** which is 4767 years old.

2 An old bone is found to have only one eighth of the carbon-14 contained in a similar modern bone. Estimate the age of the old bone.

A radiation badge. **E**

3 Why is it important to cover the photographic film in a radiation badge with a very thin sheet of paper?

4 How could you use radiation to:
  a) decide which book contains more pages
  b) discover how old a wooden carving is
  c) control how much cereal is put into packets?

5 A radiation badge monitors how much radiation a person has received.
  a) Why is this important?
  b) Explain which is more important for the health of workers:
    i) that the workers are careful when they are using radiation
    ii) that the badges are tested often.
  c) Look at diagram F. Write down the workers in order, starting with the person exposed to most radiation.

F

| Joe's film | Bakul's film | Tara's film |

6 Uranium-235 has a half-life of 700 million years and decays to lead-207. If a sample of pure uranium-235 were left to decay for 2100 million years:
  a) what percentage of uranium-235 would be left after this time
  b) what percentage of lead-207 would be present after this time?

Summary

A Write a short article for an archaeology magazine explaining how carbon dating works.

B Explain how radiation badges work and why some workers need to wear them.

L19 Atomic models

How was the structure of the atom discovered?

Imagine firing a bullet at a sheet of thin tissue paper. How amazing if it bounced back, returning the way it came! In 1907, two scientists called Ernest Rutherford and Ernest Marsden had such a startling result from their experiments, they felt as though this had happened. They were using alpha radiation to find out about the structure of the atom. Alpha radiation consists of positively charged particles made up of two protons and two neutrons.

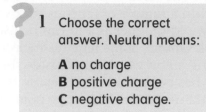

1 Choose the correct answer. Neutral means:

A no charge
B positive charge
C negative charge.

Atoms are the building blocks of all matter. Rutherford and Marsden knew that atoms contained negatively charged electrons, which could be dislodged (removed) from the atom. They also knew that atoms have no overall charge (they are **neutral**) so must have some positive charge.

At the time, many scientists believed that the structure of an atom was a bit like a plum pudding or Christmas pudding.

To test the plum pudding model, Rutherford and Marsden fired positively charged alpha particles very quickly at a sheet of thin gold foil, a few atoms thick. They expected to see the alpha particles passing through because the positive charge was spread throughout the atoms of the gold foil like a cloud. However, the alpha particles scattered in different directions. A few even returned the way they came. This could only happen if the gold contained small, positively charged particles that could repel the alpha particles.

The **nuclear model** of the atom could explain their experiment.

- The centre of the spherical atom is a positively charged, heavy nucleus.
- Negatively charged electrons circle the nucleus, but are quite far from it.
- The atom is mostly empty space.

A *The plum pudding model.*

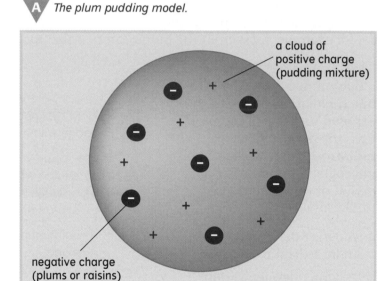

a cloud of positive charge (pudding mixture)

negative charge (plums or raisins)

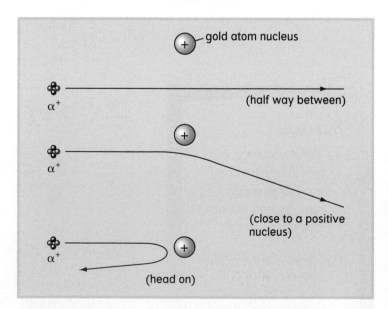

gold atom nucleus

(half way between)

(close to a positive nucleus)

(head on)

B *The Rutherford Scattering experiment. The positively charged nucleus repels positively charged particles.*

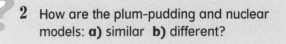

2 How are the plum-pudding and nuclear models: **a)** similar **b)** different?

More research eventually discovered which particles make up the atom.

Particle	Mass	Charge	Where it is found
proton	1 unit	+1	nucleus
neutron	1 unit	0	nucleus
electron	negligible	−1	circling the nucleus

The size of the nucleus compared to the rest of the atom is like a pea in the centre of a football pitch. At the size of a pea, the mass of the nucleus would be 230 tonnes.

 A boron atom has five protons and six neutrons in its nucleus. Five electrons circle around the nucleus.

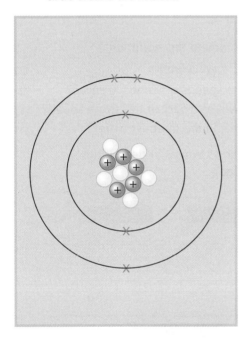

P How could you use this apparatus to make a model of a scattering experiment?

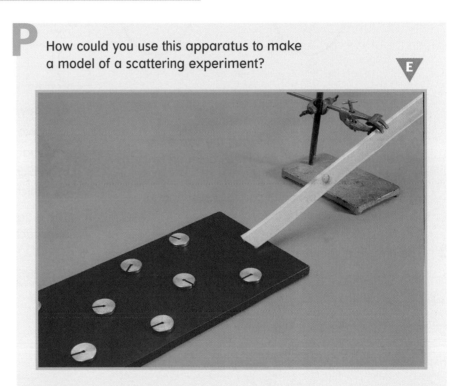

E

Summary

A Draw a diagram of a boron atom. Label the atomic particles, indicating what charge they carry.

B Explain why the atom is neutral.

C Explain why an alpha particle might come back the way it came, if fired at this atom.

3 Name the atomic particles that are:
a) positively charged
b) negatively charged
c) neutral.

4 Look at diagram B.
a) Why are some alpha particles reflected when others pass straight through?
b) Why was it important that the sheet of gold foil used was thin?

5 This question is about Rutherford's scattering experiment.
a) Alpha particles are the same as the nucleus of a helium atom. Why were helium atoms not used instead of alpha particles?
b) Electrons are negatively charged and would attract the alpha particles. Why were the alpha particles deflected more by the nuclei than they were by the electrons?

Further questions

1 Copy the wave shown in the diagram.

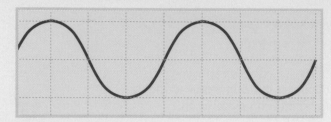

a) Label the amplitude. (1)

b) How many oscillations are shown? (1)

c) Add another wave which has the same frequency but which produces a sound twice as loud as the original wave. (2)

d) What name is given to sound waves that are too high for us to hear? (1)

2 The diagram shows the electromagnetic spectrum.

| radio waves | micro-waves | infra-red | visible light | ultra-violet | X–rays | gamma waves |

a) State *two* things that all electromagnetic waves have in common. (2)

b) Which types of waves have the most energy? (1)

c) Which type of waves:

  i) are felt as heat

  ii) are used in mobile-phone networks

  iii) can create shadow pictures to detect cracks in bones? (3)

3 S and P waves are created during earthquakes.

a) How are these waves detected? (1)

b) Describe the differences between the two types of wave. (2)

b) How do seismic waves from earthquakes provide us with evidence that the core of the Earth is liquid? (2)

4 Here is some information about three waves in the sea.

Wave	Wavelength (m)	Frequency (Hz)	Speed (m/s)
X	2	0.2	
Y	8	0.5	4
Z	1	0.4	

a) Copy and complete this equation:

  wave speed = wavelength × _____. (1)

b) What are the speeds of waves X and Z? (2)

c) Which *two* waves travel at the same speed? (1)

d) Which wave is in the deepest water? (1)

5 The diagram shows waves in deep water approaching a gap.

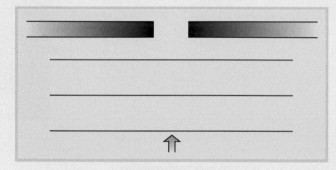

a) Copy the diagram and draw the next three waves after the gap. (3)

b) What name is given to this effect? (1)

c) The diagram below shows the same gap when the water is shallow (low tide). Copy the diagram and draw the next six waves. (3)

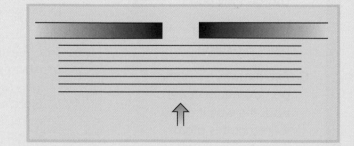

6 a) Draw a rough copy of this diagram and complete it to show what happens to the radio waves as they reflect off part of the Earth's atmosphere. (2)

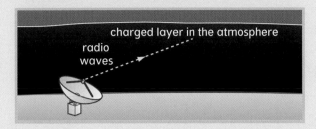

charged layer in the atmosphere
radio waves

b) Why can the atmosphere allow radio waves to be broadcast over long distances? (1)

c) Name *one* type of electromagnetic wave that can pass through the Earth's atmosphere? (1)

d) State *two* uses of microwaves. (2)

e) Which have longer wavelengths, microwaves or radio waves? (1)

7 The diagram shows what happens to sunlight as it passes from air into a raindrop.

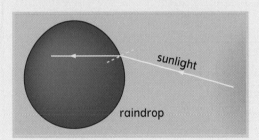

sunlight

raindrop

a) What happens to the speed of light as it enters the raindrop? (1)

b) What is this effect called? (1)

c) Total internal reflection occurs at the back of the raindrop, reflecting the light. State *one* other use of total internal reflection. (1)

d) What effect causes the sunlight to separate into different colours? (1)

e) What is a rainbow an example of? (1)

f) When dispersion occurs:
i) which colour changes direction least
ii) which colour changes direction most? (2)

8 Cordless telephones use either analogue signals or digital signals.

a) Draw diagrams showing i) an analogue signal and ii) a digital signal. (2)

b) Explain why digital telephones usually produce better quality sound. (3)

9 Radioactive isotopes can be injected into the body and used to detect medical problems. Give *three* reasons why an alpha source with a half-life of 50 years would not be suitable for this purpose. (3)

10 The table below shows the percentages of Uranium-235 and lead in a sample of uranium-235 undergoing radioactive decay.

Time (million years)	0	500	1000	1500	2000	2500
Uranium-235 (%)	100	61	37	23	14	8
Lead (%)	0	39	63		86	

a) Copy the table and insert the two missing values. (2)

b) Plot one graph to display the two sets of data. (6)

c) Use your graph to find the half-life of uranium-235. (2)

d) A sample of igneous rock was found to contain 64 g of uranium-235 and 36 g of lead. Use these values and your graph to find the age of this rock sample. (3)

11 a) Write down *two* safety precautions that should be taken when using a gamma source in the school laboratory. (2)

b) Explain why alpha radiation is least dangerous outside the body. (1)

12 Copy and complete these sentences.

Atoms have a small central _____ made up from _____ and _____, surrounded by negatively charged _____ .

The total number of protons and neutrons in an atom is its _____ number.

Atoms of the same element have the same number of _____.

Isotopes are atoms of the same element with different numbers of _____. (7)

Periodic Table

Key:

Mass number A
H hydrogen
Atomic number (proton number) Z
1

Group 1	2											3	4	5	6	7	0 or 8
																	4 **He** helium 2
7 **Li** lithium 3	9 **Be** beryllium 4											11 **B** boron 5	12 **C** carbon 6	14 **N** nitrogen 7	16 **O** oxygen 8	19 **F** fluorine 9	20 **Ne** neon 10
23 **Na** sodium 11	24 **Mg** magnesium 12											27 **Al** aluminium 13	28 **Si** silicon 14	31 **P** phosphorus 15	32 **S** sulphur 16	35 **Cl** chlorine 17	40 **Ar** argon 18
39 **K** potassium 19	40 **Ca** calcium 20	45 **Sc** scandium 21	48 **Ti** titanium 22	51 **V** vanadium 23	52 **Cr** chromium 24	55 **Mn** manganese 25	56 **Fe** iron 26	59 **Co** cobalt 27	59 **Ni** nickel 28	64 **Cu** copper 29	65 **Zn** zinc 30	70 **Ga** gallium 31	73 **Ge** germanium 32	75 **As** arsenic 33	79 **Se** selenium 34	80 **Br** bromine 35	84 **Kr** krypton 36
85 **Rb** rubidium 37	88 **Sr** strontium 38	89 **Y** yttrium 39	91 **Zr** zirconium 40	93 **Nb** niobium 41	96 **Mo** molybdenum 42	98 **Tc** technetium 43	101 **Ru** ruthenium 44	103 **Rh** rhodium 45	106 **Pd** palladium 46	108 **Ag** silver 47	112 **Cd** cadmium 48	115 **In** indium 49	119 **Sn** tin 50	122 **Sb** antimony 51	128 **Te** tellurium 52	127 **I** iodine 53	131 **Xe** xenon 54
133 **Cs** caesium 55	137 **Ba** barium 56	139 **La** lanthanum 57	178 **Hf** hafnium 72	181 **Ta** tantalum 73	184 **W** tungsten 74	186 **Re** rhenium 75	190 **Os** osmium 76	192 **Ir** iridium 77	195 **Pt** platinum 78	197 **Au** gold 79	201 **Hg** mercury 80	204 **Tl** thallium 81	207 **Pb** lead 82	209 **Bi** bismuth 83	209 **Po** polonium 84	210 **At** astatine 85	222 **Rn** radon 86
223 **Fr** francium 87	226 **Ra** radium 88	227 **Ac** actinium 89															

Common ions

Positive ions

Name	Formula	Name	Formula
ammonium	NH_4^+	calcium	Ca^{2+}
hydrogen	H^+	copper(II)	Cu^{2+}
lithium	Li^+	iron(II)	Fe^{2+}
potassium	K^+	lead	Pb^{2+}
silver	Ag^+	magnesium	Mg^{2+}
sodium	Na^+	zinc	Zn^{2+}
barium	Ba^{2+}	aluminium	Al^{3+}
		iron(III)	Fe^{3+}

Negative ions

Name	Formula	Name	Formula
bromide	Br^-	nitrate	NO_3^-
chloride	Cl^-	carbonate	CO_3^{2-}
fluoride	F^-	oxide	O^{2-}
hydroxide	OH^-	sulphate	SO_4^{2-}
iodide	I^-	sulphide	S^{2-}

Glossary

absorbed (in biology) Digested food is taken into the blood from the small intestine.

absorbed (in physics) When energy is taken up by a substance.

acceleration How quickly the velocity, or speed, of an object changes. Acceleration (m/s^2) = change in speed (m/s) / time (s).

acid gas scrubber Removes acidic gases (e.g. sulphur dioxide) from industrial smoke, before they are released into the atmosphere.

acid rain Rain containing sulphuric acid and nitric acid. Acid rain has a pH of less than 5.6.

activation energy The minimum amount of energy that particles need in order to react.

adaptation / adapted A feature of an organism or cell that allows it to do something successfully. These organisms or cells are said to be 'adapted' to their job or function.

aerobic bacteria Bacteria that respire using aerobic respiration.

aerobic respiration Respiration that uses oxygen.

air resistance A force that acts on any object moving through air. The faster the object, the bigger the air resistance in the opposite direction.

alcohol Ethanol is an example. A chemical produced by the fermentation of sugar by yeast.

alkali metals Elements listed in Group I of the Periodic Table. All are very reactive and react with water to produce the metal hydroxide and hydrogen.

alleles Different forms of a gene for the same characteristic (e.g. alleles for blue eyes and brown eyes).

alpha radiation Radioactive particles given out by the nucleus of an unstable atom. Alpha particles are fast moving helium nuclei that carry a 2+ charge. They do not travel far through air and are stopped by paper.

amino acids Proteins are made from chains of amino acids joined together.

ammonium compounds Compounds of ammonia containing the NH_4 ion.

ammonium nitrate A salt used in fertilisers. It is made by neutralising ammonium hydroxide with nitric acid.

amplitude The maximum vertical distance that a wave moves from its rest position during a vibration. The bigger the amplitude of a sound wave, the louder the sound and the more energy being carried.

anaemia A disease caused by a shortage of iron in the diet. The person cannot make enough red blood cells.

anaerobic bacteria Bacteria that respire using anaerobic respiration.

anaerobic respiration Respiration that does not require oxygen (e.g. fermentation).

analogue signal A signal which varies continuously in amplitude and frequency, like music.

angle of incidence The angle between a light ray and the normal as the ray heads towards an object.

angle of reflection The angle between a light ray and the normal as the ray leaves a mirror.

anhydrous Literally 'without water'. There is no water locked up in compounds which are anhydrous.

anion A negatively charged ion. It is attracted to the anode in electrolysis.

anode Positive electrode in electrolysis.

A_r The symbol for the relative atomic mass or RAM of an element.

artificial insemination Placing semen (containing sperm) into the womb (uterus) of an animal.

artificial selection The selection and breeding of plants or animals by man to produce offspring which have useful characteristics (e.g. plants that are resistant to disease). Also called selective breeding.

asexual reproduction Reproduction involving one parent that produces genetically identical offspring.

atmosphere A mixture of gases that surrounds the Earth.

atomic number The number of protons in an element's atoms.

atom The smallest particle of an element. It has no overall electric charge.

average rate The average (mean) speed of a chemical reaction.

background radiation Radioactivity that we are exposed to all the time.

bacteria Very small single-celled organisms with no nucleus.

balanced When things are balanced there is no change in the movement of the object.

balanced symbol equation When the number of different atoms on either side of a chemical symbol equation are the same.

base A substance which reacts with an acid.

batch process When you wait for a reaction to be over before removing the products.

beta radiation Radioactive particles given out by the nucleus of an unstable atom. Beta particles are high energy electrons that carry a 1– charge. They are stopped by thin sheets of metal.

Big Bang theory Theory that when a tiny lump of matter exploded the Universe was created.

biodegradable Something that breaks down naturally in the environment.

biomass The total dry mass of an organism or organisms.

black hole A collapsed star with a huge gravitational field strength so that not even light can escape being pulled into it.

body cell Any cell of an organism, other than its gametes (sex cells).

boiling point When a liquid is at its boiling point it is as hot as it can get. It is evaporating as fast as it can.

bond A chemical link between atoms. All chemical bonds are very strong.

braking distance The distance a vehicle travels from when the brakes are applied to when it stops.

breed A group of organisms within a species that have various characteristics in common (e.g. a Poodle is a breed of dog). (Usually refers to animals.)

brine A solution of sodium chloride in water.

cancer When cells start to grow uncontrollably.

carbohydrase An enzyme that splits apart carbohydrates.

carbon cycle How carbon is cycled between living organisms and the air.

carbon dioxide A colourless gas. It is produced by respiration and used up in photosynthesis.

carnivore An animal that eats meat.

carrier An organism that carries one allele for a disease, but does not have the disease itself. They can pass the faulty gene on to their offspring.

catalyst Something that speeds up a chemical reaction without being changed at the end of it.

catalytic converter A device fitted to car exhaust systems that reduces the amount of toxic gases released into the atmosphere. It contains catalysts.

cathode Negative electrode in electrolysis.

cation A positively charged ion. It is attracted to the cathode in electrolysis.

cell division When a cell divides to form new cells.

CFCs Chemicals that were used in fridges and aerosol cans and damage the ozone layer, which protects us from harmful UV rays.

chain reaction A reaction where the products react further (normally with the reactants) so that the reaction goes on and on.

characteristics Features that an organism has (e.g. freckles).

chloride A salt of hydrochloric acid, containing the chloride ion.

chromosomes Thread-like strands found in the nucleus of a cell. Chromosomes are made of DNA and contain the 'instructions' for a living thing.

clones Organisms produced by asexual reproduction or genetic engineering, which all have identical genes.

collision theory The theory which explains how different factors affect the rate of a chemical reaction.

combustion A chemical reaction that involves a substance reacting with oxygen and releasing a lot of heat. Sometimes called burning.

comet An object made of frozen gases and dust that orbits the Sun.

community All the organisms living in a particular habitat.

compete / competition When organisms need the same resource they 'compete' with each other for it (e.g. plants compete for light, water and mineral salts).

compost Dead material which has been broken down by decomposers. It will release mineral salts into the soil.

compound A substance which is made up of two or more different elements, chemically bonded together.

compression An area of a longitudinal wave where particles are squashed together.

compound ion An ion which contains more than one element (e.g. SO_4^{2+}).

concentrated A solution that contains a lot of the solute.

concentration The amount of solute that is dissolved in a litre of solvent.

constellation A group, or pattern, of stars in the sky (e.g. The Plough).

consumer An organism that eats other organisms.

continuous process When you continually remove the products of a reaction as it is occurring rather than waiting for it to finish.

continuous variation Variation in a characteristic that can have any number of values (e.g. human height but not the ability to roll your tongue).

contraception Birth control to prevent a baby being conceived.

contract Get shorter. Muscle cells contract by getting shorter and fatter.

cosmic radiation Rays of high energy particles that reach Earth from outer space.

count-rate A measure of the radioactive decay of a substance.

covalent bonding When atoms join together by sharing electrons in order to gain a full outer shell of electrons.

critical angle The angle of incidence at which a ray of light travelling from glass or water to a less dense medium is refracted so that it runs along the edge of the material.

crossed Fertilisation between two selected individuals.

cutting A side stem taken off a plant. It is allowed to sprout roots to make a new plant.

cystic fibrosis A genetic disease which causes sticky fluid to build up in the lungs.

decay When microbes feed on the remains of a dead organism and it rots away.

deceleration How quickly the velocity, or speed, of an object slows down. The opposite of acceleration.

decompose (in chemistry) Split up a substance by a chemical reaction.

decomposers Organisms that break down dead organisms (e.g. bacteria and fungi).

deforestation When large areas of forests are cleared.

denatured When an enzyme has changed shape and is damaged so that it cannot work any more.

dense Made up of very closely packed particles.

detritivore Animal that feeds on detritus.

detritus Rotting leaves and other parts of plants.

diatomic gases Gases which exist as molecules made up of two atoms (e.g. hydrogen, H_2; oxygen, O_2).

diffraction The spreading out of waves as they pass through a gap or past the edge of an obstacle.

digestion Breaking down food into smaller units that the body can use. (Proteins are broken down into amino acids, carbohydrates are broken down into glucose and fats are broken down into fatty acids and glycerol.)

digital signal An electrical signal that is made up of a series of pulses.

dilute A solution that contains only a little solute.

discontinuous variation Variation in a characteristic that can only have a set number of values (e.g. the ability to roll your tongue but not human height).

disease resistance When an organism has natural protection against a disease.

dispersion The splitting of white light into the seven colours of the visible spectrum.

displacement reaction Competition reaction between elements. A more reactive element displaces a less reactive one from its compound.

Distance–time graph A graph showing the distance something has travelled against the time taken.

DNA Substance that makes up chromosomes. Short for deoxyribonucleic acid.

dominant A dominant allele always shows itself in the offspring.

drag The force of friction that works in air or in a liquid.

driving force The force that makes a vehicle move.

echo The reflection of a sound wave.

ecosystem A habitat and all the animals and plants living there.

egg cell The gamete (sex cell) produced by a female.

elastic potential energy The kind of energy stored in something that has been stretched or squashed and which can bounce back to its original shape.

electric charge Positive or negative electricity.

electrical discharge tube A device that conducts electricity through a gas by forming electrons and ions.

electrode Conducting rod that is dipped into a solution during electrolysis.

electrolysis Splitting up a substance by electricity.

electromagnetic radiation When electromagnetic waves are given out by an object.

electromagnetic waves Transverse waves that travel at 300 000 000 m/s. They include radio waves, microwaves, infrared, visible light, ultraviolet, X-rays and gamma rays.

electron structure The arrangement of electrons in shells around the nucleus of an atom.

electrons Tiny negatively charged particles.

element A pure substance made up of one type of atom.

ellipse An oval shape.

embryo splitting / transplanting When the cells of a very young embryo are separated from each other so that each can develop into an organism. They are put into a womb (uterus) to develop.

emitted Something given out by an object said to be the emitter.

empirical formula Formula of a compound with the lowest whole number ratio of the elements that is possible.

endoscope A long, narrow medical instrument used to look inside the body.

endothermic reactions Reactions that take energy from the surroundings.

energy level Position of electrons in an atom, sometimes called an electron shell.

energy transfer Changing energy from one form to another.

environment The surroundings where an organism lives, including all the living and non-living factors.

environmental variation Features of an organism which are due to environmental factors (e.g. having a scar).

enzymes A substance that speeds up a chemical reaction in the body (a biological catalyst). Each enzyme works best at a particular temperature and pH.

equilibrium position When a reversible reaction reaches a point where the rate of the formation of products is the same as the rate of the formation of the original reactants.

eutrophication When bacteria multiply by feeding on dead material and use up all the oxygen in water.

evaporation When a liquid changes into a gas.

evolution How the organisms living on Earth have changed.

exothermic A chemical reaction which gives out heat energy to the surroundings (e.g. burning).

expand When the size of a substance increases due to being heated. The particles gain energy and move further apart.

extinction / extinct The process by which all the members of a species die out and become extinct.

fair test An experiment in which only one variable is changed at a time to allow a fair comparison.

fats Food substances needed as a store of energy and for insulation.

fermentation When yeast respires without oxygen and converts glucose into ethanol and carbon dioxide.

fertilisation The joining together (fusing) of male and female gametes.

fertilised egg cell Produced when the nuclei of a sperm and an egg join together.

fertiliser A chemical put onto soil to replace lost mineral salts and so make plants grow more healthily.

fertility drugs Hormones given to women to help release of eggs from the ovaries.

fertility treatment Medical treatment to help a woman become pregnant.

fluids Substances which can flow (a gas or a liquid).

fluorescence / fluorescent When light or other radiation is given off from atoms or molecules. Something that does this is said to be 'fluorescent'.

follicle stimulating hormone See FSH.

food chain Shows what eats what in a habitat. (It also shows the direction that energy flows from organism to organism.)

food web Shows how several food chains are linked together.

force A push or a pull. Force is measured in units called newtons (N).

formula (in chemistry) The symbol for a compound showing the types and number of atoms present (e.g. H_2O is the formula of water).

formula (in physics) A mathematical equation (e.g. speed = distance/time).

fossils Remains of organisms (or signs of their presence) preserved in rock.

frequency The number of waves per second. It is measured in hertz (Hz).

friction A force which works in the opposite direction to something which is moving.

FSH Follicle stimulating hormone. A hormone that causes egg cells to mature in the ovaries.

fungi Simple organisms which do not have chlorophyll (e.g. moulds, yeasts).

fuse (in biology) Join together.

fuse (in physics) A thin wire that melts and breaks if the current in a circuit gets too big.

galaxy A group of millions of stars held together by gravity (e.g. the Milky Way).

gamete A sex cell, e.g. a sperm cell or an egg cell.

gamma wave A high energy form of electromagnetic radiation that has a very short wavelength.

gene Part of a chromosome. It contains the 'instructions' for a particular feature (e.g. eye colour).

gene bank Place where seeds are stored to preserve plant varieties.

gene therapy Use of genetic engineering to cure diseases.

genetic engineering Altering the genetic makeup (DNA) of an organism.

genetically identical Having exactly the same genes (e.g. clones).

giant structure A substance made up of many atoms or ions bonded together to form a large 3-D structure (e.g. diamond, sodium chloride). A substance with a giant structure will have high melting and boiling points because of its large number of bonds.

global warming The gradual heating of the Earth's atmosphere. It is caused by the 'greenhouse effect'.

graphite A soft form of carbon. Used in pencil 'leads'.

gravitational field strength The gravitational force on a 1 kg mass in a gravitational field. On the Earth's surface it is approximately 10 N/kg.

gravity The force of attraction between any two bodies. It increases with increasing mass of the bodies and decreases if they are further apart.

greenhouse gas A gas that traps heat in the Earth's atmosphere (e.g. carbon dioxide).

Group Column of elements with similar properties in the Periodic Table.

Haber process An industrial process that produces ammonia gas from the raw materials air, water and methane.

habitat The place where an organism lives.

haemoglobin Molecule found in red blood cells that carries oxygen.

half equations Equations showing what happens to ions and electrons at each electrode in electrolysis.

half-life The time it takes for half of the atoms in a radioactive substance to decay.

halide A salt containing halogen atoms (e.g. fluoride, chloride, bromide or iodide).

halogen A non-metallic element found in Group 7 of the Periodic Table.

herbicide A chemical used to kill unwanted plants (weeds).

herbivore An animal that eats only plants.

hertz The unit of frequency of vibrations. 1 Hz = 1 vibration per second.

heterozygous When two alleles in a cell are different.

homozygous When two alleles in a cell are the same.

hormones Chemical 'messengers' that make a body process happen. Hormones are secreted by glands and are carried around the body in the blood plasma.

host (in biology) An organism that is used to help another (e.g. in embryo transplantation, the cells from an embryo are put into hosts to develop).

Huntington's disease An inherited disease of the nervous system caused by a dominant allele. Symptoms include involuntary movements and mental deterioration.

hydrated Containing water.

infrared radiation Another term for heat radiation.

inherit Receive from your parents.

inherited disease A disease passed from parents to offspring in the form of a defective allele.

inherited variation Features of an organism controlled by alleles inherited from their parents (e.g. eye colour).

inhibit Prevent or slow down.

inner core The solid central part of the Earth.

intermolecular force Force between two molecules.

ion An atom or group of atoms with an electrical charge.

ionic bond A strong force of attraction between oppositely charged ions.

ionic lattice A giant crystal structure made up of many oppositely charged ions held together by ionic bonds.

ionised When an atom has lost or gained electrons to form an ion.

ionising radiation Radiation that causes atoms to gain or lose electrons and form ions.

isomerase Enzyme used to turn glucose into fructose.

isotopes Atoms of the same element that have different numbers of neutrons in their nuclei.

joule (J) Unit for measuring energy or work.

kinetic energy The kind of energy in moving things.

lactic acid The waste product of anaerobic respiration in humans.

lactose A type of sugar found in milk.

landfill site An area of land where waste materials are buried.

LH Luteinising hormone. Hormone that causes the release of a mature egg cell from an ovary.

lichen A mutualistic relationship between a fungus and an alga (simple plant). They often occur as crusty patches on tree trunks and walls.

lipase An enzyme that digests fats to fatty acids and glycerol.

living environmental factor Living things that affect an environment (i.e. the living things in an environment).

longitudinal A wave motion where the vibrations are parallel to the direction in which the wave is moving (e.g. a sound wave).

lubricant A substance used to reduce friction (e.g. oil).

luteinising hormone See LH.

malaria A disease caused by a microbe which lives in the blood. It is transmitted by mosquito bites and causes fevers and often death.

mantle Layer between the crust and the core inside the Earth.

mark-release-recapture Way of measuring a population of animals.

mass The amount of material that makes up an object. It is usually measured in kilograms (kg) or grams (g).

mass (or nucleon) number The total number of protons and neutrons in the nucleus of an atom.

matter The material that something is made up of.

meiosis Cell division which produces cells with only one set of chromosomes – gametes.

melting point The temperature at which a solid changes to a liquid.

menstrual cycle Cycle of changes in a woman's reproductive system in which the lining of the womb (uterus) is shed and replaced each month.

metals Strong shiny elements that can be hammered into shape. Metals are good conductors of heat and electricity.

methane Natural gas. CH_4.

metres per second (m/s) A unit of speed.

metres per second squared (m/s^2) The unit of acceleration.

microbe A tiny organism that can only be seen with a microscope.

microwaves Short wavelength radio waves in the electromagnetic spectrum.

Milky Way The spiral galaxy of stars of which the Earth is a part.

mitosis Cell division. The cell doubles its number of chromosomes and then divides in two.

mole A large (6×10^{23}) number of atoms.

molecule A pair or group of atoms bonded together.

monitoring Observing and recording changes.

M_r Symbol that represents the relative formula mass of a compound.

mutation A sudden change in a gene.

natural satellite A small object that orbits a larger one that was not put into space by man (e.g. the Moon is the natural satellite of the Earth).

natural selection The survival of those organisms best adapted to live in a habitat. It is the basis of the Theory of Evolution.

negative pole The pole of a cell or battery that repels negative charges and attracts positive ones.

negligible Something so small that it is not worth considering.

neutral (in chemistry) Substance that is not an acid or alkali. Has a pH of 7.

neutral (in physics) i) One of the wires that carries electricity in an appliance. ii) Something with equal amounts of positive and negative charge.

neutron star A very dense star that has collapsed due to its own gravity.

neutron An uncharged particle found in the nucleus of an atom. Its mass is similar to that of a proton.

newton (N) The unit of force.

newtons per kilogram (N/kg) The unit of gravitational field strength.

nitrates The salts of nitric acid. Nitrates are needed by plants to make proteins.

nitrifying bacteria Bacteria which turn ammonium compounds into nitrates.

nitrogen cycle Way in which nitrogen is recycled in nature.

nitrogen-fixing bacteria Bacteria which can take nitrogen from the air and make nitrates.

nitrogen oxides Pollutants in vehicle exhaust fumes and from power stations. These are acidic gases which can form acid rain.

noble gas An element in Group 0 (Group 8) of the Periodic Table. All are very unreactive gases.

non-biodegradable Something that does not decay in nature.

non-metals Elements which are not metals. They are poor conductors of heat and electricity.

normal (in physics) A line drawn at right angles to a surface.

nuclear fusion Reaction in which nuclei of atoms join together.

nuclear fission Reaction in which nuclei of atoms split apart.

nuclear model The theory or model used to explain the properties of the atom.

nucleon A particle found in the nucleus of an atom (i.e. a proton or a neutron).

nucleus (in biology) The control centre of a cell containing chromosomes made of DNA.

nucleus (in physics) The centre of an atom, made up of protons and neutrons.

oestrogen Hormone that causes the womb lining to get thicker.

offspring The immediate descendant(s) of an organism.

opaque Does not allow light through.

optical fibre Thin strand of glass that light travels through by total internal reflection. Used in telecommunications and by surgeons to see inside the body.

optimum pH The pH at which an enzyme works fastest.

optimum temperature The temperature at which an enzyme works fastest.

oral contraception The use of hormones, taken in the form of a pill, to prevent pregnancy.

orbit The curved path taken by an object that moves round another object, (e.g. a planet around the Sun).

oscillation One whole cycle of a wave.

oscilloscope (CRO) An instrument used to display waves on a screen.

outer core The liquid central part of the Earth.

ovary The female sex organ that produces the female sex cells (egg cells).

oxidising A compound that provides a source of oxygen to allow things to burn violently is said to be oxidising.

ozone A form of oxygen found in the upper atmosphere that protects us from UV radiation by absorbing it.

parallel (in physics) When the current in an electrical circuit can flow along different routes.

parent atoms Atoms from which new atoms of different elements are formed.

parents Organisms from which offspring are produced.

particle An extremely small piece of matter.

percentage mass percentage mass of an element in a compound = mass of element in the formula $\times$ 100 / relative formula mass of the compound.

period (in biology) When the womb (uterus) lining is shed.

period (in physics) The time for one complete wave oscillation to pass a certain point.

persistent Does not break down in nature.

pesticide A chemical used to kill organisms that eat growing crops.

photochemical smog A chemical fog caused by the action of sunlight on vehicle exhaust fumes.

photosynthesis Process that plants use to make their own food. It needs light to work.
carbon dioxide + water $\rightarrow$ glucose + oxygen

physical factors Non-living factors in an environment (e.g. the amount of light).

pituitary gland A gland attached to the brain. It produces hormones.

plasmids Small loops of DNA found in bacteria.

polar orbit An object in polar orbit will pass over the north and south poles once in each orbit.

population The number of organisms of one particular species living in the same habitat.

positive pole The pole of a cell or battery that repels positive charges and attracts negative ones.

precipitate A solid product formed by a reaction in which the two reactants are solutions.

predator An animal which hunts and kills other animals for food.

prey An animal which is hunted and eaten by a predator.

probe A device which can be linked to a computer to measure changes (e.g. temperature probe, pH probe).

producer An organism that makes food from simple raw materials. Green plants are producers.

products Substances formed by a chemical reaction.

properties Descriptions of how a material behaves.

proportion The size of a variable compared to the whole.

protease An enzyme that digests protein into amino acids.

proteins Important substances used for growth and repair in living things.

proton number The number of protons in an atom. Also called the atomic number.

protons Tiny positively charged particles in an atom's nucleus.

putrifying (decay) bacteria Bacteria which feed off dead organisms causing decay.

P wave Longitudinal seismic wave.

pyramid of biomass A diagram that represents the total biomass of the organisms at each level in a food chain.

pyramid of numbers Diagram showing the numbers of different organisms in a food chain.

quadrat Square frame used to estimate plant populations.

quality control The sampling and checking of a manufactured product in order to maintain quality.

R.A.M. (Relative Atomic Mass) Relative atomic mass, symbol A_r. The mass of an atom compared to the mass of a carbon atom.

R.F.M. (Relative Formula Mass) Relative formula mass is the sum of the R.A.M.s of all the atoms in a compound.

radiation badge Badge used to detect someone's exposure to radiation.

radio telescope An instrument used in astronomy to detect radio waves produced by objects in space.

radio wave A type of electromagnetic radiation that has a long wavelength. Used to carry radio and TV programmes.

radioactive Atoms that have unstable nuclei and give off one or more types of radioactivity (alpha, beta or gamma).

radioactive decay When an atom emits one or more types of radioactivity as its nucleus disintegrates.

radioactive isotope / radioisotope An atom that is radioactive. The atoms have unstable nuclei that can break apart to give off one or more types of radioactivity (alpha, beta or gamma).

radionuclide An atomic nucleus that gives off radioactivity.

rarefaction An area of a longitudinal wave where particles are spread out.

rate of reaction How fast or slow a chemical reaction occurs.

ratio A comparison of the size of two factors.

raw material A basic starting material from which a useful substance is produced.

ray A narrow beam of light.

reactants Substances used up in a chemical reaction.

reaction (in biology) The change in behaviour of an organism as it responds to a stimulus.

recessive A recessive allele only works when present on both chromosomes in a pair.

recycled When something is used again in a system.

red giant A star that has used up its hydrogen, swollen in size and cooled.

red-shift The shift of spectral lines towards the red end of the visible spectrum caused by a galaxy moving away from Earth.

reflect Bounce something back from a surface.

reflection The image formed when light from an object is reflected from a surface.

refraction When a wave passes from one medium into another (e.g. from water into air) its speed is altered. A change in the direction of the wave also occurs if it is not travelling along a normal.

relative atomic mass (R.A.M.) Formula A_r. The mass of an atom compared to the mass of a carbon atom.

relative formula mass (R.F.M.) Formula M_r. The sum of the R.A.M.s of all the atoms in a compound.

resistant When an organism has protection against a disease.

respiration Chemical reaction inside cells to release energy from glucose.
glucose + oxygen →
                        carbon dioxide + water

resultant The final, single force acting on an object.

reversible reaction A chemical reaction that can go forwards or backwards depending on the conditions. For example:
nitrogen + hydrogen ⇌ ammonia.

salts Compounds formed when an acid reacts with a base.

satellite An object that orbits a planet or a star. The Moon is the Earth's natural satellite.

seismic waves Shock waves sent out by earthquakes.

seismograph A machine that can produce a picture showing the vibrations produced by seismic waves

seismograph trace Lines drawn on rolling paper in a seismograph.

selective breeding The selection and breeding of plants or animals by man to produce offspring which have useful characteristics (e.g. plants that are resistant to disease). Also called artificial selection.

sewage Waste matter from homes, farms and industry that is carried in drains and sewers.

sex chromosome Either of the X or Y chromosomes that determine the sex of an organism. In humans a female has XX sex chromosomes and a male has XY sex chromosomes.

sexual reproduction Reproduction that involves two parents, a male and a female. Sex cells from each parent join together at fertilisation.

shells (in chemistry) Energy levels around the nucleus of an atom in which electrons orbit.

sickle-cell anaemia An inherited disease in which the red blood cells can become sickle shaped and cannot carry as much oxygen as normal.

silica Another name for silicon dioxide.

silver halides Silver salts which contain halogen atoms (e.g. silver chloride, silver bromide).

sludge Semi-solid substance found at the bottom of tanks at sewage works.

smog A mixture of smoke, fog and chemical fumes.

smoke A cloud of small particles produced when something is burnt.

solar radiation light and heat from the Sun.

Solar System The Sun and all the planets (and asteroids) that orbit it.

soluble Something that will dissolve.

solute Something that has dissolved.

solution A solute dissolved in a solvent.

solvent A liquid which can dissolve things.

sound waves Longitudinal waves produced when something vibrates.

species A group of organisms with similar characteristics that can breed with each other and produce fertile offspring.

spectrum A range of wavelengths.

speed How fast an object travels. speed = distance/time

speed of light How fast light and all other types of electromagnetic waves travel; 300 000 000 m/s.

sperm bank A place where sperm is stored for future use.

sperm cell The male sex cell.

spoil Waste material from mining.

stable An unreactive substance that is unlikely to change suddenly.

state symbols Letters written in chemical equations in brackets after each formula to indicate the state of the chemical. (s) represents a solid, (l) represents a liquid, (g) represents a gas and (aq) represents a substance dissolved in water.

states of matter The three states of matter are solid, liquid and gas.

sterile i) Unable to produce offspring. i) Free from any living microorganisms.

sterilise To kill all bacteria on something.

stimulate To cause something to happen or make it happen faster.

streamlining Making the shape of something smoother so there is less resistance to drag.

sulphur dioxide A pollutant gas produced by burning fossil fuels. It causes acid rain.

supernova An exploding star.

surface area The total area of the outside of an object or surface.

S wave Transverse seismic wave.

symbol Letter, or letters, used to represent an element (e.g. Na is the symbol for sodium).

thinking distance The distance a car travels, from when a driver realises that he needs to break until the break pedal is pressed.

tilted axis The Earth spins about its axis. The axis is not vertical, it is tilted by 23.5°. This tilt causes the different seasons.

tissue culture Technique used to grow plant cells into new plants.

tolerant When an organism can withstand the effects of a drug.

total internal reflection When a ray of light travelling towards the edge of a transparent block is completely reflected and stays inside the block. (This happens when the angle of incidence is greater than the critical angle.)

toxic Poisonous.

trace Display of waves, either on paper or on a screen.

tracer Liquid used to find things. Can be radioactive.

transferred When energy is changed from one type into another.

transmitted i) Sent out radio waves. ii) Particles or energy have passed through something.

transparent Allows light to pass through easily.

transverse A wave motion in which the vibrations are at right angles to the direction the wave is travelling in (e.g. all electromagnetic waves).

triplet Code of three DNA bases which provides the information to add one amino acid onto a chain.

ultraviolet rays / radiation Electromagnetic radiation that causes a sun tan. Over exposure can cause skin cancer.

ultrasound Sound waves with a frequency above 20 000 Hz that cannot be heard by the human ear. Used to scan body tissues and for echo-sounding.

unbalanced force When the forces acting on an object are not equal and opposite, causing the movement of the object to change.

unreactive A chemical which is unlikely to change, it has a stable structure.

unstable A substance that easily breaks down or emits radioactivity.

vacuum An empty region of space.

variation The differences between organisms of the same species.

variety A group of individuals within a species that have particular features in common. Usually refers to plants.

velocity Speed in a particular direction.

Velocity–time graph A graph to show how the velocity of an object changes with time.

visible light / spectrum The part of the electromagnetic spectrum that can be detected by the eye. Made up of red, orange, yellow, green, blue, indigo and violet light.

wavelength The length of one complete cycle of a wave.

weight A force due to gravity acting on an object.

white dwarf A small, dense star formed when a red giant collapses.

word equation A way of showing what happens in a chemical reaction using words.

work done Work is done when a force causes movement.
work done (J) = force (N) × distance moved in direction of force (m)

X-rays Very penetrating, short wavelength electromagnetic waves. Used to detect broken bones.

yeast Single-celled fungus.

yield (in chemistry) The amount of a product formed in a chemical reaction.

yield (in biology) The amount of useful substances produced by a crop plant.

Index

A

absorption, radiation 230, 233, 234
acceleration 170–1, 173, 177, 184–5
acid gas scrubbers 38
acid rain 38–9
acids 153, 160
activation energy 97
ADA deficiency 69
adaptation 8–9, 18–19, 75
aerobic bacteria 25
aerosols 37
air
    composition 112
    pollution 36–9
    resistance 182–3, 188–9
alcohol 106
alkali metals 146, 150–1
alleles 60–1, 62, 63, 72, 76–7
alpha (α) radiation 232–4, 242
aluminium 121, 240
amino acids 28, 49
ammonia 114–15, 116–17, 153
ammonites 83
ammonium nitrate 114, 116–17, 118
amoeba 50
amplitude 208, 217, 226
anaemia, sickle-cell 64–5
anaerobic bacteria 25
analogue signals 226–7
angle of incidence 212
animal populations 18–21
anions 149
anodes 149, 158
antibiotics 79
aphids 51
aqueous solutions 129
arctic habitat 8
argon 143, 241
Aristotle 132
artificial insemination 71
artificial selection 70–3
asexual reproduction 50–1, 56–7
astronauts 186
atmosphere 197
atomic models 242
atomic number 118, 134–5, 138
atoms
    balanced equations 130–1
    collision theory 94–5
    discovery 132–3, 242
    electronic structure 136–7
    elements/compounds 126–7
    formulae 128–9
    ionisation 232
    structure 134–7, 142
average rate of reaction 87
average speed 168

B

background radiation 235
bacteria
    decomposition 22
    division 50
bacteria
    DNA 68

evolution 78, 79
    food 107
    sewage breakdown 34
    soil 112, 113
baking 107
balanced equations 130–1
balanced forces 174–5, 188
batch processes 105
beer-making 106
beta (ß) radiation 232–4, 240
Big Bang 200–1
biodegradable materials 22
biological catalysts 23, 102–7
biological washing powders 102, 104
biomass 13
black holes 186, 199
bonding
    covalent 152–3, 162, 163
    energy changes 108
    ionic 146–9, 163
    metallic 144–5, 162
Boyle, Robert 133
braking 178, 180–1
bread 107
breeding, selective 70–3
brine 158
bromine 156, 157
bronchitis 36

C

cacti 9
caesium 150, 151
calculations
    formulae 122
    molar 119–21
camouflage 8
cancer 77, 229, 230
carbohydrases 105
carbon 155
carbon cycle 26–7
carbon dating 240
carbon dioxide
    carbon cycle 26–7
    formation 86
    global warming 40–3
    pollution 36
carbon isotopes 236
carnivores 10, 15, 18–19
carriers, genetic 63
catalysts 100–1, 102–7, 114, 116
catalytic converters 38, 39, 100
cathodes 149, 158
cations 149
cat's eyes 219
cattle grazing 43
cells
    radiation effects 229, 230–3
    reproduction 50–3, 54, 55, 57, 60, 66
    sickle-cell anaemia 64–5
    structure 48
CFCs see chlorofluorocarbons
chain reactions 237
characteristics 46–7
charge, ionic 146–7
chemical energy 190
chemical formulae 128–9

chemical reactions
    catalysts 100–1
    collision theory 94–5
    concentration 92–5
    energy transfer 108–9
    enzymes 102–7
    neutralisation 117
    rates 86–103
    reversible 110, 111
    surface area 98–9
    temperature 96–7, 102–3, 108–9
chlorine 152, 156, 157
chlorofluorocarbons 37
chromosomes
    alleles 60–1
    genetic engineering 68–9
    inherited variation 48–9
    Mendel's factors 59
    reproduction 50–3
cleaning, ultrasound 216
climate change 40–3
clones 50, 56–7, 66–7, 72
collision theory 94–5
comets 195
common salt 157, 158–9
communities 6–7
competition 16–17, 75
compost 25
compound ions 147
compounds 126–7
compressions 207
concentration 92–5
conductivity 145, 148
constellations 194–5, 198
consumers 10, 11, 12, 13
continuous processes 105
contraception 55
Copernicus, Nicolaus 194
corrosive substances 91
cosmic radiation 235
count-rate 238
covalent bonding 152–3, 162, 163
covalent giant structures 154–5
Crick, Francis 59
critical angle 218–19
crop yields 69, 112, 113
crossing plants 58
crystals 148, 154, 155
cuttings 56, 57, 67
cystic fibrosis 63

D

Dalton, John 133
Darwin, Charles 59, 78, 80
DDT 34
dead tissue 22–3, 24
decay, fossils 83
deceleration 170, 172, 177–9
decomposers 22
decomposition 22–3, 24
deforestation 43
denatured enzymes 102, 103
density, wave speeds 210–11
deserts 9
detritivores 22
detritus 22
deuterium 236

diamonds 155
diatomic molecules 152, 156
dieldrin 32
differences 46–7
diffraction 222–3
digestion 104
digital signals 226–7
dilution see concentration
dinosaurs 83
'disappearing cross' method 90
diseases
    inherited 62–5
    natural selection 75
    resistance 71
dispersion 220–1
displacement reactions 157
distance–time graphs 168–9, 173
division, cells 50
DNA
    bacteria 68
    code 49
    forensics 48
    inherited variation 48–9
    radiation 76–7
Döbereiner, Johan 140
dominant alleles 60–1
drag 182–3
driving force 189
drought 41
drugs, fertility 54
ductility 144

E

Earth 30–1, 194–5, 214, 215
earthquakes 206, 208–9, 215
echoes 212
ecosystems 24
egg cells 52–3, 54, 55, 57, 60, 66
elastic potential energy 191
electric charges 134
electrical conductivity 148
electrolysis 121, 148–9, 158
electromagnetic spectrum 220, 224–5, 228–9, 230–9
electron shells 136–7, 142–3, 144
    atoms 142
    covalent bonding 152–3
    ionic bonding 146–9
    metals 144–5
    noble gases 142
electrons 134–7, 232, 234, 243
elements 126–7, 129, 135, 138–43, 246
embryos 65, 66
empirical formulae 123
endoscopes 218–19
endothermic reactions 108–9
energy
    kinetic 190, 192–3
    photosynthesis 14
    transfer 108–9, 111, 190–1
    types 108, 190–3, 206
energy levels see electron shells
environmental variation 47
enzymes 23, 102–7
equal and opposite forces 175
equations, balanced 130–1
equilibrium position 110, 114, 115

eutrophication 34
evolution 59, 78–81
exothermic reactions 108–9
explosions 86
extinction 31, 81
extraterrestrial life 202–3
Exxon Valdez oilspill 35

F

faeces 25
fair tests 92
fats 104
fermentation 106
fertilisation 52–3, 66
fertilisers 29, 34, 112–16
fertility 54–5
flammable substances 91
Flemming, Walther 59
flooding 41
fluids, drag 182–3
fluorescence 228
fluorine 156, 157
follicle stimulating hormone 54
food
    chains 10, 12, 13, 14, 15
    enzymes 106–7
    webs 10, 11
forces
    see also friction
    balanced 174–5, 188
    equal and opposite 175
    resultant 176–7
    unbalanced 176–7, 184–5
forensics 48
formulae, chemical 128–9
fossil fuels 26, 36–9, 40, 42
fossils 80–3, 202
frequency 208–9, 216–17, 226
friction
    effects 178–9
    fluids 182–3, 189
    kinetic energy 193
fridges see refrigeration
fructose 105
fungi 22, 72

G

galaxies 200, 201
gallium 141, 144
gametes 52–3, 57, 60–1
gamma (γ) radiation 220, 229,
    231–4, 240
gas syringes 88
gases 129, 142–3
    mass measurement 89
    volumes 88, 120
Geiger counters 235
gene therapy 69
genes
    discovery 58–9
    diseases 62–5
    genetic engineering 68–9
    inherited variation 48–9
    plants 56
geostationary orbits 196–7
giant structures
    covalent 154–5
    elements 126
    ionic compounds 148–9, 163
    metals 145
    sodium chloride 128
global warming 40–3
glucose 105

graphite 155
gravitational field strength 186
gravity 186–7, 196
Greek thinkers 132
greenhouse gases 40–3
Group 0 elements 142–3
Group 1 elements 150–1
Group 7 elements 139, 156–7
groups of elements 138
growth rates, competition 17

H

Haber, Fritz 114
Haber process 114–15
habitats
    competition 16–17
    population size 20–1
    predators 18–19
    types 6–7
haemoglobin 64
half equations 149
half-life 238–9
halide ions 146, 157
halogen compounds 160–1
halogens 156–7
harmful substances 91
hazard symbols 91, 233
heat energy 225
heavy water 236
hedgerows 7
helium
    atom 134, 136
    balloons 143
    nuclei 232–4
    stellar 198
herbicides 32–3
herbivores 10
hormones 15, 54–5
Huntington's disease 62
hydration 111
hydrogen 136, 198, 236
hydrogen chloride 153, 160
Hyracotherium 80–1

I

igneous rocks 241
incidence, angle of 212
industrial catalysts 101
industrial enzymes 104, 105
industry, raw materials 30
infrared radiation 220, 225, 230
inherited diseases 62–5
inherited variation 47–9
intensive farming 15
intermolecular forces 154, 155
iodine 156, 157
ionic bonding 146–9, 163
ionic compounds 146–51
ionising radiation 76–7, 230–9
ions 94, 128, 144
iron catalysts 101, 114
iron sulphide 148
irritants 91
isomerases 105
isotopes 135, 236–41

J

Johanssen, Wilhelm 59

K

kinetic energy 190, 192–3, 206

L

lactic acid 107
lactose 107
lakes, acidification 38
land pollution 32–3
land use, human 31
landfill 32, 43
lattices, ionic 148
Law of Octaves 140
lead 36, 231, 234, 241
leap years 195
leaves, competition 17
Lecoq, Paul-Emile 141
lichens 39
light
    photosynthesis 14
    reflection 212–13, 214
    refraction 220–1
    total internal reflection
    218–19
    waves 210–11
Lightfoot, Dr John 80
lipases 104
liquids 129, 182–3
lithium 136, 144, 150, 151, 236
long wavelength electromagnetic
    waves 224–5, 230
longitudinal (p) waves 206, 207,
    210–11, 214, 215
loudness 217
lubricants 179
lysozyme 102

M

malaria 65
malleability 144, 145
mammoths 79
marking 20
Mars 202
Marsden, Ernest 242
mass
    acceleration 184
    atomic 118
    gas 89
    gravity/weight 186–7
    kinetic energy 192–3
mass number see relative atomic
    mass
masseter muscle 174
matter 187
mean speed 168
media, refractive 213, 214
Mendel, Gregor 58–9
Mendeleev, Dmitri 141
menstrual cycle 55
mercury waste 35
metals
    alkali 146, 150–1
    bonding 144–5, 162, 163
    catalysts 100–1
    ionic compounds 146–51
    Periodic Table 139
    properties 142, 144–5
    waste 33
methane 40–1, 153
micro waves 220, 225, 231
microorganisms
    decomposition 22–3, 25
    disease 65
    food 96, 107
    fossils 83
Milky Way 200
mining waste 33
mirages 213

mirrors 212
mitosis 50
mixtures 127
mobile phones 225
Moeritherium 78–9
molecular formulae 123
molecules 94–5, 126–7
    balanced equations 130–1
moles 119, 120–1
Morse code 226, 227
movement, unbalanced forces
    177
muscles 174
mutations 76–7

N

natural selection 74–5, 78, 81
negatives (film) 161
neutralisation 117
neutron stars 199
neutrons 134–7, 234, 243
Newlands, John 140
Newton's Second Law 185
nickel catalysts 101
nitrates 112, 113
nitric acid 116–17
nitrifying bacteria 29
nitrogen 112–15
    cycle 28–9, 113
nitrogen oxides 38
nitrogen-fixing bacteria 28
noble gases 142–3
non-metals 139, 142, 146–51,
    162, 163
normal, reflection 212, 213
nuclear fission chain reaction
    237
nuclear fuel 235
nuclear fusion 198
nuclear model 242
nuclear-powered stars 198
nuclei, atomic 234
nucleons 236
nutrient recycling 24–5

O

octuplets 54
oestrogen 55
offspring 46–7, 60–1
oil 30
oilspills 35
opaque materials 210
optical fibres 218–19
optimum pH 103
optimum temperature 102
oral contraception 55
orbits 194–7
oscillations see waves
oscilloscopes 216
ovaries 54
oxidising substances 91
oxygen, air 112
ozone 37

P

p (longitudinal) waves 206, 207,
    210–11, 214, 215
pacemakers 233
parachutes 188–9
parent atoms 238, 239
pea plants 60–1
peppered moths 74–5
percentage mass 122–3
Periodic Table 135, 138–43, 246

periods (elements) 138
periods (menstruation) 55
periods (waves) 206
pesticides 32–3
pH effects 103
photochemical smog 36
photography 160–1
photosynthesis 14, 26–7, 42
pitch 216–17, 223
pituitary gland 54
planets 194–5, 196
plants
    competition 17
    food chains/webs 10–15
    fossils 83
    genes 58–61
    habitats 7
    population size 21
    reproduction 56–7
    selective breeding 70–3
    survival 9
    tolerance 33
plasmids 68
platinum catalysts 101, 116
plum pudding model 242–3
polar orbits 197
pollen 57, 60–1
pollution
    air 36–9
    fertilisers 34
    land 32–3, 38–9
    water 34–5, 38–9
populations
    explosion 30–1
    habitats 6–7
    human 30–1
    size 18–19, 20–1
potassium 150
potential energy 191
predators 18–19, 78
pressure effects 95
prey 18–19, 78
prisms 220
producers, food chains 10, 11,
    12, 13
products 86, 110, 127
proteases 103, 104, 105
proteins 49, 104
protons 134–7, 234, 243
Proust, Louis-Joseph 133
pulses, digital 226
push/pull forces 174
pyramids of biomass 13
pyramids of energy 14–15
pyramids of numbers 12

Q
quadrats 21
quaggas 70
quality control 216, 240

R
radiation 76–7, 224
    cells 230–1
    half-lives 238–9
    ionisation 232–3
    isotopes 230–41
    types 234–5
radio telescopes 203
radio waves 220, 222–3, 224
radioactivity 230–41
radon 239

rainbows 220–1
rainforests 30
RAM see relative atomic mass
rare breeds 72, 73
rarefactions 207
rates of reaction 86–103
    catalysts 100–1
    collision theory 94–5
    concentration 92–5
    enzymes 102–7
    measurement 86–7, 88–91,
        93, 96
    surface area 98–9
    temperature 96–7, 102–3
ratios 128
raw materials 30–1
reactants 86, 110, 127
reaction times (reflexes) 180–1
reactions see chemical reactions;
    rates of reaction
reactivity 136, 143, 157
recapturing 20
recessive alleles 60–1
recycling 31
red giants 199
red-shift 200
reflection 212–13, 216, 218–19
refraction 213, 214–15
refrigeration 96
relative atomic mass (RAM) 118,
    119, 122, 135, 141
relative formula mass (RFM) 118,
    119
releasing 20
reproduction 50–3, 56–7
resistance
    agriculture 72
    evolution 79
respiration 14, 23
    carbon cycle 26–7
    global warming 42
    water pollution 34
resultant forces 176–7
reversible reactions 110, 111
RFM see relative formula mass
rocks, dating 241
roots, competition 17
rotting see decomposition
rubbish see waste
Rutherford, Ernest 242

S
s (transverse) waves 210–11, 215
salts 146–51, 157
satellites 196–7
scattering experiments 243
search for extra-terrestrial
    intelligence (SETI) 203
seed banks 73
seismic waves 206, 208–9,
    210–11, 214
selective breeding 70–3
semi-metals 139
SETI see search for extra-
    terrestrial intelligence
sewage 25, 34
sex chromosomes 53
sexual reproduction 50–3, 57
shells
    see also electron shells
    fossils 82, 83
short wavelength
electromagnetic waves 228–9

sickle-cell anaemia 64–5
silicon dioxide 154
silver halides 160–1
skeleton 174
skin cancer 230
slowing down see deceleration
smog 36–7
smoke 36
sodium 150
sodium chloride 146–7, 157,
    158–9
sodium hydroxide 158, 159
soil pollution 32–3, 38
Solar System 198, 200
solids 129
solubility 148
solutes 92
solutions 92
solvents 92
sound
    analogue/digital 226–7
    diffraction 223
    reflection 212
    ultrasound 216–17
    waves 210–11
space competition 16
space probes 202
species 46–7, 78
speckled peppered moths 74
spectrum 220–1
speed
    calculating 166–7
    fluid resistance 183
    kinetic energy 192–3
    orbits 196
    waves 209
speeding up see acceleration
sperm cells 52–3
spoil tips 33
stars 194, 198, 199, 200–1
state symbols 129
sterile conditions 67
sterilisation 229, 230
stopping distance 180
streamlining 182–3, 184
structures, bonding 162–3
sulphur dioxide 36–9
supernovas 199
surface area 98–9, 182
surface area/volume ratio 8–9
survival, adaptation 8–9
symbols
    chemical/elements 127,
        128–9, 246
    hazards 91, 233
    state 129

T
temperature 96–7, 102–3, 108–9
terminal velocity 188–9
thinking distance 180–1
tissue culture 67
tolerance, waste 33
tornadoes 192
total internal reflection 218–19
toxic substances 91
tracers, radioactive 238
transparent materials 210
transplanted embryos 66
transverse (s) waves 206, 207,
    210–11, 215
TV broadcasts 224
twins 54

U
ultrasound 216–17
ultraviolet (UV) radiation 37, 76,
    77, 220, 228, 230
unbalanced forces 176–7, 184–5
units
    energy 190
    frequency 208
    speed 166
Universe 198–9, 200–1, 202–3
unleaded petrol 36
unstable nuclei 236–41
uranium isotopes 236, 237, 239,
    241

V
vacuums 210–11, 220
variation 46–7, 74–5
varieties 70–1
velocity 167, 170–1
    see also speed
    terminal 188–9
velocity–time graphs 172–3
visible spectrum 220
volumes of gas 88, 120

W
Wallace, Alfred Russel 78
washing powder see detergents
waste 24–5, 32, 34–5, 43
water, test 111
water pollution 34–5, 38
Watson, James 59
wavelength 208–9, 222–3, 224–5
waves
    see also light; radiation;
        sound
    definition 206
    diffraction 222–3
    dispersion 220–1
    long wavelength
        electromagnetic 224–5
    radiation 230–9
    reflection 212, 218–19
    refraction 213, 214–15
    short wavelength
        electromagnetic 228–9
    spectrum 220
    types 206–11, 228–9
    ultrasound 216–17
weak intermolecular forces 154,
    155
weather monitoring 197
weight 175, 186–7, 188–9
white dwarfs 199
wine-making 106
womb 54, 55
word equations 127
work 190–1
world population 30–1

X
X chromosome 53
X-rays
    medical 161, 229, 230–1
    mutations 76, 77
    wavelength 220

Y
Y chromosome 53
yeast 106–7
yoghurt 107